THE

BALANCE

BETWEEN

CHURCH & POLITICS

Dr. Donette wright

THE

BALANCE

BETWEEN

CHURCH & POLITICS

DR. DONETTE WRIGHT

Manufactured in the United States of America

ISBN Paperback: 979-8-9861473-8-3
Library of Congress Control Number: 2022918478

Follow Dr. Donette Wright
Social Media Outlets:
Facebook: Donette Wright
YouTube: Donette Wright
Instagram: @drwright_bookboss
Email: balancebetweenchurchnpolitics@gmail.com

DEDICATION

To Trinity-Ville Secondary School now known as Robert Light-burn Technical High School.

As an alumna, I am honored to dedicate this book, *The Balance Between Church and Politics,* to the Trinity-Ville Secondary School, now known as Robert Light-burn Technical High School in the Providence of Saint Thomas, Jamaica, West Indies. I want to thank the teachers and faculty who help mold me into the woman I am today. And to all the teachers and staff who have touched my life, directly and indirectly, I honor you.

To our teachers and educators in your various capacities, your work is your legacy to the students whose lives you've touched, impacted, and changed for the better.

ACKNOWLEDGEMENT

Mr. Neil Santouse

It is my pleasure to acknowledge Mr. Neil Santouse. You are not only a friend and a confidant but an amazing father, son, mentor, and leader. I want to recognize you because you have been an ideal friend. It is said that one should "seek a friend before they need a friend," and you've always been there. I pull strength from your encouragement and those early morning quotes you send me. Your voice echoes in my ears, "never quit," which is one of the motivations I needed when writing this book. I implore people always to have someone such as yourself in their corner. Continue to be the person you are, change only for the better, and remain humble. Thank you for being there during my mom's passing; I appreciate your friendship for life.

Thank You

TABLE OF CONTENTS

INTRODUCTION

The book " The balance between The Church and Politics" is a profound inquisition into the birth and metamorphosis of the Christian faith and its ever-frosty relationship with the larger society. It seeks to x-ray the endemic conflicts of opinion and loyalty between the Church and the State.

It must be thoroughly understood that the coming of the Lord Jesus Christ and the birth of the Church (His body) was never intended to compliment politics and the State as it was constituted but as a confrontation and challenge to the very fabric of human existence conduct. Therefore, the issue of balancing either the views or convictions of the Church and politics remains a daunting and delicate enterprise throughout Church history.

The conflict between the Church and politics is a fundamental one and is caused by the differences in convictions and practice between the two. Before the advent of the Church, the world was accustomed to the inequality of the human person and the domination of the poor and vulnerable by the rich and powerful. But the Church became a unique social project, counterculture, and a contrasting community with a reverse belief system that contradicts the political system.

While the Church cannot be extracted from politics because it is comprised of human beings whose daily existence is affected by the laws and policies of the political environment, the Church can only remain relevant and alive if it is steadfast and committed to its doctrines and ideals.

The book highlights the major contentions that pitched the Church against the State and the various ways the issues were handled from the birth of the Church, including the instances where politics threatened to obliterate the Church institution but sought to retain some of the Church's teachings.

The Balance Between Church and Politics aims to bring to the fore the Church's age-long heritage of influencing the practice of politics and the equality of all men before God positively.

The essence is to help this generation of Christians and subsequent ones to understand their role and relationship with their political environment in such a way that they will not compromise on the real significance of their existence as the Church and also draw strength from the rich historical background of the Church as a change agent.

It is also important to note that the Church exists within a political framework that poses the challenge of trying to balance the two ends of the sea saw for the Church to achieve its mandate of evangelizing the world.

The main reason for the Church's existence is to serve as a light to the world of darkness by illuminating - (influencing) through teaching and personal conduct the thought pattern and ultimately the behavior of all political stakeholders in a way that engenders just and peaceful communal life.

In some cases, the ideals of the Church and the objectives of politics are so closely aligned that the balancing is not contentious, but in other instances, there exists a huge wide gulf between politics and the Church that threatens the life of both in degrees proportional to the sphere of influence of each.

The balance of the Church and politics is found not in compromise by believers but in resisting the alluring temptations of political inducements, which whittles down the core values of the Church and drowns the voice of the scriptures. It is found when the Church holds up conspicuously without much ado the very objectives often reckoned with by politics but not achievable because it lacks the requisite discipline and character to achieve. Politics at its best holds up hope for a better life but seldom delivers on its promise, so the Church will strike a balance when she influences and supports politics to borrow integrity and selflessness from her to survive.

This book could not have come at a more auspicious time than now, when the Church seems to have abandoned her ideals and is lost in politics without realizing it but muses at her fixated position.

The Church has a history, antecedents, and a robust culture that she can draw strength and courage from in reclaiming her pivotal influence and life-changing role in the political life of the society.

Come with me on this insightful exposition of the balance between the Church and politics, and you will be glad you did.

CHAPTER 1

THE BIRTH OF THE CHURCH

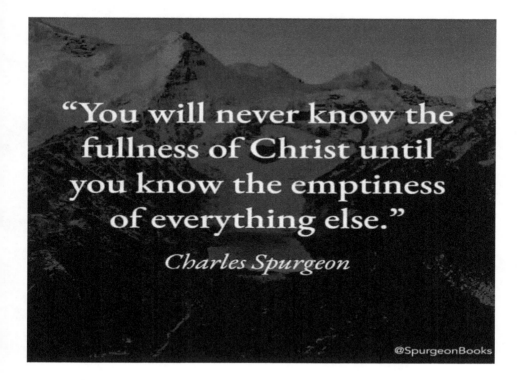

"You will never know the fullness of Christ until you know the emptiness of everything else."

Charles Spurgeon

@SpurgeonBooks

THE CHURCH

T he Church (ekklesia) is comprised of all individuals professing Christians residing in a geographic location like Jamaica (the Church in Jamaica) or refers to the amalgamation of the entire population of professing Christians in all the nations of the world.

In the first century after the death, resurrection, and ascension to heaven of the Lord Jesus Christ and precisely ten days after His ascending to heaven, the Lord empowered the one hundred and twenty disciples whom He had commissioned before His ascension and who obediently waited at the upper room in Jerusalem with the baptism In the Holy Spirit with the initial evidence of speaking in others languages they had not learned. (Acts Chapter 2)

The formal inauguration of the Church took place on the day of Pentecost (the Jewish second-most important festival of presentation of the first grain harvest to the Lord) when the Holy Spirit was first poured on all the one hundred and twenty believers gathered in the upper room.

It is noteworthy that the Lord Jesus Christ chose Pentecost day to also fulfill the prophecy of Joel 2:28 NIV: "And afterward, I will pour out my Spirit on all people. Your sons and daughters will prophesy, your old men will dream dreams, and your young men will see visions. The first fruits of the Church (the new Israel of God) were thus harvested and presented on the same day that the first grain harvest was to be presented by the Jewish people, all in Jerusalem.

Fifty days after Jesus Christ was raised from the dead, the followers were assembled in Jerusalem to celebrate the Jewish spring harvest of Shavuot (Pentecost). There, with people congregated from several lands, the new population of Christ-followers encountered an outpouring of the Holy Spirit. The New Testament depicts flames like fire sitting on their heads. Enabled by the Holy Spirit, they spoke the good news of Jesus in every language on Earth (Acts 2:4). It was an occasion of empowerment that altered a fearful and somewhat troubled group of disciples into apostles, those who are motivated to confirm their faith (Apostolos means "messenger" in Greek). That day served as Pentecost for Christians and is commemorated as the birthday of the Church.

The sound of the wind signified the incredible dignity of the Holy Spirit, whose appearing and leaving is like the wind, which can be experienced but not described. He came in the realization of the promise brought by John the Baptist (Mathew 3:11) and by Jesus Christ (Acts 1:4-5) that the believers would be baptized into one body, the same baptism which all disciples now encounter at the time of their salvation (1 Cor. 12:13-14).

The tongues of fire signified the purifying and refining work of the Holy Spirit. Through His indwelling and infilling, He bestows on them power for godly life and practical witnessing (Gal. 5:22-23; Eph. 5:18-21).

The incredible speech signified the worldwide progression of the Gospel from Jerusalem to the humanity of every dialect group, breaking down all prior barriers (Gal. 3:28-29).

Pentecost was not only characterized by three supernatural incidents, but it also accentuated a powerful sermon by an improbable preacher, Peter, the fisherman. Three components were included: a careful description, an illuminating declaration, and a challenging overture to receive the Spirit of God.

Peter proclaimed that these incidents were a realization of prophecy (2:14-21). Joel had foreseen the arrival of the era of the Spirit, an age that would climax in the tremendous end-time signs. The era of the Spirit started that day.

An Illuminating Declaration: Jesus of Nazareth is the Lord and Christ (2:22-35). This is substantiated in four ways. First, God had exhibited through wonders that Jesus is the Christ (v.22). Second, God's predestination was apparent: Christ grieved and died in a means that not only fulfilled Old Testament revelations but was commemorated by God's power in the resurrection (vv.23-24). Third, the psalmist had composed words that could only pertain to Jesus Christ (vv.25-31). Fourth, the great occasions of that amazing Pentecost day were the indication that the living Christ was performing His promises (vv.32-35).

A Challenging Invitation: The people were warned to repent and be baptized (2:37-39). The Greek term for repent means "to change one's mind." That call to repentance has prompted some people to believe God's method of salvation has altered from works, a system that encompassed repentance and baptism, to one of faith solely (Acts 8:12-17; 19:1-10).

But that's not an issue. Regretting and believing are two aspects of the same coin. This Jewish population had to "alter their minds" concerning the One they had denied. That alteration of their reasoning went hand-in-hand with their current belief.

Today someone repents when he admits his need for God's compassion through Christ. He believes when he positions his faith in the Lord Jesus. You cannot believe without regrets, and you cannot repent without believing.

In the same direction, Peter's invitation to "be baptized... for the remittal of sins" (2:38-39) is not, as some thought, a paradox of "believing in the Lord Jesus Christ, and you will be saved" (16:31). Peter did not mean that your sins will not be wiped away if you are not baptized. He said, "Repent and be baptized with a view toward or about the remission of sins." The preposition interpreted as "for" is eis, and it rarely means

18

"to." It is found, for instance, in Luke 11:32, where it explains that the nation of Nineveh "repented at the preaching of Jonah."

The Jewish population who raised the question "What shall we do?" understood Peter's proclamation about Jesus of Nazareth that He is Lord and Christ. They illustrated their faith through an allegorical, open label of themselves with the Lord Jesus in baptism. This exhibits that faith and repentance are two sides of one coin. Baptism visualizes the typical procedure in salvation as people come to an awareness of God in Christ.

Belief, repentance, baptism, acceptance of the Holy Spirit, and joining the Church were and are a package. The 3,000 people who were saved on the Day of Pentecost were saved by faith. They illustrated the reality of their belief by their baptism. They were filled in the Holy Spirit and became embodied in the Church. They "continued steadfastly in the apostles' doctrine and fellowship, in the breaking of bread, and prayers" (2:42). The New Testament did not record a single instance of anyone believing and refusing to be baptized or refusing to identify with a local church.

The Book of Acts of the Apostles was written towards the close of the 1st century by the Apostle Luke, the same author of the Gospel of Luke narrates the story of the early Church starting with this episode.

The transformation of a Jewish tentmaker called Saul also propelled the early church expansion. As the Bible stated in Acts of the Apostles, Saul had lived as a persecutor of Christians before he saw a bright light from heaven and listened to the voice of Jesus as he traversed the road from Jerusalem to Damascus. This occasion compelled him to be baptized as a follower of Jesus Christ. For the remaining days of his life, he traversed the Mediterranean hemisphere educating small populations of Christians until he ultimately took the Gospel to Rome. He preached in churches and to districts of Jews, defending his belief in Christ as

Messiah. However, he also talked to Gentiles (those who were not Jews) because he recognized that the Gospel of new life in Christ was not for his Jewish people alone but for women and men universally. As a preacher to the Gentiles, he is recognized by the Roman tongue of his name, Paul.

Paul's disagreement with the apostle Peter and the population in Jerusalem was of absolute significance for early Christianity, as the group gradually became distinguished from its Jewish roots. Paul contended that new Greek believers are not required to first become circumcised like Jews and to keep Jewish dietary and calendar-based laws to become Christians. In this, he differed from Peter, who he believed to be the apostle of the Jews. A Church council in Jerusalem about 50 A.D. concluded in agreement with Paul: Gentiles could become Christians without Jewish religious ceremonies like being circumcised first. With this ruling, the gate was opened for a new and more inclusive body of the Christian population. Paul's epistles to the new congregations of the Greek civilization have become a crucial part of the New Testament.

The Christian population is called the Church; the root word in Greek is ecclesia, indicating those who were "called out." It conveys the fact that Christians were called out from their former lives and into a different community. The Acts of the Apostles (2:44-47) depicts the life of the first Christian community: "All who believed were together and shared all things in common, sold their possessions and goods and distributed them to all, as any had need. And day by day, attending the temple together, breaking bread in their homes, they partook of food with glad and generous hearts, praising God and having favor with all the people. And the Lord added to their number day by day those who were being saved."

In its biggest sense, the Church is the universal population of all people who proclaim faith in Christ. The word "catholic" with a lowercase "c," just means "universal." In its most personal sense, the Church is any room where "two or three are gathered" in the name of Christ (Matthew 18:20). Whether global or a tiny assembly, the Church is a society of people. The descriptions of the population in the New Testament comprise powerful, organic impressions of belonging. Most honorably, the Church is portrayed as "the body of Christ." As Paul sums it, "For just as the body is one and has many members, and all the members of the body, though many, are one body, so it is with Christ" (I Corinthians 12:12). Not all organs of the body of Christ, the Church, have an identical role, yet all are partners, both sorrowing and enjoying together. This influential metaphor is expanded through the central ceremony of the community: the sanctification and sharing of bread and wine, occasionally referred to as Holy Communion, the Lord's Supper, or the Eucharist. The bread symbolizes the "body of Christ," while the wine represents the "blood of the new covenant." Just as the one bread is shared by many and wine is drunk from one cup, those who share from them affirm their oneness (I Corinthians 11:23-25; Matthew 26:26-28).

Through the preaching of Paul and different preachers, the new Christian faith thrived quickly, circulating throughout the Mediterranean community. Its primary adversary was neither the sects nor bizarre beliefs of ancient Greece and Rome, rather the followers of the monarch, who all were expected to honor. For Christians, however, the Lord was Christ alone, and this made praising the Emperor as Lord unthinkable. The rejection of the new Christian population to partake in the cult of the monarch made it seem provocative. Everywhere in the Roman Empire, Christians were victimized and murdered for their faith. However, early in the 4th century, the ugly Christian ordeal was considerably changed when Emperor Constantine himself converted to Christianity. During his regime, Christianity was not only legitimized but accepted as the official faith of the Empire.

They "continued steadfastly in the apostles' doctrine and fellowship, in the breaking of bread, and prayers" (2:42). The New Testament does not report one example of a person believing and declining to be baptized or rejecting to join himself with a local church.

A Great Response (2:40-47). Three thousand Jewish folks reformed, were baptized and obtained the Holy Spirit. They instantly began meeting together, encountering the power of the Holy Spirit's presence and exhibiting a beautiful sense of togetherness.

Coming Together For Worship. The new disciples were not left to themselves. Acts 2:42 tells us They remained steady in the apostles' teaching and fellowship, in the sharing of bread, and prayers.

This passage gives us an understanding of their worship: They convened for apostolic teaching. How significant to know God's truth.

They joined for fellowship. We can't be strong Christians if we strive to live in isolation. They convened for the sharing of bread, the Lord's Supper. We are bolstered by celebrating Christ's death for our guilt and conveying our oneness.

They joined for corporate praying. A unique blessing still happens when people pray jointly.

Encountering The Holy Spirit's Power: Fear of God dropped upon these disciples as they watched apostolic signs and miracles. Acts 2:43 reads: "Then fear came upon every soul, and many wonders and signs were done through the apostles."

Right from the very outset, the Lord demonstrated that He expects us to have a healthful fear of Him, to be scared of annoying Him. God noticed that these new believers in the baby church needed indications of His tremendous power so that they would not misconstrue His grace and assume that following Him was not vital.

Sharing: These first Christians traded their properties and rationed the proceeds according to needs (vv.44-47). We may presume from Acts 4:32-37 that they performed so willingly. It was a beautiful manifestation of unity in Christ, although God perhaps did not plan for it to be continuous. It was planned for these new disciples. Several of them would naturally have retreated to their distant residences shortly after the Pentecost festivity. These people could now live in Jerusalem for a period so that they might mature strong in their faith before going back to face resentment at home.

SEEING GOD

The incidents at Pentecost accentuate some of God's incredible personalities. For instance, God is wise, He understood that the believers needed strength and power, and He recognized how to provide them with these blessings.

God is patient; He did not abandon Jerusalem and the Jewish nation even though they had opposed and crucified their Messiah.

God is faithful; He always accomplishes His promises.

God is loving, He whose affection guided Him to forge us and to procure redemption and made certain that it would touch us by bringing the Holy Spirit to attract us, to win us, to transform us, and to dwell in us.

SEEING OURSELVES

Trusting in Jesus Christ is not sheer mental assent; it is a revolutionary, mutinous decision that entails veering away from formerly held beliefs about salvation and a veering to Christ.

A person who confesses that he believes but declines baptism and designation with a local church may be indicating that his belief is not true.

God prepared Peter, a fisherman who had illustrated a propensity to talk without thinking and who had flunked the Lord badly during the hours leading to the crucifixion. This reveals to us that the Lord will encourage us to do anything He summons us to do.

These one hundred and twenty disciples became the first fruit and bedrock of the Church, and their charge was Mark 16:15 NIV: He said to them, "Go into all the world and preach the Gospel to all creation. - The great commission.

The main duty of the Church is to evangelize the whole world with the Gospel - the good news, which is the redemptive work of Christ on the cross of Calvary for the salvation of mankind. The coming of Christ and His redemptive work has altered forever and for good the basis of human interrelationships and also emphasized God's love and forgiveness of sin for every human being who accepts by faith the redemptive work of Jesus Christ on the cross of Calvary.

The mood of the first breeds of Christians toward the existing political order was determined by their expectation of the imminent coming of the kingdom of God, whose supernatural power had started to be visibly recognized in the figure of Jesus Christ. The significance of the political order was, thus, inconsequential, as Jesus himself asserted when he said, "My kingship is not of this world." Preoccupation with the imminent coming kingdom of peace placed Christians in conflict with the State, which put pressures upon them that were in direct conflict with their faith.

ITS SCOPE

It's a new world order that the Church introduced and preached, and like every introduction of change, the opposition and resistance were immediate. As the crowd gathered to witness the profound phenomenon of the Holy Spirit baptism, some mused while some mocked the multilingual expertise of the uneducated Galileans and wondered what it was all about.

And after Apostle Peter effusively preached the first sermon that drew three thousand people to repentance, the Church unequivocally announced her arrival and mission.

The stage was set for what today is the most active force in personal character reformation, advocacy for justice, equity, and peaceful co-existence. But the powers that be saw the Church and her activities as a revolution and threat to the establishments and their influence. They feared losing out of power, position, and influence, just like Herod was troubled by the news of the birth of a new the Jews from the three Maggi.

The Church, in the preaching of the Gospel, has no doubt encountered barriers and immense inevitable opposition not because its message is poignant or self-serving but because it requires a lifestyle that is less discriminatory and humble.

The pre-Church establishments and cultural orientation of the world were enshrined in racial superiority for the Jews and social and economic imperialism. The rich and powerful maintained an exclusive social class that discriminated against and exploited the poor.

But the Church came and proclaimed the equality of every man before the only Supreme God who is above all rules and powers as known.

The Church was a unique contrast community of people, a counterculture that was both offensive and yet attractive to many.

ITS NATURE

Yes, the central message of the Church was CHANGE/ REPENT In thinking and disposition based on the life and teachings of a new King-Jesus Christ. So, in effect, the Church is revolutionary, with the major difference being that in almost all other revolutions, there is the physical exertion of force to effect a change in leadership, but the Church is an army without lethal physical weapons.

Secondly, almost all revolutions seek to overthrow the existing political leadership and their ideals and replace them with another set of leaders with perceived desirable ideology; the Church seeks not political powers nor leadership but a change in personal perceptions, thoughts, and dispositions that are influenced by the life and teachings of Jesus Christ. However, one thing that is common with every revolution is change, and it is hard to effect a change, especially large-scale change without resistance from the status quo.

Before the birth and inauguration of the Church, there was an elaborate effort to lay the new foundation for her modus operandi and standards by the head of the Church - Jesus Christ. When He taught the crowd in Matthew chapters 5, 6, and 7, the Lord succinctly established a new order that is sin qua non with the kingdom of God/ Heaven, which He represents and which is the will and purpose of God for mankind.

The Church was established to represent the kingdom of heaven on earth and to propagate its ideals. So, the Church was neither an appendage to the existing social order nor a training program that helped to improve upon the old establishments. She came with change as never seen before and a change so fundamental that she was accused of turning the whole world upside down.

REVOLUTION

A fundamental change in the way of thinking about or visualizing something: a change of paradigm. The Church was not overhauling the old system but introduced a new set of rules of engagement between mortals and between man and God.

HISTORICAL ANTECEDENTS IN POLITICS

Immediately after the resurrection of Jesus Christ from the dead, the disciples had hoped that He would overthrow the Romans that were ruling Israel and restore the kingdom to them. But that was not to be, and from that point and based on the several previous emphases the Lord laid on the imminent coming of the kingdom of God, the disciples were focused on that blessed hope as it is called.

So, because they were ready to leave any moment and be with the Lord, there was no need to get involved in the affairs of politics and earthly government. This formed the basis of the Church not getting involved in politics which remains controversial throughout the centuries.

During the revolt of A.D. 70, in which the Jews revolted against the Roman authorities ruling their country, which led to the destruction of Jerusalem and the temple as foretold by the Lord, the Church did not take part. One of the fundamental teachings of the Church is respect for every constituted authority, for there is no authority except as allowed by God. The Church in Jerusalem fled to a city called Pella in Syria for safety in A.D. 66 (that is four years) before the fall of Jerusalem.

Although the Church recognized in the early centuries that the Pagan world was the custodian of political power and the legal apparatus of the State, she rejected appointment in public service and any involvement in the political process for obvious reasons.

The early Christians were depicted by Celsus as people who rejected military service and refused to accept public responsibility nor accept any commitment to the governing of the cities. Origen corroborated this description and added that Christians were doing more for the benefit of the kingdom by creating an "army of piety" that intercedes in prayers for the well-being of the king and the safety of the State. It has been asserted that Christianity made a considerable positive impact on the growth and development of modern democracy.

The early two centuries of the Christian age saw the Church growing and separating from Judaism because of the inclusion of the Gentiles in God's new covenant relationship, which the orthodox Jews had a problem with.

Beginning with a handful of fishermen, tax collectors, and alleged youthful troublemakers in a remote province of Judea, the faith has covered all over the world to claim the allegiance of over two billion citizens of our planet.

The time of Jesus Christ and the Apostles and the way forward usually meant a sober reflection backward to the image of God revealed in the story of Jesus. Christians will forever consider the age of Jesus and his apostles a sort of model for all the other ages. It bequeathed to the Church its ever-strong faith in Jesus, the resurrected Messiah, and the hope of forgiveness of sins through him. And the age demonstrated, in the life of Paul, that the Gospel of grace recognizes no boundaries of nation, race, sex, or culture.

THE JAMAICAN EARLY CHURCH

The Church in Jamaica was firstly Roman Catholic brought by the Spanish settlers who arrived in 1509 and later the Protestants led by the Baptists who became very active and were credited with the abolition of slavery in the Caribbean country.

In 1655 a joint naval and military troop dispatched by Oliver Cromwell, Lord Protector of England, invaded Jamaica and displaced the Spanish Catholics, and destroyed their churches by fire. Cromwell was a Puritan by orientation and rabidly anti-Catholic whose Western design was aimed to "purge the New World of Papists."

The Catholic Church came back to Jamaica briefly in 1688 when James II (England's last Catholic king) brought a priest to serve the handful of Catholics in Jamaica. No sooner than King William III, the Protestant champion, ousted James in 1689 and sat upon the English throne as King, Catholicism in England and her colonies were banned and remained so prohibited for more than a century. All through this period, the Catholic Church in Jamaica was undercover.

From the seventeenth century to the 1860s, the state church in Jamaica was the Anglican Church, and the State was responsible for funding the Church. Many other missionary churches argued that it was unfair for the State to use its taxes to support a competing church whose membership was largely the ruling class.

The executive director of the Institute of Jamaica, Vivian Crawford, recently enlightened me on what is thought to have been a trigger to the events that ultimately led to the estrangement of the relationship between the Church and the State in Jamaica.

It was reported that after the capital of Jamaica was shifted from Spanish Town to Kingston, the then Governor of Jamaica, Peter Grant, requested to have the bishop's residence (now King's House), which was acquired by the State for the Anglican Church, as his official residence. The fact that this request was granted indicated that the State had stranglehold power over the Church, and, as such, this event was decisive in the Anglican Church ceasing to remain as the State Church.

Jamaica has a heritage of very strong relationships between the Church and politics, unlike the case with many other countries. The conflicts within the Jamaican Church were more denominational than between the Church and State. The State and the Church forged a theocratic alliance that ruled the country for centuries.

Whether the Church was able to wield a strong spiritual influence on the State or was subjugated by the state bureaucracy and to what extent is a subject for discussion in subsequent chapters.

CHAPTER 2

THE EARLY STRUGGLE WITH POLITICS

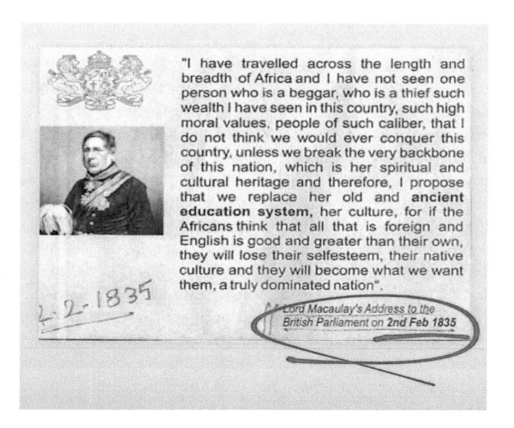

"I have travelled across the length and breadth of Africa and I have not seen one person who is a beggar, who is a thief such wealth I have seen in this country, such high moral values, people of such caliber, that I do not think we would ever conquer this country, unless we break the very backbone of this nation, which is her spiritual and cultural heritage and therefore, I propose that we replace her old and **ancient education system,** her culture, for if the Africans think that all that is foreign and English is good and greater than their own, they will lose their selfesteem, their native culture and they will become what we want them, a truly dominated nation".

Lord Macaulay's Address to the British Parliament on 2nd Feb 1835

P olitics was never at the forefront of early Christian thinking. The category of people among whose members Christianity was making progress was politically and socially extremely vulnerable, too cluttered, and obscure to take any very active interest in statecraft. Moreover, the age was so quickly passing away, and the current duty of personal preparation for the succeeding age was so urgent that declaration of the advancing kingdom of God and personal sanctification in expectation of the imminent judgment superseded all else. However, this very declaration was political with serious implications. In fact, it was both extreme and revolutionary.

Christianity was no statement of civic patchwork, no proposal of gentle social enrichment by incremental reform. It condemned the present generation, with its emperors and princes, its wealthy men and leaders, its pride and dictatorship, to permanent destruction. Jesus believed there could be no accommodation. Men could not attend to God and Mammon (Matt. 6:24). Loyalty in this kingdom implied for Jesus and his firstest followers the forsaking of all that was associated with the yearnings of the normal life (Luke 14:33). The world as Jesus understood it was condemned (Matt. 24:3-5; Mark 13:5-37). Not even the enormous accusation by the cataclysm of John of Rome and Caesarism surpasses the revolutionary resentment that echoes in the messages ascribed to Jesus by both Mark and Matthew and substantially emphasized by Luke. Nobody would overcome that judgment, neither Caesar's throne nor the Temple of Jerusalem (John 4: 21). Even the popular answer so frequently misinterpreted, "Render to Caesar the things that be Caesar's, and to God the things that be God's," was radical. It fixed God and Caesar, where Jesus deemed them, at the two poles. This era was Caesar's; the judgment and succeeding age were God's. Men must live their lives, no doubt, in this period, but they must live them as in the grim pursuit for the coming age and were to go ahead unimpeded by any of the former age's yearnings. God and his righteousness were alone worthwhile, and he who has these would also have all the other valuables of life added to him (Matt. 6:33). It was Jesus who shouted, "Let the dead bury their dead, go thou and proclaim the kingdom. "God's kingdom and Caesarism for Jesus had nothing in common. There was no reason to draw a sword to kill individuals, the harbingers of Caesar, who survived by the sword, ended by the sword, but in rightful time God must judge and rule. This fervor for God and his holiness was to thrive and circulate until all who lived as children of God had listened to the message, and accordingly, the kingdom would come as a robber in the dark, and a new world and era of righteousness and harmony would dawn. The mistitled "Sermon on the Mount" is a later collection of the constitution and ethics of that succeeding age drawn from different sermons of Jesus given at varied periods of his ministry.' The entire vision is sweeping, unalloyed, and revolutionary. It flamed a few followers with an immortal hope; it injected the multitude of the power-possessing group with equally eternal hate. The only significance of life, the only purpose of eternity, was the complete revelation of God's will. The existing age was an age conquered by its prince, and he possessed nothing accepted by Jesus (John I4:30; I6: II). Jesus had not come to share Satan's throne (Matt. 4:8-Io) or protest his supremacy in the current age but to slide the age out and inaugurate the Father's reign. The morals of Jesus on the personal sanctification of life in readiness for the succeeding kingdom. His theology is affected by his disclosure of the real character of the Father whom he adored, and his theology was the love and hope and joy elicited by that Father of mercies, who mustered all his roaming children to contrition and trust.

The Attitude of Paul

Such a gospel could not possibly be diluted into a program of incremental political amendment in the Roman Empire. And so, to the extent Jesus organized any congregation, it was solely as a group of advertisers of the succeeding kingdom. After the denial and death of such a revolutionist against all earthly government, that group commenced the life of declaration, pushed thereto by their conquering belief in the resurrection of their incredible leader. This resurrection engraved the radicalism of Jesus as real. Thus, the hostility of Saul of Tarsus. He was representative of the power-wielding class. Most of the contemporary explanations of the ethics and theology of Jesus leave us marveling at why Saul and the chief priests should so loathe him and that the power-possessing group should kill him. But when we understand that Jesus opposed the entire social arrangement in which they were so prosperous and foretold its demolition and its ultimate condemnation and that with such defeating compassion and such assuring grace, we stop to be amazed. None of us want to have our prosperous concessions ruthlessly uncovered or to see what appears to us the cores of society barraged in the name of theology. When Paul came to recognize in the risen Jesus the proof that this generation was, indeed, flying away, he also became the advertiser of a messianic judgment, and he tirelessly wandered the world striving like the earlier apostles "such as were being saved" (Acts 2:47). But his perception was associated with much more uniquely Hellenistic features, even though the idea itself remained completely Jewish. Paul, like Jesus, did not think of any incremental improvement of the Roman Empire. It was, nevertheless, appointed of God as minister of God for specific objectives. Subordination to it was an obligation, and as Rome preserved Paul against Jewish extremism, he saw in it a fortuitous "minister of

God to thee for good" (Rom. 13:4). Similarly, Paul obeyed God instead of man, and though he felt no obligation to the Roman Empire as such, he sorrowed for it. The paradox of lawlessness was at function (II Thess. 3-10), and whether the quotation plays out, as seems doubtful, in the world of political allusion or is about apocalyptic hopes, it marks the early Christian strong sense of an impending battle between the two kingdoms of the departing age and the succeeding era.

The Early Church and Politics

Two things were taking place simultaneously that greatly altered the revolutionary disposition toward the existing social and political order. In the first instance, the Messiah did not come as quickly as was anticipated. And secondly, despite Rome's periodic persecution, on the whole, her general temperament of tolerance and real insensibility of what was happening made her the regular protector against local animosity and persecution. Theoretically, Rome was condemned, and during the periods under Nero, Decius, or Diocletian, persecution burst out then the old radical apocalyptic sentiment revived. But even then, persecution was mainly local, bureaucrats were reachable by payoffs or influence, and some found it simple to compromise. The intense extremism of those who condemned their unstable brethren and the frequently renewing narrowness of parochial groups made the behavior of the credible official Church appear sane and well harmonious, and so eventually, the revolt against the social order and the extant world became a theory barely. The responsibility of the evangelical message was largely a warning for personal sanctification, allegiance to the Christian union, and the declaration of eternity. The group itself evolved into a redemptive church, with sacraments and officials, and liable for the well-being, spiritual and material, of its members. The alienation from a terrible world gives rise to an increasingly complicated ethical rationalization and a frequently altering relation of the Christian to the society he lived in.

Even Paul was confronted by the problem of Christians attending dinner parties where meat was dedicated to idols and then consumed. What was the credible Christian to do? Tertullian is deeply shaken by Christian soldiers holding the crowns that Mithras'(the Persian God of light) adherents influenced. The awareness, however, of the whole ambivalence between a Christian's life in the current era and a soldier's profession is absent, just as the internal paradox between the life of affection and the relationship between master and slave was not obvious even to Paul.

Politics were not the fundamental responsibility of the Christian organizations, and so far, as they were conscientious at all, it was just as they impacted trade and social life. Along one line alone, Christian moral awareness marked the striking contradiction between its standard and those of the pagan world around it. The recreations of the populace, its carnival, its theaters, its proms, its extravagances shocked and disgusted men awakened to a feeling of a redeemed life. Here in the center, stood the sexual concern. Judaism was never ascetic and has often been strongly emphatic on sane and normal behaviors toward the sexual relationship.

But the moral impression of the oriental world in its protest against such extravagances has constantly terminated in a vain trial at the suppression of the normal impulse itself and has upheld that repression by a principle of the intrinsic evil of life. Oriental self-denial is associated with an entire refutation of all life. This refutation stretches into politics also. The world and all its possessions are evil. It was therefore largely easy for the seriously passionate Christians, displeased with the growing agreeableness of the Christian Church to the world, to adopt the ascetic standards of the oriental and learn in them the highest manifestation of the Christian life and hope.

In the endorsement of monasticism (the rituals of monastic life - marked by self-denial and seclusion) by the established Church, a twofold behavior toward the State and the rest of life became unavoidable. The greatest Christian life comprised of the denial of life, with its politics, business, marriage, home, and even ordinary comforts. At the same time, this was not required of all, and the ordinary Christian could, without danger to his soul, acknowledge the State and the world of employment within the thresholds of ill-defined integrity. The result was a society within the Church with unconnected ideas of holiness. At the same time, the thriving organization could not for a long time remain in this abnormal situation. Firstly, tensions with the State came to be a steady menace. Moreover, as elevated social statuses came under Christian impact, the question was pressed home: What is the connection of the Christian to the virtually heathen State? Then again, the new Christian Church was evolving increasingly, hanging upon the culture of the pagan world about her, and she had to choose those ingredients she considered needful for her life and dismiss others that she felt were adverse. Now pagan culture is centered around politics and statecraft. Plato, Aristotle, and Cicero could not even be appreciated except for their political and social insights.

When Ambrose attempted to translate the forbearing code of morals into the dialect of the Christian ministry, he was constrained to make many compromises to the growing distinction between the place of the government and the need for pagan culture. Life is not overpowered by examination but by motives and interests. Most times, reflection only upholds what has transpired and analyzes the prevailing situation. As it occurred, the freedman group, among whom early Christianity had its major followers,' was rapidly becoming the actual political authority, and Christian bishops lived as the most powerful figures in the society. Ambrose is himself an example of the thriving political significance of the early Church.

The era was certainly one of vast turmoil but showed no indications of passing away. The growing congruence of the world with its culture and its political life put forward from time-to-time fiery uproars, as by the Montanists, but their watchwords were so badly chosen, their endeavors so divisive and absurd, that the authorized Church had little trouble in asserting herself as the absolute authority, and in quelling Marcion, the Gnostics, and the earlier factions.

Exchange of the Church for the State

And still, world-flight continued despite all harmony to the revolutionary objective. In assumption, at least the pagan world with its statecraft and power was terrible and was condemned. The escape from the world came to be rapidly a flight to the Church, a sanctuary from the world in her sacraments and assistance. The greatest guaranty of protection was found in monastic isolation from the world within her security and auspices. The authorized Church was mainly spiritual and not either a political or a social organization. Still, situations forced her to acclaim the social and physical needs of her membership (Acts 4:32-35; 6:1-6).

The Church became, more especially in the West, a hegemony in Imperio, a world within the nation, and having communication with the big world yet retaining her life within (John 17:15). Thus, arose within her existence a realm of politics. Leaders became essential, and internal debates about leadership often diverted her and even endangered her.

Men obtained in this way training for relationships and discovered the ability to move their fellowmen to a level that exclusion from traditional political life made hitherto impossible. No question, the Church was the only mechanism doing this. Gilds, secret cults, and the supervision of small village areas compelled men to utilize their political talents outside the world of authorized statecraft. Similarly, the Church was by far the vastly important of all these agencies and was in immediate communication with the group to which, more than any other, the destiny belonged. The breakdown of the Roman Empire, ensuring the gradual estrangement of the East from the West, and the still more incremental rise of ethnicities, was in a judgment made feasible by the training in management given to the freedman group in its administration of the metropolitan Church Paul established. Decades before the fourth century, when the Church had evolved into a political authority that the monarchy had to consider, the personal provincial Church was a prominent social factor. In Egypt, revolting monks made Alexandrian civic events often difficult to govern. In minor places, no doubt, the regional Church, and local bishop were political authorities.

Tertullian, about 212 A.D, affirms that Christians are already in a plurality in nearly every community. The fact of local aggravation may effortlessly have constrained the local Church and its bishop to safeguard themselves through political action. And still, nothing is more remarkable than the dearth in the literary vestiges of any material encouraging us to do more than guess at the connections of the local metropolitan churches to the regional administration up to the period of Nicea. Eusebius reports that just before the Diocletian persecution in 302 A.D, the rulers had dedicated to Christians the administration of gentiles.' But before that time, it is unlikely that any very effective portion in the official life of the kingdom was feasible for a Christian.

The devotion paid to the supreme standard excludes any who were not virtually ready for any and every concession of their faith.

Political Triumph of Christianity

Political life was sliding rapidly into the hands of the very group that Christianity had accomplished so much to govern and educate. So long before either the old elite or the farming commoners or the city masses were even in word Christian, the active positions in life were monopolized by a Christian minority. Indeed, it was no more the Christianity of Jesus or Paul that prevailed in the churches. Contradictions and mysticism, cult, sacrament, and doctrinal recipes had taken the place of emphasis over trust and behavior, personal allegiance to the mission of God, and faith in an imminent era of loving righteousness and family democracy.

External unity had become the greatest good, and a priestly injunction and a centralized power were practicing the old legalism authority against which Jesus and Paul had so forcefully and so effectively disputed in the case of Judaism. Still there the Church stood, the one metropolitan force apparently in communication with the whole world of thinking and action.

Her church edifices were already in the period Diocletian many and exquisite. Here men assembled while the temples were vacant. Her bishops dictated, and her organization was so robust and so worldwide that aggravation whack upon her in vain, and all other religious cults plummeted into relative inconsequentiality. Then lastly, politics came courting the established Church.

If the Church, especially the early Church, had an enemy, it was the political establishment; unfortunately for the Church, she had no option. Her relationship with the State is akin to the relationship between a drowning man and a rescue diver. While the drowning man, in his frantic effort to seize any handy object to survive, the rescue diver who is determined to save the man in danger must exercise utmost caution to avoid sinking with the drowning man and perishing without accomplishing the mission.

The Church, as the rescue diver, must necessarily mingle with the Political environment but cautiously to avoid subjugation and annihilation.

The early Church made no pretense of her susceptibility to conflict with the establishments and therefore made no effort to safeguard herself. The head of the Church had Himself expressly told the members that they should not expect any better treatment than He had received.

The Church came prepared for conflict with the kingdoms of this world; the truth is that the Church is an army raised to prey on the kingdoms of the earth.

Jesus Christ came to raise the citizens of His kingdom from among the existing kingdoms of the world, and this is a recipe for conflict which He was well aware of and with no intention of avoiding.

Matthew 10:24 NIV -"The student is not above the teacher, nor a servant above his master.

Matthew 10:28 NIV - Do not be afraid of those who kill the body but cannot kill the soul. Rather, be afraid of the One who can destroy both soul and body in hell.

Matthew 12:29 NIV -"Or again, how can anyone enter a strong man's house and carry off his possessions unless he first ties up the strong man? Then he can plunder his house.

Matthew 12:30 NIV - "Whoever is not with me is against me, and whoever does not gather with me scatters.

SOURCES OF CONFLICTS

The most veritable sources of conflict between the Church and politics are:

1. The personality of Jesus Christ: The identity of the Lord Jesus Christ was as controversial as His claims, especially to the Jews of His day. Theon God, the Son of man, and the Son of DaThed we're all used interchangeably to address Him, and each seems to mean a different thing to different people. The Son of God is His most controversial identity to the Jewish people even to date, but to the believer, there is no doubt or skepticism about the fact that He is the Son of God.

The Jews became so skeptical of the identity " son of God" that they confronted Him over the name and protested vehemently against it, but the Lord's ingenious answer to them was, " if you find it difficult to believe that I am the Son of God because I said so, why not believe me on the strength of the works I am doing of which you are witnesses.

John 5:20 NIV - For the father loves the son and shows him all he does. Yes, and he will show him even greater works than these so that you will be amazed.

John 5:36 NIV - "I have testimony weightier than that of John. For the works that the father has given me to finish — the very works that I am doing —testify that the father has sent me.

John 7:7 NIV -The world cannot hate you, but it hates me because I testify marginalization are evil.

The power and marginalization establishments were directly threatened by the person of Jesus Christ because He exercised power and authority far beyond the levels ever seen or heard of before. As His followers grew, the political marginalization came worried that He could influence the people to revolt against them, especially when there were mostly Jews while the bureaucracy was Roman occupiers.

From His birth, the political authorities saw Jesus Christ as opposition and a threat to their exalted positions and were very intolerant of Him.

The Church must necessarily inherit the same vicious treatment meted out to her head by the political establishments because, as He said, the servant cannot be greater than his master.

It was the political establishment of His time that ensured that He died an ignoble death on the cross because He was a threat to both the Jewish religious leaders and Pontius Pilate- the political authorities.

Apostle Paul appealed to Ceasar in Rome when he perceived that his trial in Jerusalem was being manipulated by the Jewish religious authorities to subvert justice against him.

Almost all the Apostles were martyred by the political authorities to exterminate the Church or subordinate her to the State against her will.

2. The Message of the Church: The message of the Church was seen as an attack on the very fabrics and foundation of both the secular and sacred world order of that time.

The message insisted on repentance- turning away from a dominant lifestyle of greed, selfishness, and exploitation of the vulnerable that was prevalent at the time. It was a huge challenge to the status quo and deviation from the norm. The call for change will always be a recipe for conflict, especially when the change demands far-reaching concessions to be made.

Those who are lords over the status quo and beneficiaries of the system will naturally be at the forefront of the resistance to change.

The message of a new king and his kingdom amid an existing political environment with ominous, powerful bureaucracy is akin to mutiny;

the only difference here is that the personality involved could not be identified with military or physical weaponry of any type and therefore does not deserving of any serious attention at least by the reckoning of the threatened polity.

The message of the Church is usually met with mixed reactions; to some, it is repulsive and demeaning and therefore rejected with impervious hatred, while to others, it is a soothing and comforting opportunity to be embraced with open arms and hearts.

The message of peace to a people under the tyranny of vicious foreign military rulers may be inspiring and welcome, but to the invaders who are benefitting from the system and therefore want to maintain the status quo, the same message of peace will be seen as antagonism and seriously opposed or stopped.

3. The Disposition of the Church: The early Church believed in the imminent returning of the Lord in judgment and rapture. Since His coming will be the end of the world, the Church saw no need to get involved in politics and any otherworldly affairs. You can be sure that this will be a source of conflict with non-profit, non-governmental organizations disrupting the established cultural and social life of the State by insisting that there is another king and kingdom to whom they owe their allegiance rather than to the common bureaucracy.

4. Concentration of Power: Before the centralization of the church structure and the inception of the pastoral primacy, the monarch was the head of both the state and spiritual kingdoms, and the Church did not balk at showing allegiance to the temporal powers. But when the superiority of the spiritual institution was established beyond question, the church fathers annexed the powers of the political world and brought them under their full control; this started the dispute between the two.

With the adoption of Christianity as the state religion and the growth of the papacy, a united Christian world was founded, and the borders of the Roman Empire and the Christian world finally coincided. The boundaries of powers of the two regimes were never clearly defined. This gave rise to the overlapping of powers.

Again, the scope of execution of the authorities of both the spiritual and secular administrations was a recipe for conflict. Any compromised arrangement was distasteful to both of them. Relations became strained, with the conflict appearing unavoidable.

5. Accumulation of Wealth by the Church: The accumulation of fortune by the church fathers may be considered another cause of tension between the two. There was a huge gap between what the Church preached and what the Church leaders practiced.

While the Church urged the members to adopt modest living and sober thinking, the leaders indulged in a very luxurious and affluent life, and to finance that purpose; it solicited and received monetary gifts from the people. And with this incredible wealth accumulated, the Church was able to participate in politics.

6. Involvement in active Politics: The Church's interest and Involvement in politics considerably curtailed the emperor's area of action and sovereignty, which ultimately led to hostile relations.

The fearsome authority of the Pope to ex-communicate any secular person, including members person of the royal family, was a source of dispute between the king and the Church. The authority of the Pope to ex-communicate was linked with dangerous consequences.

If any member of the imperial household or prince became ex-communicated, he was immediately deprived of the throne with the privileges and could no longer claim any allegiance from his citizens. The Pope was not contented with meddling in politics only; he extended his interference to the personal affairs of the king. For example, king Lothaire of Lorraine onetime decided to separate from his wife and marry his mistress. Pope Nicholas strongly opposed it based on immorality.

A long-drawn battle could not settle the conflict between the king and the Pope, and eventually, the king was compelled by the Pope to take back his wife.

The behavior and interference of the Pope were acceptable to weak emperors. But the ones with strong personalities withstood the Church, and this promoted the struggle between the two.

7. Consolidation of Royal Power: Consolidation of the imperial authority may be considered another reason for tension between the Church and government. Some historians stated that by the beginning of the fourteenth century, the monarchs were able to strengthen their power. The feudal lords and aristocrats have in the past taken sides with the Church, and towards the close of the thirteenth century, their authority was curtailed, and the Pope's impact over them moreover tended to wane. This enhanced the power and authority of the monarch, and he declined to acknowledge that he was a subordinate to the king and an agent of the Church.

The Church saw this as an audacity on the part of the king, and it became infuriated and declared a crusade against temporal power. Concerning the question of investiture, a fierce controversy arose between Pope Gregory VII and Emperor Henry IV. Being afraid of ex-communication, the emperor knelt before the Pope.

But as at, when the political situation changed, Henry IV seized Rome and sent Gregory into exile. The Church was faced with the challenge posed by the king. National monarchs also became adamant. Enhanced strength encouraged them to risk ex-communication, interdict, and other papal weapons.

8. Economic Factors: Economic considerations also fueled the acrimony between Church and political bureaucracy. Church had accumulated a huge amount of wealth over which the secular authority wanted to charge taxes on. But the Church, through its influential organization, exerted a tremendous impact upon the masses and, with the threats of ex-communication, suppressed all the moves and plans of taxation by the State.

When the king, as head of State in charge of all political and civil functions, proceeded to mint money and received taxes, the Church once again stood in the way of the secular authority.

The king's arguments that the imposition and receiving of taxes were within his jurisdiction such that the Church should have no interference with it, yet the Church refused to cooperate with the monarch setting the stage for a cold war between them.

9. The Interpretation of the Divine Right Theory: The understanding of an emphasis on the divine right theory was another cause of conflict. Emperors in the Middle Ages insisted that the origin of power and authority of the king and the Church was God, and typically the final obligation for all the actions of both Church and king was to God alone and never to the Church under any circumstances.

He was accountable to God alone for any negligence or misconducts, and the Pope should not interfere whatsoever with the roles of the king. But this position was vigorously disputed by the Church. The Church maintained that in no case could the authority of the Pope be restricted nor his decision be rejected.

10. Fight for Freedom: At the beginning of colonial slavery in Jamaica, the conversion of the slaves to Christianity was thought to be a bad idea. Farmers worried that Christianity would give rise to the slave's laziness and they would use much of the time they were required to spend working for church activities and even believed that the slaves were not sufficiently intelligent to understand the concept of Christianity.

When the slaves were eventually brought into Christianity, they were forbidden officially from joining the Church of England. The contention was that black people could not be true Christians. The idea that black slaves should not be converted to Christianity ensured the absence of real Christian impact among the slaves until the eventual coming of the Baptist missionaries in 1664.

The Baptist war, which occurred during the Christmas period of 1831, was a crucial step in abolishing slavery in Jamaica. The participating slaves in this rebellion were the members of the Baptist and their fellow Christians in other churches in Jamaica; religion played a vast role in their plans for the revolt. They used the opportunity of their gathering together for fellowship to plan and prepare for their eventual rebellion.

Though slave liberation in Jamaica was eventually decided in the British parliament, it was necessitated in part by the serious slave uprising in the Caribbean Island encouraged by Christian missions.

The sources of the endemic conflicts between the Church and Politics were varied and numerous, but it's not a surprise that it was so. Historically every century seems to have its color of the conflict, but like the teeth and tongue, Church and politics had weathered many storms together.

CHAPTER 3

THE DICHOTOMY WITH
POLITICS- POWER STRUGGLE

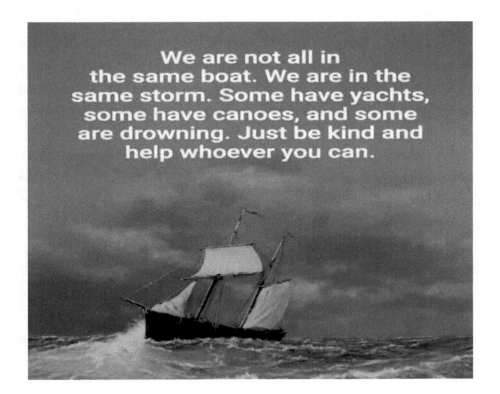

We are not all in the same boat. We are in the same storm. Some have yachts, some have canoes, and some are drowning. Just be kind and help whoever you can.

T he foundation for the division of Church and State was established in the New Testament: "Render unto Cesar those things that are Cesar's and unto God those things that are God's ."This approach was further bolstered by Saint Augustine in his book "The City of God," in which he presumed that "The City of God " is separate from "The City of Man ."The Founding Fathers were sufficiently aware of the narrative of Western Europe in the Middle Ages, which unequivocally illustrated the mischief that can happen when religion is mixed with the government.

Luke 4:5-6 NIV: The devil led him up to a high place and showed him in an instant all the kingdoms of the world. And he said to him, "I will give you all their authority and splendor; it has been given to me, and I can give it to anyone I want to.

"Given unto me," Satan is the God of worldly authority. Any time you have a line of command where one guy dictates to everybody below him what to do, that is a line of command, and Satan is the God of it. Of course, Satan knows enough not to publicize that fact; that's why God set it in the Bible.

The distinction between Church and State is if the Church is organized, the state levies people, and the church requests donations. A church that obeys biblical principles does not have a central power, so it is distinct from a state.

Throughout history, Church and State have not often been separate; not at all. It was common in antique times for the leader of society to have divine approval and be deemed a demi-god chosen by the gods. Even in Renaissance England, the "Divine Right of King's" concept died hard.

It hinges on where you live. In the United Kingdom, there is an established church, and the head of State (the Queen) is the head of the Church of England. There are 26 seats in the House of Lords for Bishops of the Church too. No other denominations are represented in parliament officially.

In the U.K., retaining an official state church for ceremonious purposes has had the outcome of making religion less poisonous and radical than it is in the U.S. because the state churches realize that they have to ceremonially represent everyone, not just members of their congregations. But that would not certainly work everywhere.

However, the impact of the Church has ebbed over the decades for various reasons. So we do not live in a theocracy.

Contrarily, the USA constitutionally prohibits the establishment of the state church. But the Church appears to have an inordinate proportion of political influence. Most of the people are religious, and 40% are extremists who are biblical realists who want the biblical doctrine of creation taught as science in schools.

Iran, for example, is a theocracy. There are religious courts, the president submits to the Ayatollah, and Islamic indoctrination is encouraged.

In addition, a State may decide to provide social insurance, a certain minimum level of education to needy people, as well as insurance against disasters, including (in most countries) sickness.

The goal of churches is to cater to people's inner life, and it still serves a very big function even now. Even proximate non-believers depend on the churches to commemorate the major events in human life, especially marriages and burials. The Church still lives for people who need the hope of eternity or to comprehend the utmost purpose of life, although options exist.

We humans are prone to mental prejudices, a wavering relationship to truth, and struggles when it gets to empathy for others. At its truest, religion prompts us to rummage ourselves and to deal with others the way we want to be treated. But put us in factions, and our tribal disposition emerges; we are the offspring of the ones who annihilated rivaling clans and grabbed their resources. We display our moral capability very differently in a group setting, often abdicating it for group cohesion. Thus, politics and religion are poisonous brews, and history is replete with evidence.

The State has an exclusive right to the use of certain kinds of force, and it is designed to acknowledge the extent to the legitimate use thereof. Every denomination claims ultimate supremacy on the truth but is not designed to admit any threshold to that. Faith admits no limit, and the use of force must do the same to possess any semblance of legitimacy.

There are numerous churches in only one State. Where the realm of the Church is of the Spirit and the conscience, individuals are allowed to align or to find a new congregation. This means the function of the Church is to attend to individuals.

Where the sphere of the Church involves action in the city square or the exercise of political authority or force, individual liberty becomes a secondary consideration, and politics disintegrates into sectarian struggle. Popular disagreements over questions of doctrine like whether or not the wafer and grape juice transmute into the body and flesh of Christ during the Eucharist have been fought over. Human beings have murdered each other over controversies on this issue. History thus educates us that it is best when doctrine remains between a man and his God, rather than between him and his fellow man, through politics.

Because religious sentiment, or non-belief, is such a critical part of every individual's life, freedom of religion affects every person.

State churches that employ government power to benefit themselves and compel their views on individuals of other faiths impair all our civil rights. Moreover, state backing of the Church inclines to make the clergy unaccountable to the people and breeds corruption within religion. Building a wall of separation between Church and State is important in a free society.

The free exercise of conscience is a basic individual right. When we strive to express religion through governmental power, that renders it inevitably a collective expression. When individuals coordinate each other's' beliefs, it involves compelling sectarian will upon that of the contrary individual. These risks twisting liberty into its contrary.

When religion and governance commix, they corrupt one another and become less effective in their several precincts. Put them jointly, and they both become worse.

Where a denomination thinks differently about the law of the land, it inclines to organize its members in the manner of an organized crime syndicate, withstanding the evil laws of the land. Can the free practice of religion be consistent with obedience to the laws? Only when the statutes are composed to the specifications of the faithful and which sect is permitted to enact the law to everyone else.

That religion, or the obligation which we owe to our Creator, and the mode of discharging it, can be instructed only by reason and faith, not by force or chaos; and therefore, all men are equally qualified to the free practice of religion, according to the requirements of conscience; and that it subsists the mutual responsibility of all to practice Christian tolerance, love, and compassion towards each other.

Belief and conscience are certainly individual things; you are independent with your conscience, within your awareness. Your beliefs implicate no one, but your activities can affect others and so should be subject to thresholds that esteem the same privileges you enjoy out of their commitment to respect you.

We are political creatures, and when in groups are prone to jeopardize our morals to align with the group. Our country is built on the premise that we associate with our country as individuals, but party and denomination compose us into groups and beget in us the will to subjugate the other that cannot be harmonized with the virtues of civilization itself except we task religion to solicit to the better elements of our nature. Probably this is what Jesus was referring to when he said to furnish unto Caesar that which is Caesar's and to maintain your affection to God.

There was a period when the significance of the separation of Church and State was comprehended and honored by the churches. Today so many churches have abandoned Christian impartiality and the division of Church and State.

Jesus taught his followers to be no part of the world and made it obvious that they should not be partial to political issues. —John 17:14, 16; 18:36; Mark 12:13-17.

Nominal Christians today reject what Jesus instructed, and not only do they not maintain separation from the world, but they are deeply active in trying to employ political influence to achieve their social agenda. They do not flinch to meddling in politics, they motivate nationalism, they endorse wars, and they try to coerce lawmakers into legislating their beliefs on others. — 1 Corinthians 1:10

The blessing of the State, by a state religious institution, is necessary," wrote the political philosopher Edmund Burke, "to operate with a wholesale awe upon free citizens" because "all persons possessing any portion of power ought to be strongly and impressed with the idea that they act in trust."

In democratic cultures like ours, which provide the people with the power to elect their government, every citizen must completely understand the gravity of their political commitments to guarantee a just and moral commonwealth. For more than a thousand years, the great nations of the West disseminated such gravity with simplicity and vitality from the altars of traditional churches. While some were representative democracies, political organizations that maintained order and administered justice have always depended on the public's common moral consensus in performing their functions. Justice and order cannot be achieved in a culture that does not concur with the meanings of those ideas. A generally proclaimed religion furnished that moral agreement for most of our nation's history.

Religion has long been expelled from the public realm throughout almost every Western country and curtailed to the sphere of individual conscience. The least formal function that religion today plays changes from the de jure institutions in decertified European monarchies like Britain and Monaco that misrepresent the de facto situation of traditional religious commination to the quantity of religiously inundated verbiage in American political language which coats an otherwise secular regime. Religion has always been with us in our history, in our common traditions, and in the churches that fleck our cities; still, one cannot help but think that it is silent in our democratic public life.

The relationship between religion and the State soars large in modern political debate. Yet it is a problem of pressing concern for the Christian, particularly those that live in a secular nation like the United States. America, in various ways, represents a rejection and a reaffirmation of the traditional function of the Church about the public authority. Despite the God or no-God opinions of fathers like Franklin and Jefferson, America was established as a nation of Christians, whose national and moral success relied on the general abidance to long-established requirements of religion and integrity. Yet by definitively prohibiting the official installation of a national church, the constitution foresaw the purging of all religious representation that is obviously or remotely supported by government revenue, a purging that currently plagues our country. If being American truly compels the belief that religion has no function in public and political life, then the faithful Christian cannot, and must not, be a faithful citizen.

The principle of the two swords, which declares that the separate blades of secular and sacred authority together govern man, earned dominance early in Western history and enacted the political and religious hierarchy of pre-Reformation Europe. While extensive disagreement punctuated the development of this theory, most disputants generally inferred that both the government and the Church would be general and companion entities, although the agreement quickly slumped in agreeing on which of the two deserved preeminence. As the fifth-century pontiff, St. Gelasius I, summarized, "There are two powers...by which this world is chiefly ruled, namely, the sacred authority of the priests (auctoritas sacral Pontificum) and the royal power (regalis potestas)." St. Gelasius promoted the clerical auctoritas above the regal potestas but still plainly recognized the distinctness and sovereignty of each of those corresponding jurisdictions. The king, with the public authority, was credited with the management of peoples' actions, while the priests, who are the ambassadors of God, with the administration of peoples' souls. Ideally comprehended, there could be unity between these two blades and their distinct responsibilities, one that would not degenerate into tyranny.

St. Thomas Aquinas enhanced this debate by distinguishing the theocratic State of the Mosaic state ruled by God Himself in the Old Testament from the existing condition of man after the birth and resurrection of Christ. The Hebrew nation of the Old Testament was established upon statutes that God Himself submitted to Moses. The tenets which governed the Hebrews were singularly and undoubtedly religious, a seamless coalition of the secular and sacred. Yet, such harmony could not be likewise attained in the New Testament world, suggested St. Thomas. The Old Law delivered to the Hebrews was concerned with external actions, often controlling through fear of penalty and incentive of reward because redemption could not yet be attained until the gift of Christ. The New statutes of the Gospel were rather promulgated principally upon men's souls and expanded into internal actions. The wiggle of the State, despite its modern benevolence and administrative capacities, is not powerful enough to permeate the inner operations of men's minds and spirits. Thus, such issues must pertain to the jurisdiction of the Church.

Where is the niche for religious authority in contemporary public life? The response, at least for Americans, is very hard. Though it compels individual belief and the individual faith of each of its followers, Christianity hypothecates a community. As Christians, our relationship with God is inseparably linked and related to our relationships with our neighbors. While we are yet a typically Christian nation, America acknowledges no institutionalized dogma; a state-sponsored effort that can be elucidated, however indirectly, as an acceptance of a particular faith has evolved execration constitutionally and is considered an impediment on those with optional beliefs.

But to deduce that public religious manifestations infringe deficiently upon the rights of others suggests that, in a reasonable nation, faith may not count at all in making decisions about political and social issues, a basal undemocratic tenet. Christianity determines our behaviors about ethics, morality, and justice, all of which certainly influence our viewpoints about politics. Faith molds the way we perceive the world and everything in it: to fully divorce our private beliefs from our notion of public policy is to perpetrate fraud of the greatest order. Eradicating all moral assumptions grounded in Christian civilization for suspicion that they are jingoism threatens the concept of factual truth in our political process. A Christian cannot tolerate living within a system that does not differentiate between right and wrong.

The remedy to the crisis of public integrity is not to endorse a theocratic Christian rule. Disorganization, as enunciated in the constitution, can exist side by side with a public affirmation of general moral principles. American Christians must hence affirm and energetically defend the idea that disestablishment does not imply secularism. Christian morality has distinguished and shaped the political establishments which we have inherited and by which we survive to abide. While church attendance goes on to decline in Western countries, the cultural and social inheritance of Christianity stays visible and vibrant. As Christians, we can and still must exercise tolerance toward those with different beliefs; yet patience does not demand that all viewpoints, while equally permitted and expressed, possess an equal stake in the truth.

Before the inception of Christianity, different religious and political arrangements were not clarified in most cultures. People worshipped the deities of the specific State in which they resided, religion in such instances being only a section of the State. But for the Jewish people, the revealed statutes and ordinances of the Scripture comprised the Law of Israel. The Christian idea of the State and the spiritual is based on the words of Jesus: "Give to Caesar what things that are Caesar's, and to God what things that belong to God" (Mark 12:17). Two diverse but not entirely separate aspects of human life and Involvement had to be established; hence, a concept of two powers emerged as the basis of Christian belief and teaching from the initial times.

In the 1st century, the Apostles, who lived under a heathen empire, encouraged respect for and submission to the ruling authorities provided such submission did not infringe on the superior and divine law, which takes preeminence before political jurisdiction. For the Church Fathers that lived in the era when Christianity was adopted as the religion of the State, the emphasis on the preference of the spiritual was stronger. They argued for the sovereignty of the Church and the privilege of the Church to preside over the actions of the temporal ruler.

With the decrease in the power of the Roman Empire in the West, civil administration became the privilege of only the educated class that was available—the churchmen. The Church, which established the only orderly institution, was reduced to the seat of secular as well as sacred power. In the East, the public administrations, centered in Constantinople, were monopolized by the pastoral throughout the Byzantine era.

From the Christians' point of view, the State and Church are distinct though both claim the loyalty of the people. While the State is vested with the political power and authority, the Church is responsible for influencing the individual members of the State to act in ways that engender peaceful co-existence, the rule of law, integrity, and selfless service by the citizens, including the political leaders.

Much of the contradictions between the Church and politics are inherent. The Church and politics are mutually exclusive in organization and mode of operation. Though they have the target audience, their stock in trade differs as well as their objectives.

Matthew 14:3 NIV - Now Herod had arrested John and bound him and put him in prison because of Herodias, his brother Philip's wife.

The dichotomy is inevitable. Otherwise, the Church is not fulfilling its sacred duty of changing how the world thinks and lives.

The relationship between the Church and State (politics) is akin to that of light and darkness, and here the light (Church) is not seasonal or confined to a time band but intentionally unleashed on the darkness for permanent illumination. This darkness has the capacity and choice to fight and resist the influence of the light.

Matthew 10:34 NIV - "Do not suppose that I have come to bring peace to the earth. I did not come to bring peace but a sword.

When someone hears the Gospel and is converted, his / her change in thought and disposition draws the attention of the immediate environment, and in most cases, this is followed by hatred and persecution.

What is surprising with the ugly fate meted out to Christians throughout the Church's history by the state bureaucracy remains the lack of any known offense attributable to them except that they preached Jesus Christ.

The intensity of hatred and animosity visited on the Church by the State leaves the sane mind wondering if they committed a felony. Without any offensive weapons nor any defense mechanism, these helpless and simple fellows were hounded and tortured most times to death or maximum punishment for merely preaching the Gospel.

Apostle Paul stated the obvious when he said that the preaching of the Gospel is an offense to the Jews and foolishness to the Gentiles.

The Offense of the Gospel

What constitutes the offense of the Gospel may be considered as:

1. The Challenge of the Gospel: The Gospel confronts the hearer with unflinching resolve and compelling truth that disarms even the hubris. There are no room to frustrate the truth and no viable argument to vitiate the truth as presented. The Gospel appeals to your conscience and often arrests it for recognizing the ignoble attitudes that were not reckoned with because of the prevalence of sin. The Gospel presents a compelling reality of the awful situation of the present conditions with an open invitation to escape from your obvious damned condition. It is an affront to the inappropriate exercise of freedom and inconsiderate insistence on selfish aggrandizement. The Gospel touches those personal habits and conducts we will rather conceal and protect from the public purview for personal pride and preservation of ego.

The Gospel does not have segregated messages that appeal to the several social, economic, and political strata of the society; it's one message that applies to both the king and his slaves and brings them to sit and eat together - it is a humbling but incredibly relaxing position to be.

2. The audacity of the Gospel: The Gospel is never altered, even in the face of intimidation and danger.

The Acts 26:28-29 NIV - Then Agrippa said to Paul, "Do you think that in such a short time you can persuade me to be a Christian?" Paul replied, "Short time or long —I pray to God that not only you but all who are listening to me today may become what I am, except for these chains."

The Gospel does not refrain from challenging age-old foundations and ancient practices irrespective of the influence they have on society, provided they are accessible. There is no power or institution that the Gospel does not seek to address. There is no outside authority or faculty to which the gospel appeals for its veracity and therefore remains genuinely incontrovertible and is presented as such by the preachers. The gospel preachers always present it with the utmost conviction that what they are saying is absolute truth.

3. Hegemony of the Gospel: When Gospel preachers who on their own have no claim to any strength or inherent special endowment or learning present the life-changing message of the Gospel with passion and dangerous commitment, the high and mighty of the society are reminded of what they went through to establish their authority and to wield power, they often react with scorn and imprudence. The power of the Gospel is not sine qua none with the power of the preacher, its authority is inherent, and that is why its effect can be replicated through the centuries and in diverse environments.

The preacher is a mere messenger who may accurately deliver the message and be a witness to the unfolding effect of the message on the recipients, but if he fails to accurately deliver the message, it will mean that he did not go with the Gospel, but something else and the results will bear witness to his message.

These perceived offenses of the Gospel by the State are parts of the reasons for the struggle. The State, represented by its bureaucracy, is worried that the Church and its doctrine will remove or drastically reduce its hold on power and subordinate them to the Church.

While the Church may not be seeking power and control over the state bureaucracy, she, however, wants to influence the personal lives of both the bureaucracy and the entire population with the message of the Gospel.

The Church does not exist in a vacuum or yet separated from the society and is therefore affected like everyone else by the actions of the State. She invariably must be interested in the politics of the State.

The State should not be wary of the Church or antagonize her; otherwise, the stench of its intrigues will drown the State, and the Church should not seek to grab the political power from the state bureaucracy but concentrate on influencing the personal life of both the leaders and the led.

The popular argument that the Church must get involved in partisan politics to "sanitize the system" is preposterous given the historical antecedents of the Church in politics. The mandate of the Church does not include making the world a better place and transforming the world into heaven on earth.

John 15:19 NIV - If you belonged to the world, it would love you as its own. As it is, you do not belong to the world, but I have chosen you out of the world. That is why the world hates you.

Any rescue diver who forgets his mission to get into the troubled waters may end up being drowned with the drowning man he got in to rescue.

Earlier on, when we considered the historical antecedents of the Church and politics, we saw examples of instances where the head of the Church doubled as the head of State like the papacy; we also saw in England where the emperor was also the head of the Church.

We also saw in Jamaica where the Anglican Church was adopted as the state Church with the constant attendant struggle for power and authority between the Church and the State even when the State was funding the Church. Usurping the political authority of the Church has always adversely affected the Church in the pursuit of her divine mandate and alienated her from the State.

Notwithstanding the early Christian eagerness for the imminent kingdom of God, they acknowledged the pagan State as the custodian of order in the world. Furthermore, Christians are admonished to obey political authorities because they are from God. (Romans 13:1–4).

In 800 A.D, under Charlemagne, the Holy Roman Emperor, the monarchy was restored in the West, and in the 10th century A.D., many temporal rulers held power in all of Europe. An era of political manipulation of the church structure and a general deterioration in clerical fervor and purity brought robust action from several reforming popes, of which the most prominent was Gregory VII.

The subsequent centuries were characterized by an impressive struggle of monarchs and rulers with the popes. In the 12th and 13th centuries, the Pope's power greatly expanded. The 13th century, though, saw the greatest philosopher of the era, St. Thomas Aquinas, influenced by Aristotle, aided in boosting the dignity of the political authority by proclaiming the State a perfect Institution comparable to the other perfect society, which was the Church. The medieval conflict between temporal and sacred power was at its peak during the 14th century when nationalism was vigorously promoted, propelled by the increased fame of lawyers who were both royalists and canon. Various theorists supported the climate of controversy that was responsible for the disaster that finally met the papacy beginning with the eviction of the popes to Avignon influenced by the French authorities and followed by the great division consequence of an attempt to bring back the popes to Rome.

Church discipline was softened, and church dignity deteriorated everywhere in Europe.

Even the attempt at Reformation immediately diminished the power of the Church further. Christianity, with its fractured situation, could not offer any effective resistance to strong emperors, who affirmed spiritual authority for their positions as both heads of Church and State.

John Calvin's insistence on the Church's superiority in Geneva was the only exception of the day. Almost all the Lutheran churches effectively became arms of the State. In England, Henry VIII severed ties with Rome and became the head of the Church of England.

By the 17th century, most people did not believe that a variety of religious beliefs and a church separated from political power was feasible in a unified country. Established religious norms were seen as the primary support for political authority. When the ideas of the variety of beliefs and tolerance of variance began to grow, they were not generally perceived to dispute the idea of the state church. The Puritans, for instance, who escaped religious persecution from England in the 17th century, insisted on rigid adherence to church ideals for the settlers in the American enclaves.

The idea of secular government, as reflected in the First Amendment of the U.S. Constitution, expressed the impact of the "French Enlightenment" on colonial scholars and the particular interests of the conventional churches in conserving their distinct and unique personalities. The Baptists, most especially, believed in the separation of the Church from the political powers as a tenet of their dogma.

In the Jamaican context, the constitution, which was drawn up upon independence in 1962, guarantees religious freedom but eschews the establishment of any religion by the State.

As early back as the 1648 "Treaty of Westphalia," freedom from dominion by the Church has always been seen as a prerequisite for a democratic society. The term "Separation of Church and State."

was popularized by former United States President Thomas Jefferson in an 1802 letter to the Baptists in Connecticut. Thomas Jefferson believed religion was an individual matter, and the Government had no place supporting a specific belief system or restricting the free exercise of belief or non-belief.

Separation of Church and State is an academic idea that defines extent, enabling nationals the liberty to practice any religion of their interest and thereby preventing the nation from officially adopting or supporting any religion in any national agency or parastatals.

Belief in religion and the colonial establishments had a great influence on the law and protection of rights, which are viewed as contrary to popular morality or disruptive of the established order. The retention of certain colonial laws and policies that govern citizenship eternalizes a structure of power, which makes the postcolonial order – supposedly structured on political autonomy empowering the constitution as the ground of citizenship incomplete.

There were no major elements of legislation dealing with issues of gender inequality, reproductive liberties, and sexuality that were passed by or deliberated upon in the houses of parliaments of any Caribbean country like Jamaica without the input of religious institutions. Considering the advancement and popularity of Evangelical ministries, and notwithstanding the growing impact of human rights organizations throughout the region, it is obvious that the Church will continue to exercise considerable influence.

In 2019, the Church and Parliament disputed over legalizing abortion in Jamaica, while Belize and Guyana witnessed landmark cases abolishing laws against sodomy activities and cross-dressing, respectively. These prosecutions and the legislative disputes exposed the complicated interrelationship that exists between religion and constitutional liberties.

Churches and other religious organizations constitute a dominant voice in each of these legislations and have assisted in forming the terms of the conversations, if not defining the outcome. The recent and continuing discussions in respect of laws governing sexuality and abortion, the prominent place of faith, and the constitutional independence suggest that the time for the investigation of these relationships is ripe.

CHAPTER 4

COOPERATION WITH POLITICS

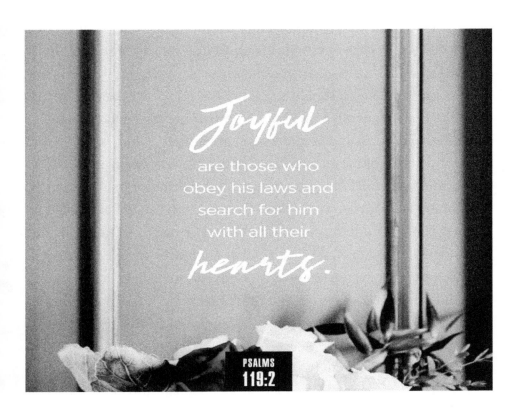

We know that Scripture illustrates several examples and manners for the people of God to associate with the governing authorities. Jesus does not invite his followers to open rebellion, although there are occasions when biblical faithfulness will require civil disobedience to the presiding authorities (Acts 4:1-20). Jesus does not order his followers to obey all ruling authorities blindly, although there are occasions when biblical commitment necessitates obedience (Romans 13:5-6). While declaring that our utmost loyalty is to God, Scripture acknowledges that faithfulness to God compels political involvement by the people of God. The aspect of this involvement is defined by the particular condition and biblical faithfulness. By the Social standards of the Church, we believe that the Government should not undertake to control the Church, nor should the church desire to subjugate the State. The separation of Church and State implies no fundamental union of the two, but it does allow interaction. The Church should continually wield a strong ethical impact upon the State, endorsing policies and programs considered to be just and resisting policies and programs that are unfair.

As we assess the religious defense of the First Amendment of the US Constitution, the unrestricted exercise, and the non-establishment of religion, we are also deeply thankful for the crucial statement issued by the 1968 General Conference on "Church and Government Relations." In acknowledging that debt, we reaffirm the significance of that declaration.

The essential purpose of universal basic education at the primary and secondary levels is to give equal and sufficient educational opportunities for all children and young people and thereby guarantee the nation an enlightened citizenry.

The Church believes in the doctrine of universal basic education, and we revalidate our support of public, academic institutions. At the same time, the Church recognizes and promises our continued commitment to the US constitutional standard that citizens have a right to build and manage private schools from personal resources, provided such schools fulfill public standards of quality. Such schools have created genuine services to society. We do not endorse the development or the empowerment of private schools with public funds. Similarly, we oppose the building or managing of private schools in ways that endanger the public school system or undermine valid public policy.

The Church particularly rejects tuition tax credits, school coupons, or any other means that directly or remotely allows government finances to assist religious schools at the elementary and secondary levels. Persons of one specific faith should be unrestricted to use their money to enhance the belief system of their specific religious group. They should not, however, require all taxpayers, inclusive of those who hold to different religious belief systems, to contribute funds to teach religious beliefs which they do not accept.

To achieve the Government's obligation in education, occasionally, Government and non-governmental educational institutions need to embark on a cooperative relationship. But public funds should be employed only for the best benefit of the whole nation. Drastic caution must be exerted to guarantee that religious institutions do not accept any aid directly or remotely for the sustenance of their religious nature or the development of their institutional facilities. Such funds must be utilized for the express objective of fulfilling a precisely public responsibility and should be liable to public accountability.

By procuring a setting for interaction at an early age between children of extensively different backgrounds, public schools have always been an important uniting force in modern plurality society. We acknowledge, in particular, that persons of every religious experience may have a perception of the nature of absolute reality, which will assist in improving the common life. It is therefore important that the public schools take extremely the religious respectability of each child charged to their care. Public schools may not appropriately establish any selected form of religion for formal exercises of worship, religious ritual, or study. At the same time, however, education should allow the assessment of the numerous religious beliefs of humankind.

We acknowledge that every person has the freedom of education, comprising higher education, proportionate to his or her capacity. Society must encourage every person to appreciate this right. Public and private establishments should cooperate to deliver these educational opportunities.

Freedom of interrogation poses a threat to established opinions, beliefs, programs, and organizations. We accept that threat in the confidence that all existence is of God. Colleges and universities can accomplish their vital missions of expanding knowledge and the understanding of truth in an environment of profound academic freedom.

We assert the principle that liberty to inquire, to communicate, and teachers should be supervised by the continence of scholarship and the significant examination of intentions in the setting of free public conversation, instead of by censorship by administrators, school committees, or any control compelled by churches, governments, or other associations. In the academic process, people have the freedom to appropriate voluntarily for themselves what they think is real, valuable, useful, and fulfilling.

Experience has illustrated that freedom to interrogate, discuss, and teach is best protected when schools and universities are not pendants upon a single source or a few sources of assistance. When an educational organization relies upon multiple streams of financial support, and where those streams tend to counteract one another, the organization is in a stance to resist unfair pressures toward control exercised from any one source of assistance. In the case of church-associated schools and universities, we think that tuitions fees; scholarships; investment incomes; bequests; payments for services provided; loans; government donations; and souvenirs from individuals, business enterprises, institutes, and churches should be pursued and received in as great a mixture as possible. Care must be used to ensure that all assistance from any of these streams is free from attachments that impede the school or university in the sustenance of freedom of interrogation and expression for its personnel and students.

The Church is very much conscious of the dangers of church-sponsored schools and universities being overly pendant upon government funding. But we are also conscious that given the autonomy thought of most school students today, there is little threat of using the government resources to indoctrinate scholars with religious beliefs. Therefore, tertiary institutions should feel free to accept government funds unless for religious instruction and edifices for worship. Also, they should always take cognizant of the threats of simultaneous government oversight that might endanger the religious environment or unique independent identity of church-sponsored academic institutions.

No church-sponsored tertiary institution should become such a pendant upon government awards, research grants, or support programs that its academic liberty is jeopardized, its commitment to social critique, including a critique of governments, inhibited, or its spiritual significance denied.

We understand that the freedom essential to the existence of a school or university in the elegant sense may be jeopardized by forces other than those implicated in the nature and origin of the institution's financial assistance. Institutional independence may be adversely impacted by governmental requirements of allegiance oaths from instructors and students, by public encumbrance, by the unrestricted flow of information, or by approbation and certification protocols and requirements intended for dictating the content of school and university curricula.

Concerning church-related institutions of higher learning, we deplore any ecclesiastical attempts to manipulate the dissemination of knowledge or inquiry, to use the academic community for the promotion of any specific point of view, to demand ecclesiastical loyalty oaths designed to protect some cherished truth claims or inhibit the social action activities of the academic community members. We call upon all members of The United Methodist Church, in whatever capacity they may serve, to be especially sensitive to the need to protect individual and institutional freedom and responsibility in the context of the academic community.

We are persuaded that there may be events and conditions in which the conventional forms of tax immunities awarded to schools and universities may be a prerequisite for their freedom. Therefore, we advise a continuation of the public scheme of granting sufficient and nondiscriminatory tax exemptions to all private schools and universities, including those that are connected to churches.

We reckon that schools and universities should assess the benefits, services, and protections that they obtain from the nation and its governmental agents and should evaluate their responsibilities to the community in the view of this support. We believe all church-sponsored institutions of higher learning must discern on their drive what help, services, and reliefs they ought to procure for the whole community, as different from their normal campus constituencies.

We acknowledge that governments realize the unique classification of religious institutions. To be in this distinct category is not freedom held by these establishments for their advantage or self-glorification but is an appreciation of their special personality designed to safeguard their independence and to help them to serve humankind in a manner not required of other categories of institutions.

We exhort churches to assess at least the subsequent factors in defining their response to the granting of protection from property taxes:

1. Responsibility to make applicable contributions for important services provided by the Government; and
2. The threat that churches become so pendant upon a government that they jeopardize their integrity or fail to exercise their critical impact upon public policy.

We believe that all the organizations and resources of the private sector, as well as those of governments, should be taken into account in the formulation and execution of social welfare policies.

We recognize that applicable government bodies have the liberty to specify minimum standards for every public and personal social welfare agency. We think that no private agent, because of its religious partnerships, ought to be excused from any of the regulations of such standards.

Governmental provision of physical assistance for church-related agencies necessarily raises critical questions for the religious institution. In recognition, however, that various health, education, and welfare institutions have been established by churches without respect to religious conversion, we suppose that such agencies may, under particular circumstances, be reasonable channels for public agendas in these fields. When the government assists in programs operated by private agencies, it has a vastly serious commitment to establish and implement standards guaranteeing the fair administration of such policies and the responsibility of such agencies to the civil authority.

In particular, we reckon that government funds should not be given to any church-related organization unless it fulfills the following minimal criteria:

- The services to be delivered by the church-related organization shall meet a legitimate community need.
- The services of the organization shall be developed and operated in such a manner as to avoid performing a sectarian purpose or agenda.
- The duties to be provided by the organization shall be accessible to all persons without prejudice to race, color, nationality, creed, or political cogency.
- The services to be provided by the organization shall be executed by established professional and administrative standards.
- Ability, competence, and honesty in the accomplishment of duties shall be the principal references in the employment of workers and shall not be supplanted by any condition of religious affiliation.

The Church recognizes that all of the integrity involved in the auspices of a social welfare mechanism by a church may not be completely expressed if that mechanism has to rely perpetually on access to government help for its existence. We are also mindful that under certain situations, the auspices of a social welfare mechanism by a church may hinder the development of extensive welfare assistance in the community.

Accordingly, the Church and the mechanism should choose which form of service to offer:

1. Channeling standardized and established services supplied or funded by the Government, or

2. Undertaking experimental or uncommon ministries and chastising government programs when they are inadequate.

We think that these two ways are difficult, if not absurd, to combine in the same mechanism and that the option between them should be created before reliance upon government resources renders an affirmation of the first way irreversible. In their endeavors to meet human needs, churches should never permit their preoccupation with therapeutic programs under their guidance to distract them or the bigger community from a mutual search for fundamental solutions. In handling the elimination of the situations of poverty and starvation, churches should have no interest in programs that partake in facilitating dependency or embody behaviors and practices that neglect to promote self-sufficiency.

We think that churches have an ethical responsibility to challenge infringements of the civil rights of the underprivileged and marginalized. They should direct their endeavors toward assisting the poor to overcome the hamstrung that makes such infringements of civil rights possible. Precisely, churches should dispute such policies and policies by welfare workers as unwarranted aggression of privacy and reject any requirement of attending church activities to entitle them to social services.

The Church also recognizes that churches live within the body polity, along with several other forms of human organization. Like other social institutions, their existence impacts and is impacted by governments. We reckon that churches have the freedom and the duty to converse and operate corporately on those issues of public policy that affect basic moral or spiritual issues and concerns. Any idea of, or action respecting, church-government relations that prohibits churches from this function in the body polity hits at the very foundation of religious liberty.

The endeavor to influence the construction and implementation of public policy at every tier of Government is always the most valuable means available to churches to maintain before humanity the standard of a society in which strength and order are compelled to serve the horizons of justice and liberty for all people. Through such social activity, churches generate new ideas, question certain goals and strategies, and help alter the emphasis on specific values in ways that promote the adoption and execution of specific policies and projects that promote the goals of a credible society.

We assume that any effort that would prohibit the Church the right to operate corporately on public policy topics threatens religious freedom. We, therefore, reject the inclusion of churches in any lobby exposure legislation.

This doesn't imply, in any manner, that we want to hide activities carried out by the Church on public matters. On the opposite, we are usually delighted by such actions. It does acknowledge, however, that the Church is already reacting to members who demand information concerning church activity on public policy topics. In effect, by legislation passed by the 1976 General Conference, the Church already has its lobby exposure requirements in place.

It is entirely another matter, still, for the Government to contend that it must learn everything concerning what a church is telling in its communications with its members.

In its most strict form, regulation such as this would hinder our unrestricted exercise of religion. It would be difficult for the Church to kowtow to certain provisions, thus exposing our church authorities to criminal liabilities.

We reckon that churches must conduct responsibly in the field of public affairs. A responsible attitude requires adherence to morally sound considerable and procedural criteria.

Churches should strive to enlarge and elucidate the ethical basis of public discourse and single out and distinguish the foreseeable outcomes of accessible options of public policy.

In partaking in the field of public affairs, churches are not naturally superior to other players; hence the positions that they assume on specific issues of public policy are not beyond question or criticism.

A credible attitude in the field of public affairs compels churches to recognize the fact that in dealing with complicated issues of public policy, good motives and high standards need to be blended with as much empirical and technical understanding of politics and economics as feasible.

Another criterion of responsible behavior arises from the reality that no specific public policy that may be ratified by churches at a given juncture in time should be considered as an ultimate representation of Christian morals in society. Churches should not infer that any particular social structure, political order, or economic philosophy represents a complete epitome of the Christian ethic.

When churches discuss with the Government, they also accept the obligation to discuss with their members. Cultivation of morally informed public impression is particularly critical in local congregations. It is important for the responsible attitude that procedures be ascertained and maintained to secure full, frank, and knowledgeable discussion by religious committees within the field of public affairs. In the present interval of human history, vigilance should be lent to the prestige of every person, and a plea should be rendered to the consciences of every person. Churches must concede and respect the position of the laity and the clergy in defining their attitude on the scene of public affairs.

The synergy between Church and State has become increasingly inevitable as progress is made in human development and economic cooperation. Religion has come to be fully integrated into the political spectrum and plays a considerable role in the overall quality of legislative and economic cooperation.

While the age-long struggle for supremacy between the Church and, later on, religion as a whole is still prevalent in varying degrees across the nations, the ability of any state to reach a workable compromise between the two determines the level o peace and religious harmony that will reign in that jurisdiction.

The most advanced countries seem to have achieved more harmonious cooperation with the Church than the developing and third world countries. It's like the more enlightened the population, the better cooperation with the components of society like the Church.

In some cases, the Church is also very sensitive to its relationship with the State and other members of the society and deliberately takes actions that engender peace. Most states also are less antagonistic of the Church and no longer seek the dominance of the Church but her maximum cooperation in both legislative and economic matters.

The State and Church seem to have learned their lessons from the bitter experience of the past and have come to realize that in all ensuring conflicts between them, the line of demarcation is always very thin. In most scenarios, there is a double identity for the central actors; the Emperor, for instance, who is prosecuting the war against the Church, may himself be a member may be of another denomination of the Church, or his close family members belong to the Church.

Cooperation between the Church and State will be greatly enhanced and mutually beneficial if each is recognized and limited to the boundary of influence. Members of the Church are citizens of the State and will be affected by the state policies while the State stands to make meaningful progress in the peaceful atmosphere created by the activities of the Church when allowed to operate unhindered.

The Benefits of Cooperation Between the Church and State

1. **Church Registration:** In most democratic environments, the Church is registered as non-profit, non-governmental, and therefore exempted from the payment of corporate tax and other levies. This has helped the Church to conserve financial resources to pursue her growth and infrastructural requirements with relative ease.

2. **Taxation:** Today, no doubt generates a tremendous amount of money that is capable of generating enormous revenue for the State if taxed. However, individual employees of the Church in most climes are required to pay their personal income tax to the State.

3. **Infrastructural Development by the Church**: The Church continues to provide strategic infrastructure like roads, bridges, and portable water supply to places hitherto without such amenities. Comparable to the State's allocations for the same purpose and sometimes even more. The most enduring physical legacy of the Church to the State remains the tremendous investments in schools and education all over the world. From Oxford, Cambridge, Harvard, and innumerable primary, secondary and tertiary institutions, the interests of the Church in human capital development from her inception.

4. **Church's Timeless Message:** The impact of the Gospel on the lives of people remains invaluable. This impact saves the State

from chaos and anarchy. While the State builds prisons and reform centers, the Church mitigates crime and criminality by the message of salvation. The Gospel remains the greatest character reformer and regulator. Imbibing the message of the Gospel reduces the crime rate and improves productivity and wealth creation.

5. **Social Re-orientation**: The State relies heavily on the Church in disseminating information on its social re-orientation programs like the issues of girls' child rights, sexuality, and gender equality. In most cases, the Church is at the center stage of championing the campaigns. The Church as a social crusader also weighs in on any state policy that is repugnant to equity, justice, and fairness, like the Church's position on abortion and child labor.

6. **It enables decisions to be made based on experience rather than perspective:** One of the attributes of personal faith, irrespective of the name, creed, and scope, is that it originates from a personal perspective. Anyone can choose to believe what is right from their point of view. But from a general standpoint, the personal perspectives cannot represent the collective interest in such matters. Opinions may differ in specific considerations, even among those with a common faith, by the separation of personal perspective as in the Church from real-life experiences of governance; society benefits by having both.

7. **It separates capability from the claim of divine right**: In the past, some rulers came to political leadership based on their claim to the divine right to power from God. There are still rulers and politicians making such claims today, the only difference between now and then being the separation factor. All the claims to the divine mandate can be spurious and misleading, and open

to manipulation. By separating State and Church in the political process, it becomes easier to elect people based on their known integrity and capability rather than on their claims to divine selection.

8. **It shields the Church from getting involved in political governance**: In administrations where the Church is entangled with the State, there is often the need to first seek the opinion of the Church before certain laws and policies can be implemented. And If the Church thinks the action is against its ethos or immoral, like requiring companies to fund birth control services and programs through health insurance, the Government could be rendered ineffective in this regard by the actions of the Church. But with the separation and autonomy of both Church and State, each can pursue its objectives unhindered. This enables the Government to concentrate on the physical body while the Church's attention is on the soul.

9. **It promotes personal choice:** Without separating the Church from the State, there is the tendency of the Government to dictate which religion someone can practice. Rival religions in the State could be fully banned or discriminated against. Separating these two authorities ensures that everyone has the liberty to pursue any faith of their choice instead of being dictated to. It also frees people who prefer not to belong to any religion or have religious faith.

10. **It curtails the Government and the Church's undue influence on families**: Without separating the powers of the Church and that of the State, schools could indoctrinate pupils into a "national religion," and households would not be able to stop it. Jobs in government establishments could be exclusively

preserved and offered only to candidates from the state religion. Even when other religions are allowed to operate, they might not enjoy the same rights and privileges. With the separation of powers between the State and Church, the citizens and families can make their choices when it comes to faith.

11. **Cooperation encourages discussion**: People will often be different from each other. They are the things that make us different and make us stronger. By separating the Church and State, we create the need for discussion, listening, and deeper cooperation. When that can be done successfully, we learn and grow as a society.

The cooperation between the Church and State is needed for the benefit of all and the overall achievement of their separate mandates.

The following are some of the demerits of the separation between State and Church:

1. **Separation establishes limitations for both**: When the Church and State are separated, both are restricted in the extent of what they can handle, and some people exploit the benefit of the positive impacts provided by both sides to create a unique life for themselves. The Church's core mandate remains to influence society with moral rectitude, and peaceful co-existence relieves the State of the burden of educating the public on social and moral responsibility. With the separation, religious education is not mandatory or implemented, which could affect the daily lives of the nation.

2. **The State can take undue advantage of the separation:** The Church not being involved in the lawmaking process can impact negatively on the State. For instance, if a group of leaders

determines to pass unfair laws that promote division, hatred, or other vices among the citizens, the absence of the Church's positive influence on the legislative process will mean that such laws will be passed without hindrance and the society will be the worse for it.

3. **Churches can benefit from the separation:** Churches can as well take undue advantage of the alienation between them and the Government by encouraging their members not to support the Government and its policies or to revolt against it. The Church can be employed to create a crisis within the community between people of one religion and others who hold a different view. As incitement emanates from the Church, followers will believe that they are "right" while others are "wrong," thereby justifying their need to perpetuate negative actions or even atrocities.

4. **It can restrict personal liberties:** Several people in the United States get employment through some aspect of a government agency at local, state, or federal levels. This ranges from teaching in a public school to becoming a federal contractor. The employment may be different. However, the attitude to faith remains still the same. If the worker is working as a government agent, then they cannot work equally as religious representatives. The separation compels the worker to decide where their allegiances are.

5. **The establishment clause may not be construed as a real separation:** In the United States, the judiciary has ruled numerous times that the establishment clause in the Constitution's First Amendment is a feasible alienation of Church and State. Some have argued that at the time the constitution was composed, the original objective of the establishment clause was extremely different. The purpose was to safeguard the Church from the

Government and not to separate it from the Government. There is no obvious wording in the constitution that authorizes a precise separation between the two establishments.

The advantages and disadvantages in respect of separating the Church and State will continue to be controversial at a certain level. By paying attention to each key point of its merit, we create the opportunity of building an egalitarian society for all people, faiths, and perspectives.

The struggle between the Church is not necessary or beneficial because they both have the overall interest of the society at the center of their respective objectives. They must strike a balance by respecting the principles of power separation as provided by most constitutional democracies.

The balance should be that the State stays out of or withdraw from direct involvement in religious affairs, including the Church but provide an enabling environment for every law-abiding citizen to join and practice any religion of their choice without let or hindrance.

The cooperation between the Church and State will be in the highest interest of both of them because they both need each other to function effectively and fulfill the purpose of their existence.

All through the centuries, there has been a topsy-turvy relationship between the State and the Church, but progressively great achievements have been recorded toward what is the ideal Church/state healthy relationship. I believe that both Church and State have at least accepted the reality of co-existing and will continue to work even harder to achieve a more peaceful and mutually beneficial environment.

The ideal situation will continue to be in perspective and will vary depending on the historical antecedents, culture, and evolving system of Government obtainable in the society.

CHAPTER 5

THE INFLUENCE OF POLITICS ON THE CHURCH

Patience is not
an ability
to wait,
but the ability
to keep a good
attitude while
waiting.

LIFEQUOTES101.ONLINE

The Church was established by the Lord Jesus Christ with her members drawn from the State and had existed amid the State and had grown and will continue to grow by drawing people from the State until the consummation of the world.

During the early days of the Church, when the individual members were apolitical due to their belief in the imminent return of the Lord Jesus Christ for the rapture, the Church and the State were so separated that they became acrimonious, especially from the State.

As we read in the previous chapters, when the waiting for the rapture began to be prolonged and with the massive evangelization and conversion of more people, political influence and cooperation with the State became inevitable.

Since It is said that man is a political animal, all the members of the Church are therefore political creatures first and foremost and will necessarily exhibit politics no matter how remotely.

The influence of politics on the Church can be divided into two categories as follows:

1. **Inherent Political Influence**: This is comprised of the diverse personal political influences brought into the Church by the respective individuals who are converted into the Church. Although they are converted, they, however, come with their political ideology or inclinations because they are political animals. They may be inclined to subdue as much as possible this political side of their being for Christ's sake, but as long as they are politically conscious, their inclinations will continue to manifest even if minimally.

The inherent political influence on the Church has been boosted by the separation of the Church as an organized body from politics because since the Church as a body does not involve in politics, the individual members of the Church are free to exercise their political inclinations.

Secondly, as the population of the Church grew, there was the need for a form of governance structure to cater to the ever-growing population, and since the members came with political knowledge, the Church quickly drew inspiration from them to set up her administrative hierarchy.

2. **External Political Influence on the Church:** The most contending influence the Church has so far experienced is the external political influence. The first reaction of the State to the Church was as a dreadful foe that must be annihilated, and that set the tone for the rancorous relationship between the two during the first few centuries of the Church.

The State's influence on the Church has been both negative and positive over the years, and some of them are:

1. Accumulation of Wealth: The Church at inception was contented in just meeting the basic daily needs of its members while they waited for the return of the Lord Jesus in glory. However, as time progressed, the Church began to settle down to the reality of the situation and started accumulating wealth and making financial investments. Though most of the Church's investment in education was initially offered to the public for free, they were later commercialized.

Through the years, the Church has been involved in commercial enterprises and accumulated tremendous wealth, and become very rich financially. Today, the Church is competing with the State in wealth creation, and the overall opinion is that the contemporary Church has lost most of its core spiritual values because of its quest for money.

2. Dearth of Spiritual Fervency: The resigned Pope Francis once said, " the Church today can neither silver and gold have I not nor in the name of Jesus Christ of Nazareth rise and walk" this is a serious indictment of the Church concerning her unbridled pursuit of wealth at the expense of her traditional spiritual heritage.

The Church now measures her achievements and well-being in monetary value like the State. "You cannot serve God and money," Jesus told the Church, but the Church seems to have found the right way around that divine injunction to her hurt.

3. Undue Competition with the World: Church leaders are competing with the political leaders in affluence and wealth accumulation to the detriment of the Church, and members of the Church are being influenced by the leadership to pursue a life of affluence at the expense of their spiritual lives.

The line between the sacred and profane is becoming thinner by the day in the Church due to the influence of the State, where almost every consideration is money-induced.

4. Politicking in the Church: Tribal, racial, educational, and financial considerations have found their way into the Church and are influencing decisions rather than prayers and the Holy Spirit. Promotions and postings in many big congregations are contentious and politicized, and that has given rise to breakaway factions and more new congregations springing up and competing for space and relevance.

Politics in the Church is assuming dangerous proportions in many cases; factions like in a political party are emerging from some congregations and threatening the life of the Church and its members alike. Some leaders in the Church are deliberately importing the intrigues of political party politics into the Church for selfish reasons.

5. Instability in the Church Hierarchy: The Church has inherited from the State the same measure of political instability that is rocking the nations of the world. From instability in leadership to structural instability that is responsible for frequent changes in Government and policies and agitations for self-rule. The Church is copying the greed for power and the schemes that are commonly used in the Government to secure power.

6. Imperialistic Tendencies: *Matthew 18:4 NIV - Therefore, whoever takes the lowly position of this child is the greatest in the kingdom of Heaven.*

Matthew 20:25- 26 NIV: Jesus called them together and said, "You know that the rulers of the Gentiles lord it over them, and their high officials exercise authority over them. Not so with you. Instead, whoever wants to become great among you must be your servant.

These words of Jesus Christ have completely lost their meaning to the Church leadership of these days, who insist on being served first and on enjoying the same privileges as the political oligarchs. Most of the Church leaders see the Church as their enclaves and administer it as personal estates.

7. Capitalism: The State has influenced the Church into adopting free-market/capitalist regimes like privatization and commercialization of economic processes, thereby reducing her original missionary work outlook drastically. Even most of the educational facilities owned by the Church are competing in cost with non-mission schools, and the same goes for health care and other essential social amenities provided by the Church.

In Jamaica, with a strong Christian background and the highest number of Churches per square mile, the political influence of the State on the Church is higher than in countries with a less Christian heritage.

How influential are Jamaican churches and their leaders over the affairs of the State, and is it commensurate to their numerical strength when it comes to controversial issues, like LGBT rights, being promoted by global trends and influential interest groups?

There exist at least two explanations for the Church's dearth of proportionate influence in Jamaica. The first reason is the misuse of the very thing that provides the Church with its strength. Jamaica is known to have the highest number of churches in the world per square mile, but it is a disunited body. The Jamaica Umbrella body of Churches, which claims to speak for more than 90 percent of conventional Christian membership on this isle, has failed to significantly leverage this power of numerical strength to impact government policy towards making the judicial practice more equitable or the economy further inclusive which two issues that immediately affect their church members on the pews.

Secondly, the Church disengaged from the aisles of power and possible influence. When pastors converse publicly on the electronic media or write in newspapers, they always major on limited religious topics rather than on economic, civil, or political ones. Apart from saying beginning prayers or blessing the dinner, pastors are rarely seen attending events in government, diplomatic, or corporate circles. It is an aberration to see priests on the golf arena, at flashy corporate events, at poolside celebrations in glitzy homes overlooking the borough, or on the cocktail course, and these are the places where the influencers hobnob, socialize, and define the course of prospective events before even they get deliberated on in the house of parliament.

Jamaican pastors, given what engages their time and where they prefer to expend their time seem to be very good at heeding the biblical injunction to "come out from among them. "It is little wonder that the July 2017 Bill Johnson survey found out that only 26 percent of the surveyed population indicated they could depend on the Church to inform them what was going on in the events of the country.

In 2006 the Centre of Leadership and Governance, The University of the West Indies, Mona, did a survey and discovered that the Church is near the top in the pecking order — below educational institutions and the family as the organization in which Jamaicans trusted the most. The low rating of the Church's impact on the affairs of the State is in the context of the Church existing as the biggest, most widely distributed, and believed membership body.

Compare the impact of the Church in Jamaican politics to the impact of the Church in the United States, where the constitution delineates a line of separation between the Church and State. In 1979 Southern Baptist preacher Jerry Falwell, together with Christian fundamentalists, dissatisfied with America's dwindling values, established the Moral Majority, which is a right-of-center campaign intended to grant conservative Christians tremendous influence in America's political life. Since its inception, the movement has influenced a key role in the election of every Republican president. Donald Trump's checkered presidency was sustained largely by the strong backing of evangelicals. Rev Robert Jeffress is the chairman of the president's Advisory Evangelical Board. The evangelical stance in the Israeli relationship is a key element behind the president's determination to move the American diplomatic base to Jerusalem. Jeffries, together with another equally conservative evangelical pastor, John Hagee, constitute the president's envoys at the commencement of the contested new embassy on May 14, 2018. That's influence!

Any personal relationship between the clergy and politicians where it does occur is always one of convenience. Politicians have something vital to the clergy, which is the influence on the matters of the State. And the clergy has something that politicians want, which is influence on votes during elections.

David Kuo, a pious Christian who was the next in command in President George W Bush's Office of Faith-Based and Community Initiatives, in his book Tempting Faith — An inside story of political temptation, speaks of the sometimes avaricious but crucial relationship between politics and religion: All through the nearly 20 years interest in politics, I have noticed the tender lure of respected Christian leaders including their supporters by politicians singed for votes but indifferent about these Christians and their faith. On the one hand, this shouldn't be startling; because politicians are always about wooing or enticing voters for them to win elections. On the other hand, Christian authorities are presumed to be considering Jesus above and beyond things. Rather, it's like they assume that political superiority is the most significant thing in lifting the Christian agenda.

The classic example of the lack of influence or commensurate influence of the Jamaican Church is the debate about horse racing on Sundays, which has shifted from the domain of the Church and racing tracks to every street and institution of higher education as Jamaica wrestles with the idea and reality of separating the Church and Government.

The Church forcefully denounces the idea of Sunday horseracing. However, the followers of horseracing, together with non- Churchgoers in general, are pointing out that the Church's view should not certainly prevail over what the Government recognizes as economically beneficial to the nation. Since the start of the debate, discussion on the separation of Church and State has assumed a renewed life on the streets, the Universities, and the Church. If the Church influences policy formulation, she would have been contacted or taken into consideration when such policy was at its incubating stage.

The lack of unity among the various Christian organizations is responsible for the low level of influence and the vulnerability of the Church to neglect and marginalization by the State.

The non-religious groups are clamoring that the Church should accept the back seat when it comes to politics, while the Church speaking through her various ecumenical associations are insistent on salvaging the moral decadence which she says is the outcome of the extensive secularism.

Yet Jamaica is confronting a mockery or contradiction because in this characteristic Christian nation, with the greatest number of churches in every square mile of the world the over and where almost every public function begins with prayers and Bible reading, one of the most current hot topics in the mouth of every adult is the separation of the Church and the nation. Or, more succinctly put, it's a debate on what function the Church should maintain in Jamaica's democratic process.

The debate in favor of separating the Church and the State in Jamaica believes that personal liberty and independence from state dictatorship is the bedrock standard of any real democracy. Freedom of opinion, expression, and religion is a basic democratic and human right. Therefore, if Jamaica hopes to deem itself a democratic society, then religious liberty will mean that religious and moral principles are the exclusive primacy of the individual. Civil engagements should not be overly influenced or steered by the Church's point of view, and the Church should recede from its previously lawfully enshrined lofty heights and submit itself to being merely one of the several interested parties in the public domain.

On the opposite, the proponents of the freedom of the Church to be neutral in public discourse adduced the issue that traditionally, Jamaica remains a Christian country. This view is buttressed by reference to the number of churches in every square mile, including the remark that the preponderance of Jamaicans is adherents of Christianity or at the least nominal believers in God. The moral decadence and social ills which affect Jamaican reality are given as the direct outcome of a departure from the venerated Christian tenets, morals, and decency.

There is nothing ambivalent on this issue of separating the Church and State. I think the moral conscience that the Church contributes is very crucial, and I have serious suspicions about the action of some people to silence this critical voice. Nevertheless, I am equally certain that beliefs, especially Christianity, should not be legislated and be left to personal freedom of choice.

Jamaica is a constitutional democratic society that guarantees the right of its citizens to make their own choices within the boundaries of the law. Therefore, I do think the position of the Church in the nation should be to ensure it puts ahead its views on all matters. But the Church should not dominate the legislative process but be one of the several significant voices in the public domain.

We must not lose sight of the very bedrock of democracy which is the dominant force of the majority, and if Jamaica has more than 90 percent of her population as Christians and given her historical Christian background, why would anyone discountenance this factor. The implications of this dominant Christian force in the State include having the majority of the state bureaucrats as Christians, and invariably their inclinations, in general, should be obvious.

It is unfair, undemocratic, and grave injustice to contemplate the idea of denying the Church her due dominant position in the political life of Jamaica, and the State will be the best for a Jamaica that is well-influenced in legislation and policy formulation by the ideals of an overwhelming majority of over 90 percent.

CHAPTER 6

THE CONTENTIONS BETWEEN
CHURCH AND POLITICS

We often hear,
"Life is short... better
enjoy it"!

How about,
"Eternity is long, better
prepare for it"!

T he phrase 'Church and State' is always used to represent the alliances between religious institutions and their leaders on the one part and temporal administration on the other.

The Church and State should ordinarily be partners in progress and complementary to each other, being that their common objectives, if honestly defined, are similar. While the Church's emphasis on the teaching of the word of God for character reformation is important to the citizens, which include the state oligarchs, the State also, in pursuit of democratic ethos, is committed to physical protection and well-being of the citizens. In many cases, like in Jamaica, where an overwhelming majority of the population are Christians which implies that the state bureaucracy will also be dominated by Christians. When we talk about the State and the Church, we are invariably referring to the same set of people.

Yet, in reality, there is competition and, most times, a very unhealthy one between the two, which sometimes leads to subterfuge and intrigue from both parties to either maintain the status quo when it is favorable or to offset the system to its favor.

The contentious issues between the Church and the State are many and varied, which include:

1. Suspicion: There is mutual skepticism about the enormous influence each one is having on the populace. The State, for instance, is afraid that the Church hierarchy can be used to subvert the State and its policies or deny the ruling party votes. The State is also afraid that the Church can be used to oppose its policies and programs, thereby making it ineffective.

On the other hand, the Church sometimes sees the Government as an ungodly representative of evil and, therefore, must be avoided, especially when the Government is not popular with the masses due to bad governance. The Church as a pious body is most times afraid of being contaminated by the usual clandestine corrupt tendencies of political bureaucracy.

2. Basic Philosophy: There is an intrinsic propensity for conflict between the State and the Church emanating from their different ideological inclinations. While the Church's ultimate belief is the destruction of the world by God at the culmination of things and they're then going to Heaven to live, the political authorities are more interested in pursuing a more peaceful and prosperous nation. So, the conflicting long-term perspectives on the future are a veritable source of enduring conflict.

The State sees the Church as anti-development and parochial, whose ideology is capable of sabotaging its common ideals and creating an infamous impression of Government in the minds of the Church members.

The Church on her own gives the impression of less concern with the affairs of Government since she is a pilgrim with no permanent interest and possessions in the nation that warrants hobnobbing with perceived obnoxious rulers with earthly mindsets.

3. Economic status of the Church: In some countries, churches are required to be duly registered as business entities and are subjected to corporation tax payment. They are further required to submit their financial statements for tax assessment while property tax Is imposed on Church buildings and other structures owned by the Church.

Any attempt to regulate the Church and her activities by the State in whatever form is a potential source of conflict and discontent.

The Church is not in the business of generating income like a normal business entity and, as such, must be distinguished from profit-oriented enterprises and allowed to operate as a non-profit, non-governmental organization and be registered for identification.

Jamaica, like other Caribbean countries, is in several ways a site of opposition to and controversy over religion, the colonial power, and the cultural and the universal constitutional rule propagated by the West. Given its record of efficient survival and battle for full liberation, made crucial by the transatlantic slave business and coming into contact with Europe, Africa, and different peoples in America, the Caribbean countries can be declared to constitute a complicated and contradictory interaction of ethnical, constitutional, political and sacred personalities. These are displayed in the relationship that exists between constitution and religion or between the Church and Government, including between the colonial and sovereign establishments of law and politics. The intricacy of these relationships furthermore reveals itself in the current civic and legal consequences in the Caribbean countries and difficulties that have attended the attempts to create modifications in the social and justice system.

Confidence in colonial institutions and religion has impacted the law, and the preservation of rights that are perceived as opposed to conventional morality or that disrupted the established order. The retention of certain colonial laws and procedures that govern citizenship eternalizes a structure of power, which has made the postcolonial order which was purportedly established on political sovereignty and the constitution as the ground of citizenship, incomplete.

In Jamaica, the Government went on to order a nondenominational religious school curriculum in all schools and funded public events to facilitate interfaith engagement and appreciation for religious diversity. It similarly took steps towards paying people from a trust account it created in 2017 for casualties of the 1963 Coral Gardens event, which claimed the lives of eight persons and hundreds wounded in clashes involving a Rastafarian farming neighborhood and security forces.

The Seventh-day Adventists Church members continued to report that they had a limited capacity to secure employment just because of their tradition of observing the Saturday Sabbath. Local news media went on to provide an outlet for religious dialogue, which is open to partakers from all religious organizations.

Furthermore, regardless of incorporation stature, religious groups pursuing tax-exemption status must be registered as charities. To be deemed a charity, an association must apply either to the Ministry of Industry through the Department of Co-operatives and Friendly Societies, located in the Ministry of Industry, Commerce, Agriculture, and Fisheries, or to the Companies Office. Upon registration, groups will as well submit their registration to the Jamaica Customs Agency in the Ministry of Finance and the Public Service and apply formally to the Tax Administration Agency of Jamaica in other to be evaluated for tax-free status.

While Christians are expected to be the biggest agents of peace, it is an irony that there exists so much dispute between other faiths and Christianity, or even within Christian denominations. The recent report of demoting the head girl at St Hilda's in St Ann simply because of her alleged religious beliefs, as she was supposed to be of the Jehovah's Witness, is very vicious. And to think that this could arise in Jamaica in 2015 is better imagined.

What is more malicious is that the academy is owned by a denomination that claims to be a Christian organization. But also, there is such an extensive religious confrontation around the world, with people being killed and properties destroyed by others who claim to believe in God. However, this is cannot a justification for abandoning religion. If the culprits in the churches and different religions were denied the opportunity, they might be more dangerous, and there would be less peace than we have presently.

In the report on ecumenism of the Second Vatican Council -- the 21st main Council of the Roman Catholic Church and the second to take place at the Vatican -- Roman Catholics were persuaded to work with the things that unite us with others and de-emphasize what divides us. While Jehovah's Witness adherents do not take part in inter-faith worship, that should not deter a trial from a resolution. The other perfects can take the prayers at the assembly, for example.

If the pupil at St Hilda's was promising enough to merit the head girl and presuming that her good personality came from her being associated with Christianity, then they should discover what unifies the Christians of her denomination with others, like the ten commandments, for instance.

One permanent solution to this discrimination is to make it mandatory for all administrators and teachers to study the rights and protections in Jamaica's constitution and to sign a statement upon engagement that they read it. By this means, no administrator or teacher can allege ignorance and plead for mercy. Although unawareness of the law is not an alibi, some judges argue in fairness that, in some examples, ignorance lessens guilt and are gracious if they have the choice, so let us curtail the ignorance.

School administrators and teachers, for the most part, are well knowledgeable of their rights but often fail to protect the rights of the students. If you are a member of the school board, I do not suggest that you entirely attempt to terminate or suspend a teacher unjustly unless you have a great passion for being arraigned to answer accusations in court.

Nevertheless, one of the extensively talked-about procedures of bringing peace currently is in acting towards 'dispute resolutions' and 'restorative justice,' whether in the Church or out of Church or in other religions.

Yet, I am curious about how all these 'conflict resolution mechanisms' can put a stop to the class discrimination that is prevalent in Jamaica and as well the religious and political racism. The Roman Catholic Church has accepted responsibility and already asked forgiveness for its part in any such discrimination during the 2000-year history of its existence. However, the Roman Catholic Church was outlawed in Jamaica for 136 years between 1655 and 1791. Yet no apology has been issued for that. Will any become or should we just "forget that and move on," as the former UK Prime Minister David Cameron suggested we do in the question of slavery?

Someone, a Christiani, reportedly was denied employment in the public sector more than 20 years ago because of the anti-Roman Catholic prejudice displayed by one of those on the interviewing committee.

While everyone that wears dreadlocks is not a Rastafarian, there were bank workers I knew who had dreadlocks before they got the job and after they left but not during the period of that employment. Yet cafeteria chefs who prepare delicacies for consumption can have dreadlocks with their heads covered.

According to Scripture, the Lord Jesus Christ said that "...for the children of this world are in their generation wiser than the children of light" (Luke 16:8). While there is vicious conflict without solution between some denominations, within some leaders and members, and in marriages, there seem to be more solutions found to disputes within workplaces and within political groups. In construction sites, for instance, any breakdown in the worker's relationship can delay the culmination of the construction, which in turn will delay payment. Therefore, conflict resolution is achieved quickly so that payment of workers is not delayed.

In the party politics of Jamaica, it is not necessarily the handling of the current issues that produce the winner, but the party with the best organized and unified internal structure. Since inside conflicts destroy political harmony, therefore the party with the more efficient conflict resolution mechanism will be competently organized to win. Political power and monetary inducement can be used to motivate people toward a temporary and perhaps phony cessation of hostility but cannot offer an everlasting peace.

Parliamentary democracies like Jamaica require all citizens and groups to respect certain privileges that properly belong to the people living in the country. One of these time-tested rights is that of religious freedom. Besides being included in our Bill of Rights, it is also enshrined in international conventions that the Government has signed. The right to practice religious liberty (religious liberty) is of primary importance and deserves to be honored every time in civilizations like ours. But, this right, like every other right, is not absolute. A major reason for this is that freedoms do occasionally come into disagreement with each other. When this occurs, one has to negotiate how to compensate for the rights in such a way that none is offended. Often, this requires a positive compromise.

The necessity to balance opposing rights makes it lawful for agents of the Government, for instance, to carry out raids in areas where religious liberty is being practiced if it is being done to prevent illegal actions or to obtain evidence to help in establishing justice.

Religious freedom, though a constitutional privilege, cannot be defined as any brand or type of religion. Besides, there is no unconditional legal right, not even the basic supreme one dubbed the 'right to life, itself the incredible 'right' for me since no state can safeguard it. A country can only endeavor to provide a remedy for its violation and that remedy, like life insurance, provides benefits only to the families of the deceased.

Within an accountable society, no organization should be allowed uncontrolled liberty to do whatever it decides since a major assignment of any government is to safeguard the well-being of its citizens in general.

The common American epithet 'separation of church and state' is best appreciated through the verbiage of the First Amendment to the American constitution, which states that "Congress shall make no law respecting an establishment of religion, or prohibiting the free exercise thereof." Meaning that no state religion is allowed or any encroachment on religious freedom. This is not an absolute either, given the United States/federal action against religious groups that endangered the safety of US citizens, despite the proliferation of several religions in the USA.

Then what of a dominant or anti-religious state? For Christians, the Bible and historical precedents provide examples of civil disobedience and non-violent opposition.

What is hazardous for a democratic nation that honors human rights is for the Government to presume the power to legislate the practice of religious freedom farther than the boundaries of the normally acceptable standards to all citizens. Whenever the states assume that they have the authority to target these religious institutions for reasons that are usually unethically justifiable or are incompatible with existing laws, they exceed their limits and should be questioned and withstood.

The instance of the apostles in the book of Acts is very familiar. They defied a declaration from the state-approved Jewish authorities (the Sadducees) 'not to teach in the name of Jesus Christ", preferring "to obey God instead of men" (Acts 5.29).

According to Tertullian, the father of Latin Christianity and author of western theology, Apostle John was deported to the island of Patmos because of his Christian witness. John depicts himself as a fellow partaker with his audience in the suffering and persistence (1.9) and as being on Patmos because of God's word and his declaration about Jesus. (1.9b), i.e., as a result of his testimony and presence being discerned as probably seditious and subversive by the State.

The Rev Dr. Burchell Taylor highlighted three components of state oppression illustrated and condemned in Revelation: (a) the conceit of power (13.1-17;11.7;14.9;17.3), (b) the use of betrayal through quasi-religious hype (13; 1.9; 2.13;14.9) utilized by the beast from the Earth, and (c) economic disservice through the state monopoly (13.17).

By the atoning death of Christ on the cross, Christians constituted a kingdom of priests. The word 'kingdom and 'priests' were politically laden terms in the 1st century- 'kingdom meant monarchy, and 'priests were holders of the State's sacred authority.

The contentious issues between the Church and State are not something that a single solution can fit into at all times because they are multi-faceted. However, with mutual respect and determination to work together for the common good, it will be necessary for the two parties to be proactive in identifying potential conflicts and taking joint steps to nip them in the bud before mischief-makers take advantage of them.

CHAPTER 7

INFLUENCE OF CHURCH ON POLITICS- WE ARE INVOLVED

Never say
mean words out
of anger. Your anger
will pass. But your
mean words can scare
a person for life.
So use kind words
or be silent.

THE
WISE
YOU

T he Church's involvement in politics became inevitable after the prolonged waiting for the second coming of the Lord Jesus Christ. The earlier justification for being apolitical by the early Church began to wane as the believers were subjected to abuse and neglect because they were, after all, not represented nor participated in the process that produced those that decided what happened to them.

When the Church began to interact with the State both at personal and corporate levels, it didn't take long before her presence and influence began to be seen and felt in the political landscape. This is to be expected because the Church is comprised of people who were from the society and, therefore, will bring to bear their innate political inclinations. With more people being converted to the Church, including monarchs and top political figures, the Church's organizational climate acquired political influence.

Secondly, when the state actors became aware that their initial attacks on and efforts to annihilate the Church were unsuccessful and counterproductive because the Church was rather winning more souls and attracting the sympathy of most unbelievers, they decided to soften the hostility and cooperate with the Church hoping to bring the Church under their control. This move accounted for the numerous numbers of kings, emperors, and monarchs that had hobnobbed with the Church in her turbulent historical journey.

However, the Church has been very resilient in protecting its beliefs, doctrine, and spiritual heritage and has influenced the State in more than one way. Today, the Church has asserted itself so well in most countries that it is always consulted or taken into consideration in both legislative and economic decisions of the State, and it has become the dictum for the Church to offer its opinion and, at times, position on national policy and programs.

The Bible and the Christian religion have likewise strongly impacted scholars and political activists. The instructions of Jesus, like the story of the 'Good Samaritan", are one of the most vital foundations of contemporary ideas of human rights and the good commonly empowered by authorities in the West. Long-established Christian education on sexuality, marriage relationship, and household life has also been powerful and contentious in contemporary times. Christianity contributed significantly to stopping practices like human sacrifice, the killing of twins, and polygamy. Christianity, in general, impacts the dignity of women by denouncing marital cheating, divorce, incest, birth control, infanticide, female babies being more prone to be murdered, and abortion. In comparison, authorized Church teachingreckons women and men to be companions, comparable and different.

Jamaica, with very rich historical antecedents of Church culture and influence the Church, has continued to influence the State in many areas, although there are arguments that the Church should do much more.

We cannot talk about the influence of the Church on Jamaica as a country without mentioning the first and foremost of the influences, which is the abolition of slavery.

The Slave Rebellion of 1831-1832: "The Christian slaves are generally quieter, calm, peaceful, and obedient than the ones who are not Christians" When John Stewart (1800-1877) wrote these remarks in 1823, he had no impression that the very Christian slaves he had written about would instigate one of the most terrible slave rebellions in the history of Jamaican. The so-called "Baptist War" that happened during the Christmas period of 1831 was a vital step towards the abolition of slavery in Jamaica. The slaves who participated in this uprising were members of Baptist and different Christian groups in Jamaica, and faith played a large role in their schemes of rebellion. Although slave liberation in Jamaica was eventually determined in the British Parliament, they acted partly because of the overwhelming slave uprising in Jamaica—an uprising instigated by Christian missions.

The Baptist pioneers were in support of liberating the slaves. They belonged to the first white folks to take an interest in the slaves in Jamaica. These missionaries came up with the idea of presenting the Christian faith to the slaves, and with time, this idea was combined with the religious opinions the slaves already had from Africa, such as "myalism." The previous colonial preachers tried to rationalize slavery by manipulating portions of Christian Scriptures that could suit the idea of slavery, so the slaves rejected that brand of faith, but the concepts of equal rights and brotherhood innate in Christian principles that they taught together with myalism's convictions against evil spirit boosted the slave's fight for liberation. Several of the white Baptist preachers advised the slaves to stay patiently, for freedom would come someday, but the slaves stood encouraged by the missionaries' indirect support of the abolition.

Among the several other white religious denominations, no such backing existed. The new blend of African and Christian beliefs created a platform for the slaves to relate with themselves. Religious gatherings were the sole place where the slaves were permitted to gather without supervision, and the church fellowships gradually metamorphosed into gatherings where political concerns were discussed. These gatherings of the young Church did not bother the Baptist ministers because they assumed that the Baptist sermons would dissuade the slaves from contemplating ideas of rebellion. However, the slaves deduced Christian doctrines as a legitimate basis for and stimuli to revolt, while the preachers comprehended it as an impediment against such action. The missionaries did not attend these religious gatherings, so there was no one to stress the importance of obedience to the slaves. They could freely communicate the ideas of liberty and rebellion.

One of the leading instigators of the revolutionary gatherings of these slaves was Sam Sharpe. He was a slave in Montego Bay and was also an adherent of the Baptist denomination. Sharpe was literate and became a reliable speaker and authority in the Baptist Church. Sharpe's owner did not disapprove of his role as a preacher but permitted him to conduct nighttime religious meetings without any white supervisor in attendance. So, Sharpe used this confidence to his advantage, using the services as a cover-up for rebellion-organizing meetings. Sharp was convinced that the Bible favored the freedom of slaves, and his lopsided interpretation steered him to mastermind a rebellion that would culminate in emancipation. Sharpe's original plan for the revolution was a sedentary resistance movement, which won much larger backing and participation among his fellow slaves than if he had attempted raising a violent revolt.

About the time Sharpe was starting up to assemble Baptist followership, and to ready himself for rebellion, the conversation on abolition was hovering around the island. Rumors were circulating that the British would shortly be liberating the slaves. It was not surprising that the plurality of the rumors was emanating from the Baptist quarters on the island. Even when a royal statement was eventually made refuting the rumors, this was not widely published. The governor had an opinion that the refuting proclamation would add impetus to the talk of liberation.

When the proclamation became well circulated, it barely served to heighten the unrest. Because of the atmosphere of expectancy, the invitation for passive resistance received an even more favorable response.

According to new research, slave uprisings became possible when the slave's yearnings were thwarted, as in the example of the Jamaican slaves and the gossip of freedom. While the slave community was readying for drastic steps, the missionaries were making an effort to persuade them not to revolt and that the issue would be resolved in England. Having done all the planning and consultations, Sam Sharpe and his fellow slaves that followed him started the rebellion on December 27, 1831.

The slaves had met several times under the impression of religious meetings and had scheduled to quit work and begin with passive resistance, although It didn't end up happening that way. The revolution began with the burning of a trashed building on one of the vast estates. Although Samuel Sharpe initially did not intend to facilitate violence and property vandalism, the rebellion advanced that way nonetheless. A group comprised of about 150 "soldiers" called the black regiment was the nucleus of the military regiment, but there were various separate groups that partook. Unfortunately for the revolutionaries, the groups were not well organized and had no knowledge of warfare. Some of the individual countries did not take part in the passive resistance but rather gloated over the destroying of property, slaughtering livestock, or partaking in other acts of hostility. The rebellion was quelled by the first week in January 1832. Much of the country was wrecked. In the St. James area of Jamaica, the destruction was worth about 600,000 pounds. Wholly, the damages were worth over one million pounds. There were only two incidents of turmoil by the slaves against whites reported, and they only struck when threatened. Although the duration of the uprising was not very lengthy, it became a very significant part of the Jamaican past. The rebellion demonstrated the progress that the slaves had attained politically and religiously, thus indicating that the slaves could begin a campaign that could quake the foundation of the Jamaican slave population. The religious gatherings established a legal protest, including a full-fledged spiritual group composed of the slaves.

Although the slaves were not entirely unified, they still posed a large danger to the whites, and the farmers were not ignorant of this. During the era of slavery, Jamaican history was characterized by rebellion and hostility from the beginning up to the post-slavery era.

Social-Cultural Influence: Christian concepts and citations are intertwined throughout the composition of Jamaican life. Common people and political administrators regularly quote biblical and different Christian sayings. Business meetings and conferences for national associations always start with prayer. Jamaicans always struggle over obvious cultural paradoxes and self-perceived moral weaknesses that seem to thwart their overt affirmation of Christian loyalty, but despite any personal shortcomings, Christianity is a primary cultural structure for Jamaican life.

Jamaicans always assert that the country has more churches per square kilometer in its towns and villages than any country on Earth, and Jamaicans are incredible entrepreneurs when it has to do with launching churches. Kingston communities, smaller towns, and even country townlets are spotted with an impressive variation of Seventh Day Adventist, Assemblies of God, Church of God, individual Pentecostal, and Baptist congregations that attract a great chunk of the population. A reasonable figure of Catholic cathedrals is also spotted around the island, as well as Anglican and Methodist chapels, but the congregations that lead the landscape are the ones with Pentecostal centered worship and revival-style messages; literal interpretations of Scripture; healings, and speaking in other languages; and regular messages on repentance and the proximity of end times. In Jamaica, these churches are mostly parochial in their outlook, and while there is cooperation between some churches, the overall religious climate is usually fragmented and always competitive.

The Jamaican Catholic Church has been remarkably entrepreneurial also, through the building of churches and educational facilities, religious groups, and service schemes for the poor and destitute. Catholic schools are exceptionally referred to among the exceedingly best schools in the capital city of Kingston and are also operated by parishes at every level of integrity and admission. The Government depends so much on the Church for not only education but likewise for assistance to the less privileged. Even with all this, the number of Catholic Church members is small and shrinking, and Jamaican Catholics unfailingly reveal that their belief is generally criticized by Jamaicans as paganism and idolatrous.

Effects of Church's Influence: Jamaica is such a religious nation that certainly has positive effects on its citizens. This is displayed in the culture and social norms of the island. It is seen in the way we dine and drink, our core values and behaviors, our dress sense, and our common lifestyle.

1. Dress - In Jamaica, you will discover that Christians are instructed to dress modestly. This implies that clothes are normally not revealing. Many Christians put on lengthy skirts or dresses, normally on or below the knees, and blouses that have enough long sleeves that the cleavage. The wearing of trousers by women is discouraged by most churches, precisely forbidden from being worn to Church by many. In some cases, for both men and women, trousers must not be trim-tight. Many churches dissuade the fixing of hair extensions in their hairs, and a few even forbid it altogether in their denominations, teaching their members to wear their natural hair at all times.

Christian groups exhort the wearing of quite restrained outfitting entailing ankle-length kilts or dresses. They use scarves to wrap the hair and dissuade or forbid the wearing of any clothing that could be deemed revealing completely, either going to Church or in daily life. It is normally very simple to say if somebody is of these denominations by their habit of dressing. This has permeated through to every facet of Jamaica as one must be dressed modestly to join certain careers and almost all government organizations; if you are believed to be differing from these restrictions, you will not earn an entry. It is commonly perceived as a mark of disrespect and low integrity to be dressed in low or revealing clothes.

2. Diet – Many Christians drink little or no alcohol and refrain from smoking. Christian organizations like Seventh-Day Adventists encourage healthy eating and normally live as vegetarians or vegans. While some Christians in certain religious groups may elect to eat just about anything, several others practice a beneficial eating lifestyle.

3. Values and Attitudes – The various religions practiced in Jamaica all seek to promote decent values and manners. These comprise abstinence from betting, love, and regard for others irrespective of their religious beliefs and how they vary from yours. Christianity, for one, standing as the most practiced faith, has the highest impact on society. Biblical precepts of good and bad are taught from the cradle as soon as parents and guardians can engage the child's attention, and this goes on throughout the years in school. They all emphasize integrity, compassion, discipline, self-esteem, self-respect, decency, confidence, strong family virtues, and honor for elders.

4. Social Inclusion - Social inclusiveness is very valuable to many individuals in Jamaica. The congregations and all worship centers provide a place of sanctuary for individuals who are regarded as outcasts or who have nobody to help in times of difficulty and distress. These establishments are ever willing to receive people who feel abandoned and miserable and give counseling and comfort to bring them in the right direction. There are so many shattered family systems in Jamaica, and the churches plug the void for people who yearn for a feeling of belonging. Many have affirmed the truth that the Church and its instructions have changed them from a life of criminality. This also is another favorable influence of the Church in the country.

5. Social Responsibility: The Church has enabled the country to abide by an understanding of civic obligation. Philanthropy is demonstrated to people in need, particularly in periods of personal and nationwide crises. We see less privileged people being given relief packages or a neighborhood group coming together to renovate the house of a church member, construct a bus terminal or paint a pedestrian bridge. Jamaicans are generally generous, and this is rooted in the influence of the Church.

As with all things, there are a few negative impacts of the Church on the State, and they are:

1. Hypocrisy - Many people in Jamaica are inclined to be identified with any church or religious organization, and the justifications are numerous. Some of the people have not come out with a very nice experience from their place of worship. Most of the worship centers are always perceived as a refuge from the outer public, but several others feel frequently humiliated and criticized for their kind of life if they are slow in conforming to the Christian ethics. Once they fall, they are immediately booted out or ostracized, which is the same thing they are fleeing from. This has pushed many backs to their former sinful way of life and to cultivate resentment against the Church.

The awful reality is that some members of the same religion or denomination will severely stress the mistakes of their fellow believers. It is quite normal for recently converted believers to be chastised for their behaviors by those who have existed as part of the organization for a long period. Most of them perceive it as looking out for each other, but their methods of bringing it across are sometimes harsh.

2. Financial Soliciting/Exploiting - While many admit the fact that money is needed to run any organization inclusive of the Church, some Jamaicans are suspicious of church leaders, always soliciting financial assistance or donations for church buildings projects which in many instances are never finished even after several years or show minor sign of improvement. Many believe that the ministers or administrators of the Church seize the money for personal use, which, unfortunately, is the case in many cases.

Some church authorities take undue advantage of the susceptible, who are always cajoled into making contributions and who are made to feel guilty for not being able to give. Others sermonize the prosperity gospel and motivate people to sow financial seeds for some sort of blessings which most times are physical things or cure. There are also so many church members whose fundamental needs are hardly met while the religious authorities are well off economically, as evidenced by the kinds of automobiles they drive and buildings they own.

3. Denominational Disputes – While this happens to a minor level in other religions, the Christian religion is awash with the denominational competition. Christians are tended to argue among themselves on who is real or who is wrong based on beliefs and knowledge of the scriptures. This amazes the skeptics who, more often than not, concluded not to pertain to a congregation at all due to the fear of joining with the wrong Church or some will move from one Church to another in pursuit of the truth. This may lead to a noticeable argument that similarly influences the viewpoint of the converts and shift into the wider society like the workplace. It can also result in adverse attitudinal changes and the whole chain of interpersonal relationships.

Regrettably, some religious organizations' drift away from true faith, especially in Christianity, has resulted in persons resorting to unbiblical and occultic exercises, which have caused the loss of lives, money, and other valuables. Admittedly, there is the independence of faith in Jamaica, but at the time of reckoning, each person is eventually accountable for their faith and religious exercises and should be prepared to deduce well from the bad.

The Jamaican Church- which is the unified Christian membership, should be vocal and have a prominent voice in government matters, encompassing the constitution and fraud prevention. The Church should scrutinize every enactment to guarantee just laws are enacted. The Church should lobby the parliament to considerably improve translucency, competition, responsibility, and integrity in official contracting and guarantee keeping with the nation's procurement processes, and eliminate waste, corruption, and inefficiency in the grant and execution of deals. The Church must possess a representative and count on matters concerned with poverty mitigation, employment generation, deficit compression and administration, reducing the tax weight on poor individuals, the conditions of the International Monetary Fund commitment, use of alternative energy reserves, infrastructural improvement, the modification of the educational structure and crime deterrence and decline.

I reminiscence on Jamaica advancing through the Catholic; elementary, primary, and high institutions of learning. Incorporated in the school curriculum to educate and cultivate us into refined and well-grounded graduates was the topic of religion. In addition to studying the ethos of Christianity, we were also compelled at the beginning of every assembly to stand erect and bow our heads in homage to pray and offer thanks to God. There were no complaints or misgiving from pupils or their parents to this formality because it was presumed or anticipated that students who received entry to these establishments were Christians.

There is certainly nothing improper with this because they are Christian institutions; a substantial number of Jamaican schools were established by Church leaders (bishops, Jesuits, priests, or missionaries). They held out the evangelizing crusade of the Church, incorporating Christian instruction as the major subject in the school's curriculum of studies. "Established on outstanding moral doctrines based on the ethical teachings of Christianity" -

There is a marked discrepancy between religious indoctrination and instruction. The Christian set-up schools enhanced the Christian principle and teachings.

Religious education is vital in schools because it is a critical ingredient for a wide and balanced education. It gives a substantial and unique contribution to the school's courses by broadening students' understanding and knowledge of several religious principles and habits as well as their impact on people, societies, and civilizations. It helps students to assess and react to a broad spectrum of critical questions concerning their spiritual growth.

Both varieties of this religious awareness have their values. Nevertheless, a spiritual predicament is possible when religion dabbles in non-religious domains.

Therefore, there is nothing wrong with the Jamaica Council of Churches (JCC) wanting an audience with the prime minister to verify what the economic and political outlook is for the nation. The Church can have a standing economic committee from its qualified and well-experienced members who can complement the political authorities in policy formulation, implementation, and monitoring.

Nevertheless, after having the meeting, it becomes necessary for the JCC to communicate the findings with the public.

A United Jamaican Church can decide through the ballot who rules the nation because it has the numerical capacity to call the shots as far as a constitutional democracy depends on the majority of people and voters having their way.

After the ballot and the election of a new administration, the Church should proceed to be partners with the political authority of the nation so that Jamaica can have peace and prosperity.

CHAPTER 8

THE BALANCE BETWEEN CHURCH AND POLITICS

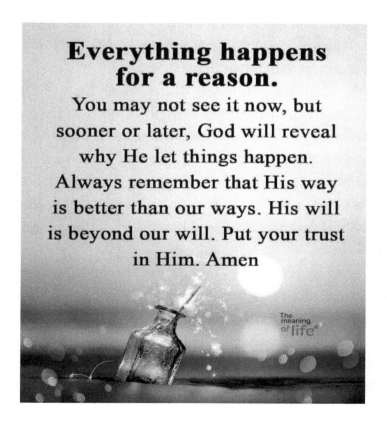

Everything happens for a reason.
You may not see it now, but sooner or later, God will reveal why He let things happen. Always remember that His way is better than our ways. His will is beyond our will. Put your trust in Him. Amen

The meaning of life

T alking about finding the balance between two vectors or entities implies a current state of imbalance or disproportion. The State and Church have an inherent dispute in their relationship, and it started with the birth of the Lord Jesus Christ, the head and owner of the Church. The state political hierarchy saw the announcement of a new king of the Jews as a challenge to their imperial authority and declared hostility with not only the person of Christ but the idea of another king. The threat of losing political power and relevance is responsible for the State's aggression against the Church, and the Church's insistence on continuing with the message of the new king and His kingdom has perpetuated the conflict. However, the perceived threat by the Church has remained a mystery, and at most potential but not forcefully enforced by the Church. The Church declared itself an army, and the State responded with force; meanwhile, the Church army was without artillery.

But is the Church a real threat to the State? From the Church's perspective, there is no danger posed by the Church to the State both then in the beginning and now. When the Lord Jesus Christ Himself was arraigned before Pontius Pilate and the same question of His threat to the Roman Empire, He said His kingdom is not of this world. So, the new king and His kingdom that the Church proclaimed are not in competition with the political powers of this world and need not be antagonized or chastised by them.

The separation between the Church and State must include a precise definition of the role of each of them and the nature of compromise needed where there is a clash of roles.

The Church's primary assignment is to influence the overall personal conduct of individual members of the State through the preaching of the Gospel. This responsibility encompasses the entire population, including the leadership of the State and the Church sees her duty as a sacred one.

It is a general belief, at least by the Church, that humanity as a whole stand to benefit from the preaching of the Gospel to such an extent that it minimizes criminal activities and social vices.

While the Church does not seek to compete for political powers and gratification with the State, it does seek for audience and dominance of the spiritual and thinking faculty of the converts, and the State recognizes this as a subtle but intensive way of gaining control of individuals.

The Church is not contending with the State on any common interests, but the State seems not to be comfortable with the presence of the Church in most climes, and this is unfortunate.

The State's main interest at all times is the loyalty and cooperation of the citizens and the provision of physical infrastructure for economic development. The State also benefits from a society that has been positively influenced morally and ethically by the Church.

The State can legislate on social responsibility and the subjection of the citizens to the State, including rights and obligations, and establish law enforcement and prosecution of offenders, but it's the Church that impacts individual citizens In such a way that alters the behavioral pattern making the individual to naturally or impulsively inclined to think and act responsibly and lawfully.

The Church and State though distinct in their structures and model, remain inseparable because of the dual identity of the citizens as both Church and State members.

Christians possessed the right to voluntarily express their religious opinions at the private level. However, Congress shall not officially authorize or appoint any specific religious organizations, such as Baptists, Presbyterians, or Anglicans, as State religion.

The balancing of independence and order is the unrestricted practice of religion by individuals without any government sponsorship of a special religious group or hierarchy, and this fits the general checks-and-balances stability created by the constitution of many Democratic countries.

The Jamaican Constitution provides and guarantees the freedom of religion and worship for all citizens. Section 17 went further to give detail on the protections given to "freedom of religion," stating:

"Every citizen shall possess the right to religious independence involving the freedom to alter his religion and the privilege, either independently or in a group with others and both in open and in secret, to exemplify and reproduce his religion in adulation, teaching, practice, and observance."

In Jamaica, Christianity is an inextricable part of society, which has helped mold the lives of our nation. It is no surprise that over 60% of the population has recognized themselves as committed Christians. Many of the island's academic institutions and philanthropic organizations are operated by religious groups.

While there is not even a single established state church or religion, the Jamaican Constitution officially acknowledges some churches. For instance, the Moravian Church in Jamaica is formally recognized by an Act of Parliament. In 2013, another Act of Parliament was enacted for the official establishment of the Church of Haile Selassie I. There is similarly official symbolic loyalty to religion; for instance, the Jamaican National Anthem includes explicit Christian references despite the substantial number of non-Christian and non-religious communities identified in the country.

Christianity is undoubtedly systematically promoted in public life, with Jamaican authorities openly expressing their faith in the Christian God in their official capacity. For instance, there is the yearly National Leadership Prayer Breakfast, with the Prime Minister always in attendance, including the Leader of the Opposition party and several Members of Parliament. This public assertion of Christianity is institutional and exists at all tiers of government. It is the conventional practice in several government offices and parastatals to begin crucial meetings and other proceedings with a prayer. No other religion receives these rights in Jamaica.

Finally, the security architectures of the State, which comprises the Jamaica Constabulary Force and the Jamaica Defense Force, have chaplains.

Section 17 of the Constitution ensures the right of each religious body or group to give religious education to people of the same faith. While at the same time guaranteeing the student's right not to be "required to accept religious education, or to participate in or attend any religious ceremony or observance, which relates to a religion or religious body or denomination other than his own."

Many public educational institutions in Jamaica long to and are operated by churches, which are empowered with state donations but expected to operate by rules made by the Ministry of Education, Youth, and Information. Referring to the US State Department, the municipal school curriculum incorporates non-denominational religious instruction, which concentrates on the historical function of religion in nation and philosophic thinking and involves group visitations to Christian, Jewish, Islamic, and Hindu places of worship. Students are not allowed any choice to opt-out of religious education. However, religious participation or exercise during school hours is discretionary.

However, an analysis of publicly accessible documents about the curriculum in elementary schools indicates that religion is understood and introduced as critical to the shaping of character and guiding one's knowledge of the essence and meaning of life. It is included as a light through which all topics are taught in an exhaustive strategy for primary education. In this regard, priority is placed on raising prospective citizens with an emphasis on morals, integrity, tenets, behaviors, integrity, legacy & civilization through the curriculum improvements and in the teaching of Religious Education, Civics, and Social Studies.

Whereas the scope of the religious education seems more natural to be designed for exploring the diversity of religious organizations' convictions in Jamaica, no consideration appears to be made of the non-religious groups; rather, students may be requested to write messages to religious organizations conveying gratitude for the work they are doing or organize a short prayer to God. Also, while seeking how to look after their bodies, the guidance recommends that teachers should lean on the Bible for tales around healthful eating and examine how healthy eating habits can enable us to give assistance to others and reverence God.

Religious education is perceived as the most prominent subject that champions and stimulates the education on religious reasoning aptitudes, distinguished civic integrity, and moral virtues such as honesty, commitment, respect, justice, sincerity, and equality. The forenamed virtues and qualities, among others, are useful in shaping the habits and souls of students, educating them on what it is to be good and honorable nationals of the greatest moral integrity.

Religion has remained an indispensable part of people's daily lives; students are therefore encouraged to be mature in their habits of beliefs and attitudes, culture, and regulations as well as those of other people. As such, Religious Education encapsulates a widened and balanced viewpoint of worldwide and Caribbean religions that enables students to comprehend more plainly how the faiths and training of these organizations have influenced, shaped and impacted daily life and culture, thereby improving students' social personalities and changing our world such that we can stay and function together in harmony.

Regulations require that religious institutions receiving government funding must accept students of all religions and follow the ministry of Education standards. Religious institutions are not exposed to any specific restrictions. Most of them are affiliated with Catholic or Protestant churches.

The balance between Church and State in Jamaica should not be defined by external factors or any general worldwide view but by the peculiar ascendancy of Christianity in the socio-cultural evolution of Jamaica as a nation.

The historical and cultural background of any country has played a critical role in defining its religious, cultural, and political ideology and shapes Church/ State relationships and ability. So, the diversity of historical orientations has given rise to several perspectives on separating Church and State and the practical implications for different States.

For example, the separation of the Church and the State in the United States created a situation where there is no state-sponsored, funded, or adopted religion, and the citizens enjoy unhindered freedom of religion and protection from religious discrimination. However, the United States President is sworn in on the Bible- the Christian Holy book and the Constitution of America still bear the phrase "A nation under God" while currency (U.S.Dollar) clearly shows the inscription " In God we trust"; all these represent Christian insignia.

In the United Kingdom, the separation of Church and State is enshrined in the sub-conscious of the citizens and the codified section of the constitution. In reality, and as peculiar to the United Kingdom, the monarchy is both the head of the Church- the Anglican Communion and the head of State and only delegates authority to the Prime Minister.

In Jamaica, they got her independence from the United Kingdom in 1962 and therefore inherited a dominant Christian influence from the colonialists and has continued to evolve as a nation; it is preposterous to expect that her development, including church/State relationships, will deviate from the norms.

It has become obvious that Jamaica, with a preponderance of Christianity, will be influenced in public and private life by Christian doctrines and ethics and attempts by either the State or advocators of the new world order or indeed other religions to rewrite the history of Jamaica's religious heritage will be seen as aggression and insurrection against the established peaceful and natural order.

Jamaica, with at least 60% of the devoted Christian population and a Christian historical background that is dated back to the 17th and 18th centuries and with no other religious group with a third of the number of Christians, the implication is that the state bureaucracy and establishments are dominated by Christians.

With most educational institutions built and operated by Christians for hundreds of years, the nation's academic environment will be populated by Christians, including the private sector. It is, therefore, necessary for the State to take into account this reality when formulating programs and policies that will impact the majority of the people.

The Jamaican State must deliberately take full advantage of its unique religious composition to achieve rapid growth and development and reduce drastically the religious tensions and civil unrest that has characterized the country.

The Balance Between Church and State in Jamaica will be found with:

Rejection of Global View- there is a tendency for the third world and developing countries to look elsewhere and adopt or copy programs that are alien to their environment when faced with challenges. Secondly, in the global village we live in today, and the fight for space and audience, cultural and historical identities are often ignored In preference for globally accepted hypotheses. International organizations and agencies are fond of theorizing and making straight jacket recommendations that fit all cases in the developing countries but end up exacerbating the situations they seek to arrest.

There is no worldwide view or position on the separation of Church and State or the balance between the two; what every jurisdiction has done is to achieve a certain variety of the Democratic ideal that is peculiar to them and necessary for a peaceful, harmonious life for all citizens.

Homegrown Policy - the historical context and uniqueness of Jamaica make it imperative for the leadership to interrogate the determinants of the policy framework for separating the Church and the State; and to put into consideration the domestic peculiarities of the country's religious culture. Our leaders, both political and religious, should ensure that the separation of Church and State takes into consideration the reality of the country's strong Christian background. It should not be compared or influenced by exogenous factors like worldwide views or the nefarious pretense of equal rights.

If there are any international declarations by either the United Nations and its agencies or the Bretton Wood institutions on the separation of the Church and State and the ideal place of balancing the two, this should not be wholly adopted hook, line, and sinker without adjustment to contain the country's unique traits.

The balance between Church and State in Jamaica is at the point where the State sincerely treats the Church as the most dominant force in the country's political sphere and concedes to her lawful influence on the socio-cultural life of the nation. The State should not be deceived or intimidated by the voices of absolute freedom (the new world order) or those shouting for the rights of the minority, no matter how vocal they are.

I am not saying that the right of minorities should be trampled upon, but in a country where more than 60% are devoted Christians and the religion has been dominant for centuries, how do you honestly prevent the influence of such a huge force without courting trouble. To entertain the thought that the minorities of whom none have 10% of the population should have equal rights and influence (equal say and participation), I think, is reasonable.

However, the balance will not hold if the Church fails to be magnanimous as its manner is and treat the minority with love and respect. If the Church wears all her garbs and exercises the fullness of her life, the State and Church will be better for it.

When a renowned American astronaut quotes Psalm 24 and is disparaged by public opinion for infringing on the so-called separation of the Church and State, it's time to know about balance. In the same way, mountain goats require a body built for balance. We also require conscious balance in the political setting, where Christians are regularly told to hush to avoid hurting the feelings of non-Christians.

The balance of somebody's civil freedoms, such as religious liberty and freedom of expression rights, and the equilibrium of a mountain goat on vertical slopes are both instances of high-demanding balancing acts. Consider the dexterity of the sure-footed wild goat.

Their hooves are built to perfect balance and clasp; the exterior hoof is forcefully reinforced, and the bottom is striped with a rubber-like material, making the entire limbs fairly like a good hiking boot.

The high-elevation agility of the mountain goat is so incredible that it regularly spends time on cursory landscapes steeper than a 40° or even 60° angle. God deliberately built mountain goats for equilibrium because habitation among alpine stones is a hazardous lifestyle.

The same truth applies to religious freedom in our society. The valid desires of the Church and State are intentionally balanced with the private rights of individuals. Securing critical religious independence is no carefree venture and is not effortlessly obtained or sustained.

The reasonable equilibrium between religious liberty and governmental interference means that the Church should not dictate over the State, and the State cannot regulate the Church. Religion is too crucial to be a government undertaking or a political ceremony.

We are often told not to mix religion and politics, and this idea has a significant fact which is that when religion is employed for political goals, it drains religion of its permanent meaning and serves as just one more suspicious method of amassing power.

However, there is yet a contradiction concealed in that phrase that most times when people say don't mix religion and politics, they are saying don't take your belief into the public domain where I may see it. In other words, keep your religion outside of your worship center because there is a "separation of church and state." The idea of separation of the Church and State is too critical a concept to be misapplied, particularly not as a means for hushing opposite views.

"No man shall be compelled to support or frequent any religious worship, ministry, or place whatsoever, nor shall be enforced. in his body or goods nor shall suffer on account of his religious belief or opinions; but that every man shall be free to profess, and maintain his opinion in matters of religion, and the same shall in no wise enlarge, diminish, or affect their civil capacities." --Thomas Jefferson.

In a constitutional democratic environment like Jamaica, the principle of balance between the Church and State is not against the dominance of the majority, which is the universal norm for democracy but state inference or adoption of any religion.

CHAPTER 9

CONTEMPORARY ISSUES OF
POLITICS IN THE CHURCH

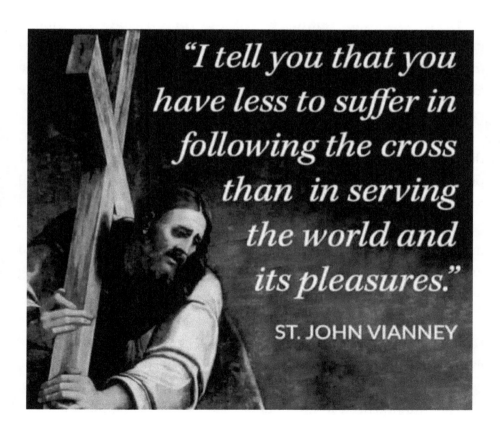

"I tell you that you have less to suffer in following the cross than in serving the world and its pleasures."

ST. JOHN VIANNEY

P olitics is simply defined as the art or science of governance, and governance is all about organizing and leading a group of people; either for a time or to accomplish some specific purposes. It involves making decisions and the process involved in arriving at the desired decision. The Church is comprised of people who require leadership and governance, and this makes politics inevitable in the Church.

Although most times, when politics in the Church is mentioned, it is seen as a derogatory and unpleasant perspective, politics in the Church generally refers to the decision-making process and organs.

Let's look at the politics in the Church from two perspectives:

1. The Decision-making Process of the Church - The Church inherited a democratic culture as seen in ***Acts 6:3 NIV - Brothers and sisters, choose seven men from among you who are known to be full of the Spirit and wisdom. We will turn this responsibility over to them.***

Leadership in the Church is as important as it is elsewhere; however, the democratic process is different from what is obtainable in secular practice. Whereas individual participation in the voting process is critical to the success of the exercise, there are no political parties formed, and campaigning or any form of canvassing for a vote is forbidden. Once the qualities of the proposed leaders and criteria for the positions being filled are agreed upon and communicated to the eligible member-voters, voting is done under the guidance of the Holy Spirit.

The Church's political process is not competitive nor involves the spending of money by the candidates and is therefore devoid of any of the acrimonious tendencies like attacks on the personal character of others, especially the opposition candidates witnessed in secular politicking. The politics practiced in the Church echoes the original intentions for leadership, which are selfless service to the led and serving as the model for good governance.

Temporal political democratic principles like justice, equal rights, freedom, and accountability were derived from the Biblical and, especially, from Jesus Christ's teachings on service and leadership. And the most enduring democracies to date are those jurisdictions whose constitution and historical antecedents were greatly influenced by the Christian faith, and they have achieved greatness by adopting the biblical leadership model for centuries.

2. Politics in the Church - These talks about the external political influence on the Church. Since the Church does not exist in a vacuum but amid a very powerful political environment, it has come under intense political exigencies of the ever-dynamic climate through the centuries.

Though the Church was meant to be resilient to the influx of political influence, the stack reality is that it has taken political knocks here and there with some bruises and red-eye to show for it even though not knocked out.

From the first century's bold resistance to political influence-"The Acts 6:9 NIV: Opposition arose, however, from members of the Synagogue of the Freedmen (as it was called) —Jews of Cyrene and Alexandria, as well as the provinces of Cilicia and Asia —who began to argue with Stephen," to the 21st-century compromises, the undeniable effects of extraneous political influence, are regrettably manifest.- "St Mary's Cathedral has become the first in the country to be permitted to conduct gay weddings, a month after the Scottish Episcopal church general synod voted overwhelmingly to allow its churches to host the ceremonies.

The vote resulted in canon law being changed to remove a doctrinal clause stating that marriage was between a man and a woman". ---- The Guardian.

Temporal political institutions are urging the Church to shed weight -make your doctrines affordable or replace them with popular opinion. After all, religion was made for man and not the other way around. The Church must realize that - Matthew 5:13-14 NIV: "You are the salt of the earth. But if the salt loses its saltiness, how can it be made salty again? It is no longer good for anything except to be thrown out and trampled underfoot. "You are the light of the world. A town built on a hill cannot be hidden. The Church cannot retain your identity after you have lost your character. Neither can it be reckoned with besides her character.

The political authorities will rather be contented to make the Church another political party to compete with, defeat, and exercise control over. They have resorted to the strategy of Balam, who could not place curses on Israel (God's people) after being hired and handsomely rewarded with additional perks by Balak, the son of Bosso. Balam advised Balak to throw a big party and invite the people of God to come and entertain them with much wine and intoxicating drinks and that when they are high on alcohol, they are sure to misbehave and commit sins, thereby attracting curses to themselves without him having to curse them.

The Church has come a long treacherous way with the temporal political systems of the world and is still managing to stand, albeit with life-threatening wounds, but the world seems afraid of a healthy, vibrant Church and will stop at nothing to ensure it is completely defeated and rendered ineffective.

SOME CONTEMPORARY POLITICAL ISSUES IN THE CHURCH

1. ABSOLUTE FREEDOM (The New World Order)- The propagators of the idea of freedom without borders and consideration

for the interest of others are insisting that whatever seems doable is right and part of fundamental human rights. If you choose to go stack naked in broad daylight, it is your right and should not be criticized. They ignore the fact that human beings were not created without boundaries, and right from the garden of Eden, God placed a limit for the first man, Adam forbidding the eating of the fruit of a particular tree.

God created us with the sense capable of knowing what is right or wrong, but this sense is blurred when we depart from following God and seeking to know Him. The farther away from God we wander, the more ignorant of His will we are, and then the efforts to fill the void created by His absence with whatever looks plausible, no matter how awful and elusive they are.

The idea of absolute freedom is an abuse of knowledge and privilege and impracticable in the long run; for instance, if I chose to drive against the traffic on the road because I have a valid driving license and therefore the right to drive, I may not go far before realizing the danger I pose for other road users.

The whole essence of having constitutions, both written and unwritten, is to explicitly communicate the agreed boundaries of the exercise of freedom within the given jurisdiction. In legislative democracies, which is prevalent in most developed and developing countries, laws are made, and punishments are prescribed and meted out to people who go beyond the limits of the law. How then do we think that the limits set by God to help regulate the human preponderance for excesses can be infringed upon without consequences?

The Church of Christ must rise to the challenge of this type of influence from the political environment where a group of people can form an association of people who want to walk around nude for the reason of their rights and freedom. The Church is strictly under the law of Christ, and it is not punitive or cumbersome and does not require improvements.

2. LGBT - Lesbians, gay, bisexual, and transgender are issues with the political spectrum that are gradually creeping into the Church with an intensity that is already rocking the fabrics are the Christian faith.

Opinions on abnormal sexual orientation are as diverse as the number of denominations and have become a matter of preferences and political relationships between the denomination and bureaucracy.

While some believe that the Church needs to bend to accommodate every manner of being accused of discrimination that is not Christ-like, others think everyone member of the Church has the right to live in whatever way that is their choice, and the Church doesn't have the right to either reject or criticize them.

But the Church is not a social gathering or a political party where everyone joins and participates in activities. Nobody is a member of the Church who is not first born again. Membership of the Church should not be legislated and politicized and cannot be made compulsory.

The only genuine and recognized authority from which the Church derives its rules and regulations are the Bible and not the current leadership of any denomination, and the Bible is very clear on the issue of lesbians, gays, bisexuals, and transgender.

One thing that has become evident is that the temporal authorities are not and have never been comfortable with the Church because they are like darkness and light; and will continue to do everything they can to obliterate or at least render the Church of no effect and one of the most subtle ways to achieve this is by infiltrating the very base of the Church's strength which her doctrine if they succeed in corrupting the Church's doctrines by interpreting the scriptures to suit their selfish ignoble purpose and applying same to support their whims and caprices thereby misleading the gullible who unfortunately are in the majority.

Compromise on the integrity of the Gospel and the Church is the only platform where the State and the Church can ever be friends.

3. LEADERSHIP TUSSLE - We are beginning to see the unhealthy rivalry between Church leaders either of one denomination and another or of the same denomination. This has engendered an unhealthy competitive spirit within Christendom. Some Church leaders engage in mudslinging against their compatriots in different denominations with an air of spiritual superiority and sagacity. The quest for a higher position of authority has brought fierce and unethical struggles for power and positions in the Church. Seeking power for reasons other than selfless service is creeping into the Church courtesy of secular political influence on the Church.

3. MISUSE OF JUSTICE: Justice expressed in the Bible is rendering righteous judgments. In other words, justice is working what is true according to the criterion of God's will and personality as he has expressed it in the Bible. The term justice first appears in the Bible when God declares that he chose Abraham and his offspring to bless the countries "by working righteousness and justice" (Genesis 18:19). The principle of justice is not "contemporary society standards"; it is God's justice. Justice and righteousness start with God's character. What God demands humans to do communicates his will and personality. It is God's righteousness that makes human liberties right. What humans consider their rights are right only if God declares them right.

The term justice in the Bible is exchangeable with judgment. Justice is primarily the act of judging or rendering a judgment. Therefore, we can interpret justice according to the Scriptures as rendering a judgment according to God's righteousness. Or, more clearly, rendering righteous judgments. This description has two parts: a standard - God's will and character as Bible reveals, and an action - assigning the standard or rendering a judgment founded on that standard—i.e., doing justice.

King Solomon demonstrates what it is like to wisely render a righteous decision. After Solomon distinguished which prostitute was saying the fact about her newborn, all Israel "stood in amazement of the king, because they recognized that the judgment of God was in him to accomplish justice" (1 Kgs 3:28)—that is, execute righteous judgments. Executing justice is speaking a righteous judgment: Proverbs 29:4 NIV: By justice, a king gives a country stability, but those who are greedy for bribes tear it down.

Justice by the Bible definition contrasts with justice defined by our secular age in which justice = rights. Our worldly age gives the fruit without the root—the fruit of freedoms without any criterion of righteousness for assessing which liberties are right. As such, people are known to elevate whatever they crave with the wording of rights. Justice virtually becomes "I merit what I want," with the one condition that others' freedoms should not be violated either, leaving a jumbled bunch for the judiciaries to sort out among the numerous conflicts that necessarily arise. So, if one man likes to marry another man, it is his right. "Justice" offers it. If a woman wishes to eliminate her pregnancy, it is her right. "Justice" mandates it. If a man elects, he likes to have surgery to change to a female, "justice" dictates it. If someone wants to seek euthanasia and "die with dignity," "justice" guarantees it. Whether this description of justice is the most reasonable we can achieve in a pluralistic nation or not is a matter for reflection.

The fact here is to recognize the distinction between a biblical perspective of rights and trendy Western culture's view.

4. POLITICAL ADVERSARY: Politics results in passionate controversies between Christians, and whenever there is disagreement on how to apply the word of God—that is, they differ in what justice entails. The other side may look like it's encouraging an injustice, which in turn can make people suspect if the other side is Christian.

People may always be right in their viewpoints and their politics. However, the fallen heart ever thinks it's right; it always believes its motive is just. Adam and Eve's determination to take part in the fruit needed a self-justifying assertion, and we all have been self-righteous and self-justifying eternally since. And self-rationalizing people are inclined to be sure that their beliefs are just. That's why we are beguiled to disdain and critique our fellow church members whose politics differ from ours.

The first rationale why Christians passionately differ on politics is that Christians ardently mind justice and assume that their political beliefs promote what they view as justice.

But most political decisions depend on wisdom, and God is the only all-wise. Political judgments are hard because we all require wisdom to several degrees. Even when Christians decide on biblical doctrines, they will frequently think differently about the techniques and tactics and timing, and more.

Knowledge is both a stance and an ability. It's the attitude of fearing the Lord, and it's the ability to make effective and righteous judgments. Life is filled with complex and arduous decisions; sensible people competently apply the Scriptures because they fear the Lord. Wisdom understands that there's a period to answer a nitwit according to his foolishness and a time to abstain (Prov 26:4–5). Like automobiles need fuel, political decisions need wisdom.

Consider once again the event of the two harlots each asking King Solomon that the baby belongs to her. Solomon ordered for a sword and ordered, "Divide the living child in two and give half to the one and a half to the other" (1 Kings 3:25). That indicated the real mother. And it needed wisdom: "And all Israel heard of the judgment that the king had rendered, and they stood in awe of the king because they perceived that the wisdom of God was in him to do justice" (1 Kings 3:28). The goal was justice; the means was wisdom.

Likewise, the goal of politics is justice; and the means is wisdom. Some examples may help illustrate the most controversial political issues that depend on wisdom: abortion, political alliances, and political parties.

Abortion. - The Bible prohibits abortion because the deliberate killing of an unborn someone is murder. Pastors and congregations, accordingly, should adopt a stance on abortion, both in their sermons and in their membership judgments. They should excommunicate any member who unrepentantly encourages abortion, whether by privately encouraging women to attempt them or by politically supporting abortion.

But Christians are not in agreement on all the political reasons for rejecting the injustice of abortion. Many Christians take an incrementalist policy. They support programs that forbid abortion except in the case of rape and incest because they believe that such policies have a better chance of legislating and that they will eradicate the large majority of abortions. Others oppose such an incrementalist policy as yielding. Rather, they adopt an all-or-nothing strategy. Who is ethical strategically? It's difficult to be sure, of course, because we depend on our knowledge. The Scriptures might have doctrines to rely on, but it doesn't apply directly to political situations like that.

Responding to those difficult questions needs wisdom. The disclosed wisdom of God in the Scriptures is different from the wisdom of man, and that's what we need to make virtually every political decision. Political decisions depend on comprehending how to pertain the Bible to the enormous and complicated set of situations that shroud every political judgment. They compel a person to correctly comprehend biblical principles and accordingly apply those tenets according to social dynamics, lawful precedent, political suitability, historical circumstances, economic forecasts, ethnic anxieties, criminal justice appreciations, and so much further.

Political alliances-. If you like to get things accomplished in a democratic system, you will need to make alliances with people with whom you don't necessarily agree on all issues. That's the reason for political parties. There are not always sufficient people whose thinking is exactly as we do on all issues, so we have to team up with people who agree with us on a significant clump of issues to get anything done.

But this strategy of forging political alliances raises ethical questions. Are we guilty of any unfair statute the other partners of our political party arranged to enact into law? What if the opposition party proves even more unjust? Does it make matter if the injustice we're addressing is a small objection versus a big one —and how big is big? Does it matter if we're contradicting evil oratory versus evil strategies? And what if one coalition leaves us as Christians, but our witnesses look artificial, while the other means taking sides with those who openly contradict us? We need wisdom.

Political parties. The issues are becoming more com complicated with the ever-changing political landscape. It may be acceptable for a Christian to favor a particular political group today but may not a decade later. The floor can shift under our feet shortly. Imagine that you had resided in Germany in the early 1920s, and a Christian companion notified you that he entered the National Socialist Germany Workers Party—the Nazis. You would have concerns, but your Church perhaps would not excommunicate him. But later in the early 1930s, what the Nazi Party symbolized would have become obvious enough that voices in your Church would most probably insist on ex-communication, as experienced by the 1934 Barmen Declaration in which the professing Church publicly condemned all Nazism. How more seriously would this be the case much later by the 1940s? Politics are not fixed, and with every day that passes, we need a new tonic of wisdom, and Christians will have to be changing viewpoints all along the way.

The several sheds of politics in the Church cannot be addressed by one solution-fit-all type of position but require dynamism and a proactive approach. The Church can no longer remain aloof or pretend not to be directly affected by the myriad of evolving challenges. However, there is one common source of an acceptable solution to checkmate these challenges and preserve the integrity and sanctity of the Church, and that is the wisdom from the word of God.

CHAPTER 10

THE CHRISTIAN AND POLITICS

"Hold everything earthly with a loose hand; but grasp eternal things with a deathlike grip."

Charles Spurgeon

The believer who is involved in the material history of the world is involved in it as representing another order, another master (then the prince of this world (Satan), another claim (than that of the natural heart of man). Thus he must plunge into social and political problems to influence the world, not in the hope of making it a paradise, but simply to make it tolerable — not to diminish the opposition between this world and the Kingdom of God, but simply to modify the opposition between the disorder of this world and the order of preservation that God wills for it — not to "bring in" the Kingdom of God, but so that the Gospel may be proclaimed, that all men may hear the good news of salvation through the death and resurrection of Christ. – Jacques Ellul

Should Christians be involved in politics is a frequent question asked in almost all generations and all climes? The answers are as varied as the number of respondents in most cases. However, the truth is that Christians are already part of the political system and, therefore, involvement in politics may be passive.

The pertinent question might be how involved in the political process Christians should be, how active or participatory we should get; decisions are made by those who show up, and everyone participates in the effects of those decisions.

The notion of politics being dirty is the point of resentment among Christians who would rather preserve their pious heritage than be mired by politics. But the concept of politics is not dirty and putrefying.

Christians, when correctly educated and motivated, change the attitude of political debate. They usually bring the moral principles of God's kingdom into the civil realm and thereby become representatives of His common mercy — of His care for those that believe together with those who don't.

Politics involves making agreements and decisions on how a group of people can live peacefully together, even in a diversified culture. Like every other human endeavor gets corrupted by the practitioners, politics is not exempted and to avoid participation is to tacitly give credence to the corrupt tendencies.

When the good men stay away from taking actions that will shape society for good, they advertently improve the chances of the wicked to continue to hold sway. The initial reason for Christians staying aloof in the political process was the imminent returning of the Lord Jesus Christ to take His bride (the Church) away.

Since the waiting for the second coming is elongated, and we are not sure when exactly it will be, we have to take necessary steps to minimize our suffering and humiliation by the world until we are raptured. Those who are afraid of the truth and benefit from the dark and dirty side of politics will invariably be opposed to the potential challenge of Christian participation in politics by insulating their dark political environments with every form of an agent of darkness to ensure that the light of the Christian involvement is effectively checked.

Christians' participation in politics should be deliberate and conscientious such that alliances and cooperation with other political actors will not jeopardize the integrity of the Christian. God minds about our spiritual beings, but He similarly cares about our nutrition, water, employment, and housing. When God instructs us to love our neighbors, He implies to love them completely. That signifies we'll care about legislation that protects unborn children. We'll care about programs that protect marriages and families. Loving our neighbor means we'll normally be worried about the corrupting ethical influences that trickle into public schools.

Christians need to get included because we believe in a God who cares with passion about his universe and his creation and, therefore, how it is governed. The Bible is immensely political in that it is all about the way God asks people to conduct themselves and act towards him and relate with each other. This includes economics and law because these are instruments that are necessary for building justice. So many times, it is an injustice that subjugates God's earth, and this repents him.

But if we are not part of the decision-making process through active participation, how can we possibly influence policies and programs.

Atheists, as citizens, obey the laws; they participate in the vote, pay their taxes, and give a helping hand to indigent neighbors. But good citizenship needs more. Good denizens feel constrained to offer a moral report of their country. Good citizens like to commend their country's integrity to citizens of the successive generation, and they wish to transmit that government to citizens still unborn. It is contended that those who believe in the God of Abraham, Isaac, Jacob, and Jesus prove to be honest citizens. The reason is that their allegiance to the political authority is qualified by a commitment to a higher order. Their maximum loyalty is not to the authority or its founding charter but to the City of God and the holy contents that guide our way toward that future for which we were created. Such citizens were precisely conceived for dual citizenship.

Christians, as citizens, are under divine obligation to work through civic authority for the promotion of justice and human welfare. It's an all-encompassing responsibility. After all, it is politics that determines whether we are at war or at peace. It impacts the nation's job creation, wealth innovation and distribution, and property ownership rights. It defines our freedom of speech, writing, and worship. Even the situations of family life always depend on government programs, encompassing the quality and scope of public education.

Christian citizens are generally committed to the good of everyone, and particularly to those who belong to the household of faith (Galatians 6:10). Such good deeds include lauding and condemning policies that impact the needy and powerless. We educate church membership to accomplish good work in clinics, schools, and inner-city communities, so why should we exclude politics? Our good jobs there, as we do in other realms, give honor to our Heavenly Father.

In every civilization, religion inclines to be significant to people who mind politics; likewise, politics always matters greatly to those who are interested in religion. And frequently, these are the exact people.

What then are unique and specific roles that might be the point of Christians' participation in politics?

1. Hold Government Accountable: *Romans 13:4 NIV: For the one in authority is God's servant for your good. But if you do wrong, be afraid, for rulers do not bear the sword for no reason. They are God's servants, agents of wrath to bring punishment on the wrongdoer.*

The Scripture tells us that government authority exists for our good. If the one in government does not know the master's missive since he is a servant and there is no one available to clarify what God wants, how can government bureaucrats serve Him well?

1 Peter 2:13-14 Submit yourselves for the Lord's sake to every human authority: whether to the emperor, as the supreme authority, or to governors, who are sent by him to punish those who do wrong and to commend those who do right.

How, unless they accept counsel from the sacred community, can mayors, senators, or presidents comprehend God's view of right and wrong or good and evil except they are Christians themselves.

Throughout history, God has summoned His people to be advisors to earthly rulers. Daniel told King Nebuchadnezzar, the most powerful ruler at the time: *Daniel 4:27 NIV -Therefore, Your Majesty, be pleased to accept my advice: Renounce your sins by doing what is right, and your wickedness by being kind to the oppressed. It may be that then your prosperity will continue."*

Joseph, as Egypt's second-in-command, always advised Pharaoh. Moses engaged the Egyptian ruler and commanded liberation for the Israelites. Mordecai advised King Ahasuerus of Persia. Queen Esther also, was important in King Ahasuerus' court.

Also, John the Baptist in the New Testament was sharp in confronting bureaucrats about morals, even berating Herod the tetrarch "for Herodias, his brother Philip's wife, and all the terrible things that Herod had done" (Luke 3:19). These bad things comprised Herod's actions as a government official.

In Acts 24, Apostle Paul talks to the Roman governor Felix about morality and self-control and the impending judgment. It's a sure bet that Paul made Felix accountable for his demeanor as a civil official. And he caught the governor's attention: According to verse 25, Felix was stunned and sent Paul away.

2. Christians Bring Uncanny Values: In a world that gives plausibility to every idea but grants certainty to none, the only reputable consistency in language and meaning that subsisting is the eternal word of God which is the basis of the Christian doctrines. Once God is excluded from civic life, we are left with two main actors: the individual and the nation. And with God out of the scene, there exists no intervening structure to create ethical values. Without the Church, there is no countercheck to the State's ambitions.

When politics is interrogated or criticized based on values, the issues, whether acknowledged or not, become religious ones. Therefore, when genuine religion is excluded, the void will be filled by phony religion, the kind of religion that has been bootlegged into social space under different names.

Law, if it must be esteemed as legitimate, must be supported by ethical judgment. In a democratic environment, government and society must drink from the same ethical well. Government has the responsibility to make moral decisions, and these are decisions of the utmost nature. But without the religious influence, worldly aptitude is given the impetus of religion.

Disposal of the transcendent drains meaning from the law, and without a supreme reference point, there is no justification and definition for obedience, and that implies the State must strive for more coercion in exercising power.

Christians, accordingly, must join the civic realm. This is because the Church must convey moral values. As James Boice once stated, "Religious people are the only citizens who advance the nation in the direction of justice and righteousness." Christianity not only contributes to individual interests but the arrangement of society with freedom and justice for all. Christianity, only as taught in the Scriptures and declared openly in the kingdom context by Jesus Christ, gives both a transcendent ethical influence and a transcendent arrangement of society without a harsh theocratic system. Society's good health and safety, therefore, depend on a strong religious impact. We don't need more laws because, without an ethical citizenry, rightful existing laws can be exploited immorally. Society needs people who are ready to abide by God's moral standards. That's the obvious way to reduce the advance of evil. It is similar to how the ethical principles of God's kingdom make progress and community life becomes governed by the character and image of the celestial city.

Civil government is well benefits from a population of citizens whose lives conform to the law behind the law. The entire human society needs a community that understands that some stuff is right while some are wrong and which sticks to the God-given judgment that permeates all creation (see Proverbs 8 and Proverbs 22).

3. Christians Provide Restraint: The Church is better than a model, but its presence in society, is a moderation of the kingdom of man. Contrary to common misconception, it is not the government's business to annunciate a moral vision. That responsibility belongs to different social institutions, primarily the Church. When the government steps beyond the limits of its planned authority, the Church serves as an effective source of ethical resistance.

But the Church does not restrain for its own sake; it does not resist amassing power or enlarging its followership; it resists for the public good. The same sentiment was noticeable in the late 1800s when Southern Presbyterian Church taught Christians, both those in authority as well as that outside must employ their Christian conscience, inspired by God's Word, in the civil sphere. Christians are expected to participate, not to impose their morals on the population as a whole, but to campaign for justice, show reverence for life, and help the powerless.

Christianity was the world's most fundamental preservative. When non-believers are not courageous to speak up out of love for their nation, Christians speak up for the love of God; when integrity and civic honesty break down, divine authority steps in to impose sane living, discipline, understanding, justice, and harmony among citizens.

4. God Wants Us to Get Involved: Romans 13:1-7 and 1 Peter 2:13-14 are not sheer gist for academic curiosity. Those words are not in the Bible for our confidential edification; they are there to prepare and educate us on how to relate with government officers and to clarify how God values the government's functions and responsibilities.

Effective government is key in the quest for justice. And real justice emanates from a sovereign God. Without justice, there can be no nation, no shared virtues, and no common standards. Christianity is the soul of Western civilization. - Christopher Dawson. Any time the soul is gone, the body dies. God's people must be prepared to deal with moral issues, they must gauge public policies by biblical principles of justice and holiness, and they must advise leaders when they —legislators, mayors, governors, and presidents deviate from God's intended way.

In instructing us to be "salt" and "light" on the earth, Jesus is exhorting us to impact our society rather than separate ourselves from our community. Some well-meaning believers believe that any measures to exercise pressure on the attitude of non-Christians are unfair. However, we preach the Gospel primarily with passion, faith, and the intention to change the behavior of non-believers.

Anything more than evangelism is off-limits. As a result, Christians should not engage in politics. This reasoning is indicated by the erroneous assumption: "I believe in such and such, but I can't impose my morality on others."

Any time a congress passes legislation, it is invariably an imposition of morality.

Statutes against robbery compel the morality of the innocent over the dishonest. Laws against hustling compel a sexual morality. Proclaiming anything lawful or unlawful is a declaration of morality. Law is based on morality, and morality is based on religion.

If Christians forsake public service, what happens to society's values, ethics, and moral principles? If Christians wash off their hands and turn back, who stands up for the needy and powerless? Throughout history, we have noticed the result of Christian influence: in the abolishment of slavery, championing for universal literacy; better education; and legislations that protect children, daily and factory laborers, and women. That sort of influence does not show up from silence or isolation. It comes from commitment.

The United States does not represent the kingdom of God, and Christians today must appreciate, as Martin Luther did in his time, that having a Christian government is out of the question even over one land because the wicked will always be in the majority over the good. Therefore, trying to form a government according to the scriptures would be like keeping wolves, lions, eagles, and sheep together in the same fold and allowing them to freely mingle.

But elected Christian officials have a fundamental right to act based on their principles, provided that before being voted in, they have clarified to the electorate their specific value system. On basic moral issues, the representative's decision and conscience take priority over regional and even federal majority priority. Voting on matters such as capital sentences, abortion, embargo, censorship, and several other moral questions would be influenced. Of course, the ensuing political price might be huge.

5. Politics are Unavoidable: As sojourners and exiles (1 Peter 2:11), it can be beguiling for Christians to assume an attitude that earthly governing structures are insignificant to the mission of advancing the Gospel. But when you ask a preacher in an undercover church or a missionary striving to enter a closed country if politics are insignificant. Religious freedom, passports, and visas are not superfluous luxuries but are always critical for pastors and missionaries striving to proclaim and teach the Gospel.

Augustine's book "City of God" advises on this point. Believers are inhabitants of the "City of God," but in this part of eternity, we are also citizens of the "City of Man" and hence must be respectable citizens of both communities. There are biblical illustrations of how citizenship in the secular city can be adopted to advance the spread of the heavenly. Paul's plea for his Roman citizenship (Acts 16:37, 22:25) is an example of this.

Because politics have implications for real-world Christian activities like evangelism, missions, and preaching of the Gospel, Christians are supposed to join in the political process by utilizing their legitimate authority, championing laws and policies that enhance human flourishing.

Politics entails compromise but so do other business activities and participation in orderly labor and professional establishments. Compromise is crucial to a civilized culture. The critical question is whether concession entails yielding on fundamental ethical principles. Whenever it does, the Christians must pull out. If there is no further acceptable option, they must quit their positions. Of course, the same standard applies to everyone else, but for Christians, this problem is highly noticeable and may arise very frequently.

6. We should love our neighbor: When challenged by religious leaders on the law, Jesus clarified that loving God with Spirit, soul, and mind was the greatest commandment (Matthew 22:37). He added that the next in importance was: "You shall love your neighbor as yourself" (Matthew 22:39).

Disciples of Christ are called to love and support their neighbors (Matthew 28:19-20). When a question was raised about the qualifications of neighbor, Jesus told the story of the Good Samaritan (Luke 10:25-37), implying that irrespective of nationality, background, social status, or occupation, friendly love is owed.

Politics is among the most crucial areas in which Christians exemplify love for neighbors. In fact, how can Christians say that they care about others and not be involved in the profession that most profoundly patterns basic rights and liberties? Looking after the destitute, thirsty, naked, sick, and downtrodden is significant to Jesus and should also be to His disciples as well. Jesus said, "As you did it to one of the least of these you did it to me" (Matthew 25:40).

Fulfillment of the biblical law to love neighbors and compassion for the "least of these" should be an emphasis for every believer. Also, a holistic strategy is necessary. Loving neighbor involves enrolling at a homeless refuge, as well as influencing legislation that facilitates human socio-economic development. Good administration and statutes are not minor factors in the wealth and freedom of a nation.

For instance, the plurality of North Koreans is kept in economic captivity by vicious political pressures, whereas South Korea's nationals are given freedom and a policy that facilitates prosperity. The nation of North Korea needs more than food cuddy and better hospitals; they require political leadership and programs that appreciate human rights. Supporting these transformations in totalitarian governments is significant for loving our neighbors in tyrannized areas.

Keeping to the golden rule involves pursuing laws that defend unborn children, strengthen marriages and families, support the helpless, and procure alternatives for flourishing. Politics is a vehicle for creating tremendous change and must be employed by Christians who care about their neighbor.

Rather than turning away believers from any relationship with a civil administration, the scriptures indicated there is a degree of obligation to engage in civil matters. Rather than having political rulers imposed upon us, we possess the God-given chance to elect our leaders.

Ought God's people not be instrumental in impacting the selection? Whatever the case, some set of moralities is going to administer or influence the nation. Considering what the Scripture conveys about the personality of God, do you believe He minds whether our rulers encourage the murder of the unborn child or the damage to the biblical meaning of marriage?

It just makes the point that Christians should be at the vanguard of electing leaders who will preside according to God's directions and will develop policies more probable to attract God's favor.

CHAPTER IV

CHAPTER 11

THE JAMAICAN CHRISTIAN AND

POLITICS - PARTICIPATION

The day people realize that if
they are in large unified
numbers, they can demand
anything from their Government.

Is the day the Government is in
big trouble, that is why they
keep you divided.

~ George Orwell

T he preponderance of Christianity in Jamaica is historic and part of the colonial heritage. After independence from British colonial rule in 1962, the country's constitution guarantees the freedom of worship. Jamaica is a representative parliamentary Democratic monarchy which means that the citizens are actively involved in choosing the political leaders of the country at all levels of government.

Jamaica has 60% of its population as Christians, with the remaining 40% distributed among several other religious groups. This country is reputed to have the greatest number of churches per square mile in the world. For all intents and purposes, Jamaica can be called a Christian country without any fear of contradictions.

The liberty to vote is the fundamental principal bedrock of democracy.

The freedom to vote might have been the most significant instrument of the power of the people or was at least a critical partner in a broader transformative system that helped in conferring legitimacy to the parties, elections, leadership, and constitutions.

The right to vote, even though critical to democracy, has not been adequately understood as a major justification for constitutional, social, economic, and democratic development in Jamaica.

Adult voting started in Jamaica in 1944 and spread to the other islands from then to 1962. In those eighteen years, it developed a democratic revolt among twelve little Caribbean nations and eleven of those nations between 1944 and 1954. This era launched mass politics in the Caribbean. The Caribbean multitudes had come into the political scene of democracy for the first time in record. Mass elections mixed with multiple parties create mass politics.

In a broader context, adult suffrage was a characteristic of the twentieth century. One commentary had it that the democratic ideal of the multi-party election with universal adult suffrage became the dominant political form of the nation-state in the 20th century. In 1900 no nation had accomplished this, but after a Century vast number of countries have. Within the last 25 years of the century, 113 countries introduced multi-party elections".

ADULT SUFFRAGE IN JAMAICA- Universal adult suffrage gives the right to vote to every adult irrespective of gender, race, educational status, and economic and marital status. Each country fixes the adult age according to its peculiar cultural and socio-economic circumstances. In most countries, the suffrage (eligible for voting) age is 18 years, but in Jamaica, the suffrage age was 21 years before independence. We should all recollect and commemorate the truth that Jamaica was the first largely black nation in the whole world to attain this milestone, whereby never again would only a few of the elite and the affluent have the freedom to elect political representatives. Rather, that right would apply to everyone who is 18 years and above, whether they are cane-cutters or factory laborers, domestic servants, or jobless, no matter how indigent or disadvantaged.

This is what Universal Adult Suffrage must represent to people if we are striving for their participation to start again to advance society through a democratic political and electoral process.

The Electoral Advisory Committee had to be established in 1979 to resuscitate and preserve a discredited voting process in Jamaica, and this has become the important challenge facing the Electoral Commission and, certainly, the country. How do we develop meaningful electoral reform and campaign-financing strategies to win back the enthusiasm of the society for Universal Adult Suffrage -- the freedom to vote in a free and fair election?

In a new national political survey, 80 percent of the poll said they preferred a direct vote for prime minister, and 82 percent preferred the liberty to recall incompetent members of congress before the successive general election. Similarly, 70 percent of the voters feel that politicians are criminals, 80 percent believe the same about the police, and 50 percent of public servants.

These impressions are buttressed by the common belief and proof that those who fund elections can alter the results, and these elections have become a battle between the hard-core followers of both main political parties. If we are pushing to revitalize confidence for suffrage in Jamaica and several other nations of the world, there will have to be a pact for fresh far-reaching modifications in the political and electoral processes of these nations.

Campaign finance reform is non-negotiable and must be clear and straightforward, with laws in place to keep officials answerable for any violations. Privileged, personal interest financing of elections has already subverted the democratic system beyond restoration in many nations and forced critics and observers to contend that democracy is for sale to the biggest buyer in today's political setting.

The Jamaican populace has communicated again through the surveys, and it is obvious that most of the youthful and more informed voters are no longer encouraged to merely vote for a party but for substantive strategies, programs, and vacancies for national and self-development.

There is a need to lay more priority on policy choice voting or more referendums and opinion polls to develop policy, as is the unfolding trend in the more stable democracies of north European welfare capitalist nations.

This life-changing event has led to the passion for the freedom to vote among older citizens who were incapable of doing so at a point in time and support for the leaders of political parties and decision-makers whom they now considered as their rulers in political independence. Accordingly, voter turnout and excitement for elections in newly sovereign states were much greater than today, as the advantages were noticeable and accessible.

IMPERATIVES OF VOTE - While so much more remains to be achieved and Jamaica must now stride to the next phase of electoral reform, much has been accomplished by programs executed by subsequent adult suffrage governments. In the health sector, for instance, after 280 bizarre years of minority colonial rule, the infant mortality rate was 99 out of every 1000. Today, after 70 years of adult suffrage, it's 14 out of 1000.

Seventy years ago, the life expectancy of Jamaicans was 53 years; today, it is close to that of developed countries at 73years. In the education sector, in 1943, only 3 out of every 100 Jamaicans could find placement in a secondary school; today, the enrollment rate is 91%. In 1943 Champs only seven boys' schools participated, but today the expansion of secondary education has meant more than 111 boys,' and 104 girls' teams took part in 2022, representing 165 secondary schools in Jamaica. Then there was no single university; today, more than 1 out of 4 qualified Jamaicans are enrolled in Jamaican tertiary institutions. The top hierarchy of the public service, the private sector, and social life excluded women and can only be attained by either whites or light-skinned Jamaicans. Today, the use of the right to suffrage has opened up roles so that those with darker tones and women are highly represented in every area of Jamaican life.

Yet, very few Jamaicans are exercising their freedom to vote. The main explanation is the assumption that progressively whoever you elect makes no considerable difference in the living conditions of the majority. Moreover, irrespective of whoever wins or loses the election, it is usually a small group of grass-roots party activists that benefits disproportionately, and a few big campaign contributors are compensated with the award of contracts, board memberships appointments, and other openings in a way that contributes to rendering Jamaica the second-most economically lopsided nation in the Western Hemisphere.

Adult voting, therefore, requires to be an occurrence to acknowledge a real achievement and also to proceed to the next stage of reviving popular involvement in the freedom to vote. The main strategy toward that feat is the execution of reforms, recommended by the Electoral Commission of Jamaica (ECJ) in collaboration with the National Integrity Council (NIA) as well as other civic organizations, to make the freedom to elect more meaningful: By compelling political party registration, to encourage the electorate to learn more about what is happening in their political parties and promote the opportunity of funding their operations; Through campaign finance restrictions, to guarantee funding is more transparent and less monopolized by the big money of corrupt or commercial-minded politicians so that the common interest of the electorate will be served and reduce if not eliminate the number of all those who seek to pay the piper, and detect the tune.

VOTER REGISTRATION - To be eligible for voting during the elections, it is expedient that we follow the lawful procedure released by the Electoral Commission from time to time.

Any Jamaican national who has the following qualifications is entitled to enroll to vote;

-Is a Jamaican national of eighteen years old or above and resides in Jamaica or

-Is a Commonwealth national who is eighteen (18) years of age or older and who resides in Jamaica at the period of enrollment, and who has remained a resident for not less than twelve months before the date of enrollment.

-Is not jeopardized by any legitimate incapability to vote, such as being of an unhealthy mind, condemned, or under a suspended judgment.

The Electoral Commission of Jamaica (ECJ) publicizes two voters' registers each year. One schedule is publicized on May 31, and the next one six months after on November 30. Enrollment is done continuously, and individuals desirous of being included in the list can simply go to their ECJ Constituency Office and indicate.

When there is voters' apathy, as is the case here in Jamaica, it implies that Christians are not exercising their civic right to vote and be voted. We established in the previous chapters the necessity of Christian participation in choosing who makes laws and regulations for us. The need for being part of the political process cannot be overemphasized but suffice it to say that the spirituality of the believer is not diminished by involvement in the political process if they play by the rules.

Isn't it appalling that in a country with more than 60% of a Christian population, the only political party identified as Christian - the Christian Democratic Party of Jamaica, does not have an elected candidate in the parliament, and indeed the last time it fielded a candidate was 1972? This is a classic example of the fact that Jamaican Christians are largely ignorant of their civic responsibilities or are not genuinely enthusiastic about improving the quality of life of the average Jamaican.

Recently a local church pastor was dismissed from the pulpit for contesting in the local government elections as a chairmanship candidate. His only offense was that he is a Christian, yet the churches spend hours daily praying to God for better and more humane leadership in our nation. I doubt if we, in all sincerity, believe that God will send angels from heaven to come and replace the current crop of corrupt and inept leaders we have, or else we don't believe or expect our prayers to be answered.

The ballot, they say, is stronger than the barrel, and those who prevent peaceful change make unpeaceful change inevitable. The only way to give force to your thoughts is to cast your vote where and when it matters most. It is sheer laziness to continue to complain about corruption and poverty and yet refuse to do the very least one can afford for a change.

Yes, admittedly, there is widespread corruption in the public service of our country and even in the private sector, but when good men and women stay away from politics and power, the evil men and their antics reign supreme. The amicable solution to bad and corrupt leadership is to effect changes through the ballot.

Rather than suspending a pastor for participating in partisan politics, I think the Church should vet his manifesto and ensure that it represents the values and changes we all want to see in the governance. Furthermore, the Church should hold the elected pastor accountable for the implementation of his campaign promises and the manifesto of his party.

The Church's concerns are understandable given the stench of corruption and other sinister activities shrouding the political arena in this country. However, there should be a deliberate and noble strategy for Christians in Jamaica to meaningfully engage in politics with the view of making a positive impact and arresting the rot in the system.

It may be advisable for any courageous Christian, whether clergy or laity desiring to engage in partisan politics, to discuss with the Church leadership in a very dispassionate way so that there can be a mutual understanding of both the intentions and operational guidelines of the candidate. This will enable the Church to make such inputs that will enhance the candidate's acceptance and preserve the Church's integrity. This kind of reasoning together will also allow both the candidate and the Church to obtain the necessary permissions from the relevant authorities where this is applicable.

Since Churches are registered where required as non-profit and non-partisan organizations, it is instructive for any clergyman seeking to engage in partisan politics to formally inform and discuss his ambition which, of course, is his fundamental right with the Church authority so that all the statutory protocols and requirements may be observed and followed to avoid embarrassment to the Church.

The Church should start now to review its stand on active participation in politics, If necessary, and change some of its regulations that constitute a hindrance to the Church as a body and individual members from taking an active part in the political process of our country. With our dominant numbers in this game of numbers, we should be the single force to reckon with in the political landscape of Jamaica.

The two factors responsible for the lack of proportionate influence of the Church in Jamaica's political life are:

1. The misconception of Biblical position on this- before now, the belief that politics is not for Christians was responsible for the isolation of participatory engagement in the political terrain. However, we have made the clarifications based on Biblical injunctions that God expects that we influence society for good, and the most basic way of doing this is to influence the decision-making process through active participation. The salt though available in the kitchen, is not beneficial to the cook and food unless applied, so we are in a tasteless state of our country. So also, is the light. As long as it remains obscure, and do not affect the darkness, therefore, we have no godly justification for avoiding the political process in our country.

We hold the key to the change we all yearn for in the leadership of the country, and as long as we abstain from using the numerical key embedded in our fundamental rights to vote and be voted for, we lose the moral right to hold the present leaders accountable and to complain or protest against bad governance.

Remember that it took Christian slaves to kick-start the protest that eventually led to the abolition of slavery in Jamaica, and the historical antecedents of our country give credence to the inextricably hold of Christianity on our socio-economic development. This is a Christian country, and we need not be ashamed of or apologetic about it but make the most useful hold on it for the good of all.

2. Lack of unity among Christians - The inability of the various denominations of the Christian faith to come together for political engagement has denied us the full benefits of our numerical strength in the political landscape of our country. The maxim "United we stand, divided we fall" cannot be truer elsewhere as it is in the current predicament of the Church in Jamaica. Imagine the outcome of any election where the Church is united in favor of a candidate whose manifesto was influenced or even agreed on with the Church.

When we talk about politicians in Jamaica, we are invariably talking about Christians because more than 60% of our population are Christians, although much of the time, power corrupts those who were good Christians before they were elected. But the Church owes it as a duty to constantly remind those corrupt politicians of the tenets of their faith and the fact that a very good turn deserves another. In the unity of purpose, the Church has a better chance of choosing and influencing the course of development in the country using the ballot.

Generally speaking, we acknowledge that this reduction in voter turnout, which has prevailed consistently in the recent elections, is largely due to a youthful electorate who did not transform from an active colonial administration to being able to choose one's government. Moreover, the reality that elections became quite brutal, corrupt, and seemingly hopeless for most voters, over time, discouraged many from taking part in elections in the last 30 years. This also has meant a continuous deterioration of the trust capital between the political leaders and the population and fewer dividends of democracy delivered by the government.

The Church cannot vote as a body but can influence the choice of the individual voting members and can as well influence the manifesto of the political parties who are aware of the Church's stand on economic, social, and reproductive health issues, for instance. The Church, whether or not it is fielding candidates for election, must show consistency in standing up to defend Christian morals and principles in such a vocal way that politicians will know that compromising on these issues can be very costly, at least politically.

When the Church produces Prime Ministers, Governors, and legislators who are known to be uncompromising with their faith, the country will witness less corruption and criminality while economic development will be accelerated. For when the righteous are on the throne, the people rejoice, but when the wicked is in control, the people suffer.

Mass participation in the political process by Christians should, as a matter of urgency, be vigorously encouraged by the Church leadership. The Church should sensitize the entire membership and educate them to present themselves for elective positions where they are qualified to run for offices. They should form alliances with like-minded believers in different denominations and take an active frontline role in party politics. This is the valid and godly way of contributing to good governance and ensuring peaceful change when and where necessary.

CHAPTER 12

JAMAICAN CHRISTIAN AND CRIMINALITY

The story of a Christian family - The pastor and his wife with three children are all workers in the local Church where they worship. The three children (a boy and two girls) were in the ushering department of the Church while their mother was the women leader. One day, the father complained that the money he kept somewhere in the house was missing but could not suspect any member of his household because he was convinced that they were Christians. Within three months, the incidence of theft had occurred more than seven times, and the parents could no longer keep quiet. The children aged between fourteen and eighteen years were summoned by the parents and confronted with the sad reality of theft, but one after another, they denied culpability, and the parents were devastated and confused. How did we come to have children who are thieves in a Christian home?

Jamaica has a long history of Christianity and is reputed to have the greatest number of churches per square mile in the world, as well as more than 60% of her population, are devoted Christians. How come we have such a crime rate that is ranked one of the highest in the world. The world bank statistics for homicide rank Jamaica's crime rate at almost 50% in 2021, the highest in Latin America and the Caribbean.

Several areas of Jamaica, especially cities such as Kingston, Montego Bay, and Spanish Town, experience increased degrees of crime and unrest. Jamaica has witnessed one of the greatest murder cases in the world for several years, according to United Nations estimations. Former Prime Minister P. J. Patterson defined the problem as "a national challenge of unprecedented proportions."

As contained in the latest police crime statistics, 112 people were murdered in Jamaica over the first 23 days of 2022. This is 15 more homicides or a 15.5 percent rise when compared with the corresponding period in 2021.

The Jamaica Constabulary Force (JCF) announced that there had been more than 1,200 homicides in just over ten months of this year, considerably higher than the same period last year.

CORRUPTION - Corrupt practices are prevalent in every sector of Jamaica's life.

According to the 2012 Transparency International (TI) Corruption Perception Index, Jamaica is ranked number 83 out of a total of 176 nations and provinces with a score of 38 on a scale of 0 to 100, where 0 means 'extremely corrupt' and 100 means 'perfect.' No public institution is immune from the destructive corrupting impact of people who are intent on accumulating wealth and maintaining titles and jobs at any cost.

From government ministers right down to the ordinary man on the road, people are the embodiment of corruption in its numerous aspects and appearances. Shockingly, the Jamaican Church has not fled from or resisted corruption inside its domain, as revealed by rather continuous allegations of pastoral impropriety in dealing with church funds. This prevalence of corruption is causing devastation to the communal Jamaican soul. As succinctly and accurately stated by the National Security Policy for Jamaica, "The main threats to Jamaica's peace and prosperity are violent crime and corruption."

Corruption is inflicting a very disastrous effect on the Jamaican nation as a whole and individual household in particular. Virtually on a daily basis, we hear news of families in unrest because some household members cheated other members and pathed with their cash or other valuables. Children are being exploited in some households as means of income where frantic families permit them to be exploited as sex objects by influential men called "dons" and some others of prominence in society. Some parents authorize their lads to own illicit firearms, which they wield to steal money from others and squeeze money from firms.

The secret theft of electricity from the central national power grid is something that various families engage in and condone. This exercise is so common that the national power company has had to install complex technology to reduce electricity thievery. Betting is now recognized in many households as a means of exiting poverty instead of as a scourge to society's advancement.

Viewed from a theological and ethical perspective, it appears the problem of corruption has saturated human society since the fall of man in the garden of Eden. It is obvious in the Scriptures that we humans are created as sacred managers of the established order (Genesis 1:28). But, since the fall and the subsequent nefarious and polluting effect and dislodgement of humans, the management of the established order is mired in intrigue and treachery in relationships.

Corruption was the norm to the extent that the psalmist's very significant testimony on corruption to the point of making people appear perverted: "The fool hath said in his heart, 'There is no God.' They have done abominable works, none doeth good. The Lord looked down from heaven upon the children of men, to see if there is any that did understand and seek God. They are all gone aside, they are lost in wrongdoing they have become filthy: none doeth good, no, not one. They are all workers of iniquity no knowledge? who eat up my people as they eat bread and call not upon the Lord". (Psalm 4)

At no point throughout the account of Israel's history and the Church did God condone fraud in any shape. He was constantly speaking out to condemn it, cautioning his children and chastising those who adamantly refused his prudent and fatherly advice through His prophets and servants. One of the most distinguished prophets that God sent to proclaim His position on criminality was Micah. He confronted God's people through the words: "He has shown you, O mortal, what is good. And what does the

Lord require of you. To act justly and to love mercy and to walk humbly with your God" (Micah 6:8). Similarly, something that is less emphasized in the Micah rebuke is that God goes on to angrily speak out against their "ill-gotten treasures" of fraud, their "dishonest scales" and "false weights" in their business habits, and their violence, prevaricating and deceptive communication (Micah 6: 10-13).

God demanded a reaction to corruption that pertained to justice, mercy, and humility. His resentment in the face of the injustice of fraud was noticeable.

That God in the Old Testament cautions his children against various acts of crime is undeniable. Bribery is forbidden, according to Proverbs 17:2: "A wicked man accepts a bribe behind the back To pervert the ways of justice," Deuteronomy 10: 17: "For the Lord, your God is God of gods and Lord of lords, the great God, mighty and awesome, who shows no partiality and accepts no bribes," and 2 Chronicles 9:7: "Now let the fear of the Lord be on you. Judge carefully, for with the Lord our God there is no injustice or partiality or bribery." Stealing and robbery are denounced in Hosea 7:1: "When I would heal Israel, the corruption of Ephraim is revealed, and the wicked deeds of Samaria; for they deal falsely, the thief breaks in, and the bandits raid without."

The Old Testament similarly speaks out against fraud. This is visible in Ecclesiastes 7:1: "Extortion turns a wise person into a fool, and a bribe corrupts the heart." Ezekiel 22:12 says, "In you are people who accept bribes to shed blood; you take interest and make a profit from the poor. You extort unfair profit from your neighbors. And you have ignored me, proclaims the Sovereign Lord." The preceding verses render an apparent relationship between bribery and swindling, which are illustrations of corruption.

There are also commands in the New Testament against fraud in its various appearances. Peter cautions his readers against the crime that is exemplified in the form of greed: "With eyes full of adultery, they never stop sinning; they seduce the unstable; they are experts in greed—an accursed brood. They have fled the upright way and wandered off to come after the manner of Balam, son of Bosor, who loved the fees of sin (2 Peter 2:14-15).

Peter tells his listeners that they are no more to be recognized for the crime in the world: "Through these, he (Jesus Christ) has given us His great and precious promises, so that through them you may participate in the divine nature having escaped the corruption in the world caused by evil desires" (2 Peter 1: 4). He also cautions them against being enmeshed in the web of crime that overpowers the world: "If they have escaped the corruption of the world by knowing our Lord and Savior Jesus Christ and are again entangled in it and are overcome, they are worse off at the end than they were at the beginning" (2 Peter 2:20). In essence, crime is practically human brokenness and the manipulation of bonds that are devoid of the love of God in Jesus Christ.

People who exploit others for greedy gain demonstrate that they have not been reached by the strength of God's love in Jesus Christ. Their lives are filled with the relationship demolishing acts of "unloved." Wherever there is no love, there is a crime that streams from hearts of self-aggrandizement and selfish purpose. Corruption is disastrous for human unity and the nation for which we were created. Wherever there is love for God and neighbor (Luke 10:27), corruption cannot exist. As Bishop Dr. Paul Tan Chee Ing (n.d.) has suitably noted: "Corruption in any form and any shape – be it bribery, underhandedness, cronyism, palm-greasing, dishonesty, etc., – breaks the covenant of love according to which we are to love God and neighbor as ourselves" (Lk 10:27), which we live to love through serving others as Jesus served, which we must live and thus be fulfilled and satisfied. crime is the infringement on the covenant of love that "binds everything jointly in perfect harmony" (Col 3: 14)

Some questions must be addressed about the culture of unrest that spreads throughout Jamaican society. One of them is that its pervading is so severe that people feel it is normal to engage in criminal practices and a lifestyle of fraud. It appears criminality is an aspect of the Jamaican culture and mentality to the extent that some people do not appear to believe that there is anything improper with it. It can be regarded as a condition in which the abnormalities have been formalized, and digressions from the normal are allowed as common practice in society.

The substandard and outdated legal procedure adds to the persistent dominance of crime in Jamaica. Politicians and prominent people who are apprehended perpetrating acts of criminality normally do not face the full weight of the law. If they are arraigned at all, they are discharged with a sheer slap on the wrist, as it were. Besides, some people are downgraded instead of being fired when they are indicted for bribery, corruption, and chicanery. This does not portend well for a nation that is being submerged in the ocean of crime and trouble.

The problems of unemployment and the uneven distribution of prosperity will remain breeding grounds for criminality. Numerous people who are incapable of securing jobs are generally perceived as those who are more susceptible to polluting influences because they are frantic for a means of income, which is critical to their survival. Many people have said in various contexts and on several occasions that they had to "tief to eat ah food," which implies that they felt they had to steal so that they could give food to their households and survive. Others have swindled people because they felt that they possessed no other alternative in a nation that fails to give opportunities for them to labor for a decent living. Still, another problem to address is the irritating problem of poverty that appears to be indomitable. This contributes to the culture of criminality. How can the Jamaican government deal with the pervading poverty to lessen the experiences of poverty-related crime?

The Church strives its best through public programs to assist people to exit the dehumanizing trap of deprivation, but it appears the Church is incapable of making the kind of impression that it hopes to make so that people would not veer into a life of crime. Further, the needy and downtrodden would invariably be easy targets for complicated acts of criminality, such as bribery, underhandedness, and exploitation, committed by the wealthy who are persistent in becoming wealthier at the expense of the susceptible and dispossessed.

Are there wrong core doctrines in the Church and false core beliefs in society that should be denounced concerning the culture of criminality? Yes, some tenets should be condemned. One of them has to do with the idea that the standards of the Church and Jesus are excessively perfectionistic and idealistic. Several people in the Church and society would affirm that the regularity of pastoral improprieties points to the need for the Church to redefine what it names criminality.

An additional core assumption in the postmodern and increasingly post-Christian public is that morality is comparative. Accordingly, right and wrong are not related to absolute commandments and declarations of ethics. Several people would contend that it would be reasonable to bribe someone in some situations or to steal or deceive someone else if the purpose is not self-aggrandizement or selfish gain. Even though the Scriptures are open about the ungodliness of criminality, some people would insist that the Bible is an old book that does not deal with the intricacies of the problems that postmodern humans encounter. Some would argue that the same Bible that denounces criminality supports genocide in the book of Joshua and elsewhere.

Corruption in the community is the idolizing of money, materialism, and power. This must be denounced because it is not only against the will of God for us humans, but it is harmful to the health of society and the unity of the community. There can be no space for any shape of criminality because of what it accomplishes to the heart of society. It indicates selfishness instead of selflessness that has facilitated the growth of civilizations and the establishment of kingdoms.

The Church will be in peril of teaching syncretism if it agrees with the beliefs and lifestyle choices of any society which adopts an alternative anti-theistic worldview and modus operandi. Several people allege that the Church is rendering itself insignificant by its insistence on defining the differences between right and wrong and good living and bad living. If the Church elects to be indifferent to the atmosphere of political and civil corruption because it wishes to stay in favor with the political establishment, it is in threat of forfeiting its essence and becoming a destructive combination of a scriptural society and a politicized entity. This has occurred before and may be going on in many nations around the world.

One of the culturally entrenched improper practices that must be specified concerning compromise to time is giving money to people in high positions of public or private employment to get things executed. This has been such a common but ignored practice that some Jamaican have engaged in for so long that it is practically an integral aspect of the culture.

Should we cave into this tradition because of how widespread it is? I do not think we should, although it would be extremely difficult to reverse this culture. Nonetheless, I think that with time and God's intervention through a transformed and sanctified church, we would be spiritually strong enough to make an impact on Jamaican society.

The additional culturally embedded improper practice has to do with leaders hiding the improprieties of their fellow leaders, whether those committing the acts of criminality exist in the Church or government employment. This practice of concealing the evils of others is a twisted and distorted understanding of "love covering up a multitude of sins." It is also related to the unwritten law that leaders should rise to and protect other leaders. Will it take an eternity to deal with this bad practice that appears to be entrenched in Jamaican culture? It will take some time, but it can be handled effectively when the people who have the courage and influence take the critical steps, create the basic institutions, and enforce the requisite statutory requirements.

A Jamaican politician onetime declared on national television that some people in Jamaican society are "beyond redemption." This has probably led some people to think that it is almost ridiculous to free society of criminality. Adopting this viewpoint on fraud could be taken as an acquiescence to the spiritual immaturity of society or to the academic immaturity of the individual who has expressed it. The impression that we may have to anticipate or condone corruption because some people are "beyond redemption" must be dismissed, although one may want to understand the basis behind it or the essence of the context that has warranted it.

Another Jamaican Prime Minister once said, "The law is not a bond but an instrument of social engineering." Whereas he may say that he brought in that statement in a background in which he was pushing for the rights of the vulnerable and defenseless by initiating new legislation, what he meant was partly true. Certainly, the law should never be inactive, but it should be heeded. It was under the administration of that same prime minister that fraud was recognized to have been prevalent. Likewise, there is the procedure in Jamaica, whether in the category of government or within the Church, for leaders to constitute committees to handle corruption and misconduct or to create responsibility and a department to grapple with issues related to corruption. Yet, in many instances, the culture of fraud never changes considerably. Footprints are made, but they seem not to be huge enough to create an impression of the level of fraud in society.

It is a reasonable thing to seem to be combatting corruption through committees, offices, and organizations, but the resources and independence must also be given so that there can be a tangible decrease in the experiences of corruption. One account concurs with this viewpoint in remarking that" the organizations (some of which are the enforcement agencies)" lack the resources required to effectively engender transformation. It is understood that these organizations can play a more useful role in mitigating crime in Jamaica if they are empowered with adequate resources and support".

The notion that systems of supervision can be extremely limiting and bureaucratic is reasonable, but this should not be a license to circumvent systems and processes. Bureaucratic procedures are suppressing progress and should be re-tooled in light of the desireè for ease of executing deals and accessing services in all areas of society. Though, evading bureaucratic hierarchies is not an excellent thing to do. Attracting attention and even suggesting alternatives to the disservice of stringent and strangulating bureaucratic structures would be the reasonable thing to accomplish in such situations.

Policies should exist to regulate processes and govern human behavior in institutions and business settings, but they should be more about helping people and their demands instead of demoralizing them to the level of fostering corrupt practices. Leaders should ascertain ethical requirements and legal practices in an endeavor to engender an environment of order and good demeanor in people.

This is a reasonable practice. Though, when those same authorities manipulate those policies and refuse to be governed by the same protocols of conduct, they fail and reveal a life of duplicity that should not define them on any status in society.

Jesus was strict that leaders in every community should be respected not just in utterances but also in actions. He engaged the phony Pharisees who did have good procedures of behavior regulator but who did not abide by those policies that were sometimes difficult to others. "Then Jesus said to the crowds and his disciples: 'The teachers of the law and the Pharisees sit in Moses' seat. So you must be careful to do everything they tell you. But do not do what they do, for they do not practice what they preach. They tie up heavy, cumbersome loads and put them on other people's shoulders, but they are not willing to lift a finger to move them.'" (Matthew 23:1-4)

Some positive cultural ingredients should be applauded concerning attacking the culture of fraud. Jamaicans are naturally copious talkers, and this is revealed in the several talk shows that exist on radio networks daily. This is one of the outlets through which numerous people voice out against corruption in every region of society. This is a favorable practice, although simply speaking out against fraud is not an assurance that it will be dealt with. Another artistic practice that is deserving of applause for its role in dealing with the culture of fraud is the use of the print media as routes through which it is attracted under the microscope. Several people write articles, columns, and Letters to the Editor relating the need for the issue of corruption to be repelled and defeated through government, corporate, and religious action, whether cooperatively or individually. Media pressure has made contributions to the public and private officers being arrested in the web of fraud to be fired and or brought to justice. This is an honorable element of the Jamaican cultural terrain. Jamaicans think that they can obtain the awareness of leaders and officeholders in society through peaceful or violent revolt. Surely, "The development of more or less voluntary protest and demonstrations as a way of pursuing redress to injustice is a strategy of non-traditional participation that has burgeoned in Jamaica in the recent year.

Whatever the catalyst, such mass actions have in common a belief that less aggressive shapes of representation are unsuccessful and end up unanswered. This is one of the potentially adverse elements of Jamaican life, but it can stand as the means through which fraud is dealt with as well. What is intriguing about many of the uprisings is that they are executed to condone corruption instead of crushing it. This is observed when the police kill gunmen, and the parents and other family members of these gunmen come on the streets in revolt even when they are aware that their cherished ones are corrupt. However, there have been occasions when protests against fraud and injustice have yielded fruit in that the revolters got the awareness of the appropriate societal leaders who agreed to listen to them and handle their concerns and problems with enthusiasm and palpability.

All the organizations and structures of society are stakeholders in this war against the culture of criminality that threatens to gulp the nation. They must be committed to action for social transformation. The Church must play a prominent role in this respect. Church leaders in every denomination should be united and speak with one voice on this matter. The umbrella church organizations in Jamaica have helped communicate the Church's standpoints on many social problems. Other stakeholders comprise human rights associations and activist associations that concentrate on ensuring justice in society. Federal organizations and groups, which are authorized by parliament, such as the Office of the contractor General, should go on to play their parts in this regard.

There are various potential platforms for adaptive communication about action for social change, particularly where the culture of lawlessness is concerned. One of such outlets of information is the Church. Leaders in this important social institution can employ their sermons to communicate clear and persuasive arguments against the rule of corruption. Bible study periods and Sunday school lectures can be developed to address these issues over one year in the churches. This can help sensitive people to the necessity not just to resist crime in their lives but to get involved actively to stand against corruption everywhere. Church websites, blogs, and social media network pages can be platforms through which the Church can increase awareness of the issue and rally Christians to respond.

Additional main means of information are the other groups in the community, such as the home, the education strategy, companies, and non-governmental associations. The people's

value system, attitudes, and governing principles are first propagated and reinforced within the atmosphere of the family. This is the most basic focus of crime-abhorring values and practices. Households must cultivate the ideals such as integrity, fairness, respectability, respect, compassion, honesty, and wholesomeness. Parents must not only discuss these values; they must similarly exemplify them consistently.

The education policy should reinforce what is taught and practiced in households instead of neutralizing it. The school curriculum should be developed and executed in such a manner that students are trained and appreciated for honesty and reliability and penalized for dishonesty and shadiness. Companies and non-governmental associations should also take a position against crime by establishing and promoting ethical codes of conduct and organizing seminars and workshops on the best ethics in corruption deterrence and management. The radio chat shows can be employed to spread the Gospel of morality and chasteness and to mobilize against corruption in every sphere of society. The daily papers should go on to be excellent instruments through which the war against crime and the course of social transformation through milieu information can be understood. Organizing community associations and town hall discussions can be significant means of increasing awareness and counteracting the deadly toxin of corruption.

The best resources accessible for contextural communication about the change program being formulated concerning crime are persons in the Church and outside who have been engrossed in it but have also been rescued and discharged from its debilitating and disastrous tentacles. Churches, parachurch institutions, and non-governmental associations should set earmark sufficient funds to drive media campaigns against crime. This campaign should incorporate publicity on radio and television, and in publications, flyers on corruption, the internet, and related means encompassing e-books, novels, and e-magazines. The resources are accessible and should be employed in setting the message within the Jamaican environment and against the pernicious and paralyzing culture of corruption.

It is obvious that because of the existing danger of the culture of fraud, now is the moment for effort against the devastating and sinister danger of corruption. We should not delay our efforts to tackle this unsightly scourge in our society. Specific timelines may be necessary concerning the seminars, workshops, community meetings, church services, Bible studies, and media campaigns, but they should all be outlined within the general context of the urgency now because corruption is threatening to destroy this nation and overwhelm even those who are far from involvement.

There are obvious impediments to anticipate in the battle against corruption through ambient information with a program for social change. The first barrier has to do with the pervading nature of the culture of fraud itself. It will be a hard battle to conquer the well-ingrained forces of crime within and without the Church. They occur in all categories and would withstand efforts at undermining or eradicating the culture through which they make a living. The intrinsic corruption of human disposition brings itself evident in their activities and lifestyles and illustrates what Paul warns Timothy about the "love of money as the root of all kinds of evil" (1 Timothy 6:10). These people are resolute on protecting their "turf" at all prices, even if this entails perpetrating massacres and mayhem.

This narrative of the culture of violence in a Christian nation is an indictment of both the leaders and the led and ironic reality of failure.

Luke 6:43-44 NIV - "No good tree bears bad fruit, nor does a bad tree bear good fruit. Each tree is recognized by its fruit. People don't pick figs from thornbushes or grapes from briers.

Luke 6:47-49 (NIV) - As for everyone who comes to me and hears my words and puts them into practice, I will show you what they are like: They are like a man building a house, who dug down deep and laid the foundation on the rock. When a flood came, the torrent struck that house but could not shake it because it was well built.

But the one who hears my words and does not put them into practice is like a man who built a house on the ground without foundation. The moment the torrent struck that house, it collapsed, and its destruction was complete."

What type of foundation is the Jamaican Church built on? becomes a critical question. However, there is always an opportunity to amend and fortify faulty foundations when they are discovered. And I think that the Church in our country, Jamaica needs a refurbished foundation if it must overcome the myriad of abnormalities facing it.

CHAPTER 13

CHRISTIANITY AND WORK ETHICS IN JAMAICA

A bad system doesn't appear wrong to those who benefit from it. They do everything to defend it to the detriment of larger society

"Ethics is knowing the difference between what you have a right to do and what is right to do." - Potter Stewart.

Christian ethics teaches us how to live both in public and private. Christian ethics teaches what the entire Bible teaches us about which acts, behaviors, and personal attitudes receive God's acceptance and which ones do not.

The basic source for Christian ethics is the moral nature of God: God delights in his spiritual character, which is incredibly good, changeless, and infinite. His moral principles for human beings' ebb from his moral nature, and therefore they pertain to all people in all civilizations for all of history. However, the Bible also includes many temporary injunctions intended only for particular people at a certain time.

God is love, so He instructs us to love (1 John 4:19). He is holy, and He bids us be holy (1 Peter 1:15). He is gracious, and He instructs us to be gracious (Luke 6:36). He is trustworthy, and He instructs us not to carry false witnesses (Titus 1:2; Exodus 20:16). God's moral nature and the historical truth that he has provided us with moral injunctions provide the ground for a Christian answer to the issue of how we can shift from " declarations" to practice in ethics.

Christian morals are founded on the Bible. One of the goals of the Bible is to instruct us on how to live a life that delights God (Col. 1:9–10; 1 Thess. 4:1; 2). Since it is the Word of God, the Bible is a greater authority in morality than myth, reason, knowledge, desired results, or biased intuitions of guidance. While these other aspects can never precede the truth of the Scriptures, they can yet be beneficial for us in making prudent decisions.

Christian morals are fundamental to the declaration of the Gospel: Some Christian preachers today downplay or ignore any warning for unbelievers to repent of their sins, but evangelism in the New Testament constituted a call to repentance. Just before He ascended to Heaven, Jesus instructed his disciples "that repentance for the forgiveness of sins should be proclaimed in his name to all nations, beginning from Jerusalem" (Luke 24:47). Likewise, Paul declared openly the need for repentance to pagan Greek scholars in Athens, cautioning them that the ultimate judgment was coming: "The times of ignorance God overlooked, but now he commands all people everywhere to repent because he has fixed a day on which he will judge the world in righteousness by a man whom he has appointed; and of this, he has given assurance to all by raising Him from the dead" (Acts 17:30-31; 11:18;) "Repentance" in the New Testament is not simply a "change of mind" but involves both sorrows for one's sins and sincere innermost determination to turn away from sin and turn to Christ in faith (Hebrews 6:1; Acts 16:31).

And how would unbelievers repent from their sins if they do not understand what God's spiritual standards are? I do not think that sweeping revival is possible for any nation apart from widespread, genuine repentance for sin. Therefore, gospel preaching today must incorporate an aspect of teaching God's ethical principles, which implies teaching Christian ethics.

Christian morality teaches us how to live for God's glory: The goal of morals is to live a life that glorifies God ("do all to the glory of God," 1 Cor. 10:31). Such a life will have (1) a personality that glorifies God- a Christ-like character, (2) impacts that glorify God - a life that reproduces substantial fruit for God's kingdom, and (3) an attitude that honors God - a life of submission to God, lived in an intimate relationship with God.

Though we are justified by faith alone in Christ and not by works, substantial teachings about living the Christian life in New Testament indicate that our daily-life compliance as justified Christians is a critical ingredient of the Christian experience.

Obeying God provokes several blessings in our daily lives. God purposed that our obedience to Him will not be a disadvantage (1 John 5:3) but bring us tremendous pleasure. For this justification, when Christians are not "conformed to this world," we realize that obeying the will of God is a way of life that is for us "good and acceptable and perfect" (Romans 12:2).

Intentional sin brings various destructive effects in our daily lives. It is no longer too fashionable to discuss sin today, but it is a big topic in the scriptures. Digging into the meaning of the English word "sin" (and similar words with a related origin such as "sins" or "sinner") reveals that it appears 440 times in the New Testament alone. We cannot neglect such a crucial topic without serious consequences.

There are several harmful consequences mentioned in the New Testament that come from intentional sin in the life of a believer. These effects include alienation from our daily communion with God (Ephesians 4:30; 1 John 3:21), the knowledge of God's fatherly dissatisfaction, and the practical experience of his fatherly punishment (1 Corinthians 11:30; Hebrews 12:5-11), and a failure to bear fruit in our ministries and Christian lives (John 15:4-5). Christians should pray every day for the forgiveness of sins (Matthew 6:12; 1 John 1:9), not to plead justification now and then, but for restoration of our fellowship with God that has been hampered by sin.

God does not expect us to commit a "lesser sin.": Though various evangelical morals books do argue that from time to time, we face situations of "impossible moral conflict" where all available options are sinful, and we must merely elect to commit the "lesser sin," this argument is not found in Scripture. It is opposed both by the life of Christ, "who in every regard has been tempted as we are, yet without sin" (Heb. 4:15), and by the promise of 1 Corinthians 10:13, which says that God will always make a "way of escape."

This "impossible moral conflict" opinion easily serves as a slippery slope that, in real practice, motivates Christians to sin more often than not.

With the acclaimed culture of corruption pervading the entire country, it is only left to be imagined what the concomitant impact this will have on the work environment. From the civil service, which is inept and compromised, to the private sector, which is generally reputed to be the engine room for driving employment opportunities and other economic development parameters, the workforce that is enmeshed in sordid acts of retrogression and stifling productivity is the bane of our country. The greatest asset of any country, including ours, is not the beautiful beaches or the enticing scenery of our topography. It is not even the many natural resources countries are endowed with. It is the people: the men, women, and the youth whose acumen, dexterity, and undaunting commitments and determination to succeed at turning mundane natural resources into earning assets. They are the ones who unleash the tremendous innate human doggedness and problem-solving perspective to serve the multilayered challenges ever confronting humanity, from the gigantic dams to the portable solar energy panels and from the combustion engine to the atmospheric friendly electric cars, the indomitable spirit of men and women who faced the common challenges of humanity with the determination and candor to solve them not for self but all.

We all must realize that corruption in any form or shade is a killer of critical thinking and, therefore, progress. It first destroys the perpetrator's innate sound reasoning faculty and distorts the thought pattern in such a way that his or her full potential is grossly compromised. For instance, when a civil servant engages in bribery to approve an expenditure for the public good, he or she is blinded to the details and quality of the work done, and we all will be adversely affected when exposed to the use of such a public facility. The bribe taker who can no longer be bothered about the quality of work done under his or her purview cannot make any further contribution quality-wise to enhance the benefits derivable from his being employed by the public. This is one of the major reasons why the corruption index is inversely proportional to the economic development index. i: e the more corrupt a country is, the more backward economically and more violence-prone it is.

Most times, violence is a revolt against a system that is perceived to be unfair and unjust to the majority of the population, you can cheat some people sometimes, but you can't cheat all the people all the time.

As the children of God sanctified with the Word of God, we must accept God's moral instruction in full compliance and wisdom. Everyone who has been shown compassion in Christ, it is our great pleasure to "walk in a way worthy of the calling" that is ours in him (Eph. 4:1).

Ethics is related to the manner we ought to conduct our lives. Therefore, it is an essential part of biblical revelation. From Genesis to Revelation, we discover tenets, precepts, commands, cautions, guidelines, and counsels that are meant to direct our lives toward that which is honest, decent, and God-honoring. The apostle Paul instructs us that the Scriptures were given not just to show God's way of salvation but furthermore to equip us in righteousness and train us for "every good work" (2 Tim. 3:14–17).

At the very beginning of creation, God himself presented ethics when he frequently proclaimed his own work "good" (Genesis 1) and went ahead to give Adam and Eve responsibilities to accomplish and standards to live by. Again, after liberating Israel from enslavement and choosing her as His unique possession (Ex. 19:1–6), God started his relationship with the people He chose, giving them a moral agreement to govern their attitude toward him and within themselves (Ex. 20:1–17). This fundamental code was broadened in the remainder of the first five books of the Bible.

Centuries later, when Jesus arrived on the stage to usher in the climacteric phase of the redemptive record, he also started by handing out an ethical manifesto to lead the conduct of his disciples (Matthew 5–7). Named the Sermon on the Mount, this pact took ethics to an entirely new dimension while similarly reasserting the significance of what the Old Testament law and the prophets had always intended. At the center of Jesus' ethics is the call to love God and neighbors (Mark 12:28–31), a call that echoes throughout the entire New Testament (1 Cor. 13:1–3; James 2:8).

Besides, the Bible condemns those who devalue ethics by naming good evil and evil good (Isa. 5:20) and means that the right morality must express itself in the right attitude (James 2:14–26). It matters particularly to God that we think rightly and acts likewise.

The implications of not living according to or circumventing the ethical standards may not seem obvious, especially for the perpetrators and casual observers but are not too far from the consequences God pronounced for disobeying Him in the case of Adam and Eve. (Gen.2:17)

Corruption corrodes the fabric of society, leaving a superfluous and dangerous competitive environment where almost everyone else thinks he or she can survive by fighting for space.

Meanwhile, the ambiance and capacity for critical thinking, motivation and innovation had been stifled by the false sense of financial success given by proceeds from corrupt practices. When someone becomes wealthy from embezzlement of public funds or drug peddling and related criminal sources, the primary concern of such a person is how to conceal the looks and avoid arrest and prosecution but not how to innovate and improve on any economic development process.

Secondly, most parts of the proceeds from corruption are kept away from the defrauded jurisdiction to safe havens, thereby inflicting additional economic woes on the economic entity that has suffered both misappropriations and denial or economic asset depletion.

There is another aspect of corruption in the workplace that is inimical to the economic development of our country. When the perpetrators of criminality, especially embezzlement of public funds, have successfully retained their loot, they often say that they have acquired wealth for their children and unborn generations, and often you don't see there in any productive enterprise. Rather they are just enjoying the looted public money. In this case, they are exempted from contributing to the growth and development of the country, their innate abilities are never harnessed, and how can the country make meaningful progress when its human capital is dangerously compromised.

The country's Gross Domestic Product (GDP) is the major indices for measuring a country's economic development status and comparisons with other nations. It is the aggregate of the value of products and services that are generated in a country in a given period, usually yearly.

The illicit proceeds of crime and corruption are mostly hidden from the public glare and account and therefore not incorporated into the GDP figures and, in fact, are a distortion because it does not represent goods or services.

When the chairman and chief executive officer of a corporation divert the company's resources to buy a house in America, his investment in America was done undercover and shrouded in secrecy and, therefore, will not be officially recorded in the trade between Jamaica and America. So while the American economy is nevertheless boosted through employment generation and capital inflow, our country is further weakened economically. The company's profits, if they ever make any, are seriously depleted with the attendant reduction in their income and corporate taxes, and the jobs of workers in the company are jeopardized.

If the work ethics are compromised by corrupt tendencies, it will adversely affect the output both qualitatively and quantitatively. This is the bane of our country Jamaica and most countries in the Caribbean where corruption and crime are holding sway.

Churches and Christians hold the key to the fight against corruption and crime in this country because the same ethical standards for normal Christian living, like honesty, hard work, commitment, and patience, are also the same qualities required in the workplace and for economic progress.

The Church has in the past provided the pathway for education and economic development. Most educational facilities in developed and developing countries were provided by the Church. From Oxford, Cambridge, and Harvard, and many more first-class institutions had their root in the Church.

The main problem with Jamaica is not that there are no churches or Christians but that the Christians are not living like Christians. With the number of churches and a predominantly Christian population, the crime rate and the economic woes do not reflect the universally acclaimed Christian virtues. The leaders who are invariably Christians are taking decisive measures to halt the rot and reposition the country for sustainable economic growth.

The Government got a wake-up alarm when its debt burden peaked at virtually 150 percent of GDP in 2013. With the help of the International Monetary Fund, the World Bank, and the Inter-American Development Bank, the country undertook an ambitious reform policy. These steps have paid off. Jamaica is presently one of the few nations that have successfully reduced its public fiscal deficit by the equivalent of half of its gross domestic product in a little time frame.

The fiscal reversal and economic transformation were feasible because of the robust responsibility across political parties over two contending administrations and electoral cycles. The country, moreover, critically profited from a boosted social consensus for change and the powerful backing of the organized private sector.

When the leaders decided for once to set aside their parochial and dubious interests to focus on the good of all, the result was improved economic development for all. The corruption perspective index at this time will be very low comparatively.

The nation has generated fundamental financial surpluses of at least seven percent of GDP for the previous six years and continues steadfast in its dedication to financial discipline. This fiscal discipline and the outcomes make Jamaica a prime performer and respected internationally.

For this silent economic revolution to go on and bring tremendous prosperity to all its population, Jamaica will require to further improve the investment environment, bolster economic and climate stability and invest further in its people to create a robust human capital base. These are critical complements to the sustenance of a vital macro-economic framework and would help stimulate economic growth and job generation. There are convincing signs that Jamaica is making an effort in these areas.

Considering the business environment, the National Competitiveness Council has approved a blueprint to fast-track reforms to enhance the business climate. Jamaica is listed in the top 20 nations in the world for its detailed credit reporting policies and is ranked among the best globally in the sector of starting a business, according to the World Bank's 2019 'Doing Business report". It takes just two processes and three days for a prospective entrepreneur to register and formally run a business.

There have been improvements in public-private partnership investments. For example, the Norman Manley International Airport public-private partnership was lately completed with advisory assistance from the International Finance Corporation — the private sector arm of the World Bank Group.

Jamaica is likewise in the front-row among Caribbean nations in facilitating climate and financial stability in the face of natural catastrophes.

To further help Jamaica in its steps to strengthen the economy, build stability, and aid human capital development, the World Bank will broaden its funding by US$140 million. This financing will be for a sequence of two operations to enable Jamaica to be better equipped to alleviate the financial consequences of natural disasters when it occurs and build a robust infrastructure and more projects to strengthen social security.

Although unemployment is at a new low, several young people are fighting to find employment. For Jamaica to go on to grow and thrive, it also requires developing the capabilities for the workforce of the future, particularly in the areas of technology and digitalization. This needs a sharp emphasis on creating the right conditions for the youths to aspire and be successful in the contemporary business world and close partnership with the organized private sector in this respect. By overhauling the education curriculum and equipping the existing institutions of higher education, and building new ones with a focus on science and high technology, the quality of the human capital resources will be greatly enhanced.

From the foregoing, we can see that corruption in any form or shade is not among the Christian work and has a double jeopardy effect. The first victim of corrupt practice is the perpetrators whose innate potential is locked up, and freedom of innovation stifled. The second victim of corruption is the State that is denied both its productively employable assets and the very potential human capital that is now corrupted. For Christians, have effects and consequences both here and hereafter. While you can evade accountability here or bribe your way through, you certainly will be accountable to God when the time comes.

Maintaining healthy ethical standards in the workplace and personal life enhances productivity in the economy and catalyzes wealth creation and a better standard of living for the citizens. It is the bedrock of mutual trust and social capital that is sin qua non for an attractive and market-driven competitive business environment.

Cost of transaction reduction and ease of doing business is part of the benefits of playing by the ethical standards.

There was a time in the history of the Church when the State and its enterprise depended on the Christians for integrity and commitment. The Christian sect called the Puritans lived in the strictest sense as Christians and became well sorted out in the business arenas. One disciple of puritanism says, "The only kind of luck that any man is justified in banking on is hard work, which is made up of sacrifice, persistent effort, and determination.

Honestly wins - This must be not only the kind of honesty that keeps a man's fingers out of his neighbor's till, but the finer honesty that will not allow a man to give less than his best, the kind of honesty that makes him count not his hours but his duties and opportunities, and constantly urges him to increase his efficiency- J. C. Penny (1875- 1971)

The Christian's work is embedded in his faith, and it is natural for him to be honest, hard-working, and patient. These are the qualities on which great nations and enduring institutions are built.

However, this post-Christian civilization in which the churches have no monopoly on morality or an autonomous voice in the public domain requires us to acknowledge that there are areas where we as Christians have no mastery. Therefore, we must live and function in cooperation with others. We must work together in the areas of Government, economics, and public policy. The good of civic society is not a solely Christian responsibility but a good that has its root in Christianity and to which Christians should devote themselves.

On John Calvin's 500th birthday, July 10, 2009, the BBC News website ran a story on the interest of youthful Dutch businessmen and women in Calvinism- the symbol of the puritan work ethics, a faith formerly prevalent in their land and on which the prosperity and robust accountability and integrity of Europe were built. Why was the reader urged to contemplate, might this outdated form of ethical revolution be making a comeback in the soul of worldly, contemporary Europe where church attendance is virtually invisible? An explanation could be inferred from the headline: "Economic Crisis Boosts Dutch Calvinism."

The appearance of this article was a joke on the apparent disagreement between contemporary Euro-sophistication and its abandoned religious past. What these youthful women and men alleged to have discovered in Calvinism were ethical certainties, a moral compass in a world that seems to grant plausibility to every idea and certainty to none. They have seen that lives committed to working and embellished by the pledges of material compensation were proving hollow. Where people believed they would find satisfaction, there was only apprehension.

It's no doubt that the Dutch pastor who was interviewed for the publication says the enticement will prove to expire, and should the financial circumstances be favorable, most people will return to their earlier habits of thought. Yet we are faced with something very significant to consider in the presumptions of this story: the connection between ethics and the economy and the position of Christianity in the temporal world.

The feeling of dislocation experienced by the Dutch nationals interviewed, which includes an ineptitude to make ethical connections between their job and what might make up a significant life, also permeates our society and puts forward old questions in new shapes. As we strive both to comprehend the nature of the economic and ethical crisis that has challenged us and to find a meaning for faith amid the storm. As people of faith, if we are to confront the problems of the economic upheaval, we need to comprehend more truly the historical origins of the issues.

As Christians, we must appreciate the value of civic society as a place where a majority of voices and opinions can and must occur simultaneously. This does not compel us to surrender our moralities in any form. Rather it challenges us to learn means of speaking and behaving that allow us to translate our principles into the public sphere. This was the reason that the Puritans were exceptionally self-disciplined. Spurred on by their pastors to "make their calling and election sure' according to 2 Peter 1:10, they lived to be 'not slothful in business, fervent in spirit, serving the Lord' (Rom. 12:11). The outcome was that the Puritans were hard-working and practical in their strategy for their career, without taking any period off for leisure or private entertainment. They were certainly in the world but not of it. They now carried the Biblical standard of estrangement from the world in its freedom and indiscipline into the world and pertained it to their own daily life and work.

Such a disciplined approach to their economic engagements, of course, meant that they amassed a lot of savings which is the fundamental requirement for investment.

Puritans believed that they should retain earnings as low as reasonable to earn a better profit and that the impoverished were poor because of their extravagant habits and carelessness so that generosity for the needy was not to be granted without consideration. Out of this behavior and philosophy on life, capitalism evolved in the Industrial Revolution and has reached down to our period, even though presently, the spiritual elements of the ethos have faded away, and it is a frantic scramble for money.

Our country can build on the recent economic achievements and sustain them if our pastors and preachers of the Gospel will teach and urge the Christians to translate the tenets of our faith into the work environment and live by the truth of the word of God.

CHAPTER 14

CHURCH IMPACT ON SEXUALITY IN JAMAICA

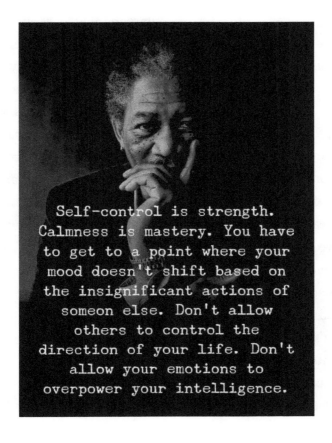

J amaica, like every other country, is not immune to the very aggressive sex culture that has become a source of concern for both parents and governments. The active involvement of teenagers and unprepared young people in sexual activities gave rise to the need for sexual education and orientation in schools and colleges.

The Church is the bastion of morality and the apex advocate for ethical standards in society. Instructions on Sexual values and morals are not marginalized in the scriptures and form the foundation for teaching and practice.

Sexuality has become a hydra-headed moral issue of an alarming proportion that requires emergency actions

40% of Jamaican women have been pregnant at least once before they reach the age of 20years, and more than 80% of juvenile pregnancies are incidental. Sexual activity starts at a premature age for many Jamaicans. Amongst adolescents aged between 15 and 17 years who were interviewed in the "1997 Reproductive Health Survey", 38% of females and 64% of males accepted to have had sexual intercourse. The younger the children are when they start sexual activity, the less probable they are to practice contraception, thus heightening their risk of pregnancy and sexually transmitted diseases.

Sex education aims to teach young adolescents to understand their reproductive health systems and safety and how to abstain from sex, and how to engage in safe sex.

As far back as 1994, the Women's Center for Jamaican Foundation had initiated the Grade 7 Project for sexuality and family life education. The Women's Centre is well noted for its pioneering works for Adolescent Mothers, and the development of the Grade 7 Project was informed by the center's background in delivering educational, health, and social aids to pregnant adolescents and adolescent mothers. The Grade 7 Project can be regarded as both a chastity promotion and a hazard reduction and safer sex intervention. Its stated goals are to postpone the initiation of sexual interaction among young adolescents and promote the use of family planning amongst those who decide to become sexually functional by giving information about reproductive health, sexuality, and family planning. And by influencing behaviors about family planning, sex, and adolescent pregnancy.

The Grade 7 Project was implemented in 10 "new secondary" and "all-age" schools across Jamaica from 1994-to 1996, in place of the sexuality education curricula usually offered. About 60% of Jamaicans aged 12-14 attend all-age or new secondary schools, which are secondary institutions that generally do not prepare students for university education. Also, adolescents at these schools, who tend to be from lower socio-economic strata, have performed poorly on a placement test at the end of elementary school and failed to gain entrance to any traditional technical high school or high school.

Health care providers and policymakers have grown increasingly alarmed over the levels of STDs and pregnancy among adolescents and are seeking new solutions to these problems. Improving adolescent reproductive health and reducing the rate of teenage pregnancy are now among the top of Jamaica's health priorities. Hence, the Government of Jamaica has announced plans t strengthen the family life education program. As well as improve access to reproductive and family planning services for adolescents.

Early motherhood is often connected with a young woman's inability to finish her education, thereby impeding her future job chances and, by extension, her child's economic well-being. Among young female students in Jamaica who became mothers before their fourth year of secondary school, less than one-third came back to complete their school after the birth of their baby. Enhancing adolescent reproductive health and curtailing teenage pregnancy rates are among the nation's top emphases arising from the "1994 International Conference on Population and Development (ICPD)". The Government intends to formalize and enhance family life education policies and, among other activities, increase access to reproductive and family planning aids for adolescents.

Youthful sexual activity and pregnancy in Jamaica are thought to be attributed to poverty, low academic levels, the dearth of father figures and role models in the home, and a social setting of conservative sexual standards that coexist with and contradict the implicit approval of early childbearing.

Despite the significant number of sexually active adolescents in Jamaica, existing policies addressing reproductive and sexual health restrict medical attention to several evidence-based services (e.g., HIV testing) for persons younger than 16 years. Even though the "Jamaican Access to Contraceptives for Minors policy" declares that persons younger than 16 years have the liberty to access health care without parental approval, laws and policies such as the "Sexual Offences Act and the Child Care and Protection Act" drastically restrict the implementation of these procedures. Under the Sexual Offences Act, sexual engagement among persons less than 16 years is unlawful, rendering any person, including juveniles themselves, who has or plans to have sex with anyone younger than16years the perpetrator of a crime. The Child Care and Protection Act penalizes health care providers for giving sexual and reproductive health assistance to teenagers without first receiving parental consent. This law leaves health care providers in the situation of having to choose whether enabling access to contraceptive benefits for persons less than 16 years is a crime of abetting child hurt and misuse or a professional duty of curtailing STI transmission and unwanted pregnancy. Due to such regulations, health care providers have a legitimate reason to withhold care, given the prevarication around their function in promoting sexual crimes of minors. Besides, young persons may be reluctant to pursue sexual and reproductive health care, worrying about the legal implications for themselves and their collaborators.

The country has recognized the need to tackle the issue of illicit sex and the attendant challenges among the younger adolescents. However, the approaches adopted by the various agencies and the organized private sector like the Women's Center for Jamaican Foundation are predominantly geared towards mitigating a cancerous hydra-headed epidemic that is the scourge of this generation.

Legislation can achieve little, as we have seen in the law that forbids persons younger than 16 years from sexual activity and criminalizes the extension of sexual and reproductive health care services to this age group.

Influencing behaviors about sex, as mentioned in the Grade 7 Project, should start in the homes. The average Jamaican is a Christian, and the average family is Christian-oriented. Character and personality are formed between ages 0 to 6 years in every child. Therefore, it is the parental nurture and influence that has the potential to stem the ugly slide in sexual abuse.

As Christians, we have been taught the truth about sex, and God's position is unchanged. While the society and Government may be interested in a less promiscuous adolescent age group for social and economic reasons, the Church is much more interested in the overall spiritual health of the body of Christ.

While the society and Government want to be able to plan for the future and wellbeing of the citizens with minimal distortions and provide social amenities for the existing population and make a reasonable projection for the future, the Church and parents are keen on raising a family and generation of people without sin who serve the Lord Jesus Christ.

There is no conflict of interest between the Church and the Government concerning the sexual health and, indeed, the overall health of our young population, but a classification of interest.

The Church and Government can work together to achieve the common good for God and humanity. This is possible if there is a congruent policy on sex education. For instance, the Bible teaches abstaining from sex for unmarried people, but the Government promotes safe sex. If the Government supports the Church in emphasizing no sex rather than safe sex by including a no sex program and policies in the basic education curriculum for all primary and secondary schools, it will reinforce the seriousness and resolve to deal with the problem.

The Government and many non-governmental organizations are heavily involved in promoting an all-inclusive sexual oriented society and are indeed pushing the Church to expand (distort) its scriptural frontiers to accommodate sexual deviants of all manners. But the Church is not and should not be an all-comers affair. Therefore, the pressure on the Church to redefine its lexicon just to accommodate sinful humanistic tendencies is both untenable and counterproductive.

Premarital sex is recognized as a sin, and those who transgress this instruction of the Christian faith may earn huge sanctions from the Church or may surely be ostracized from fellowships. One would accordingly believe that young people who are associated with the Christian faith would be more inclined to postpone sexual intercourse until wedlock. But, association with the Christian faith alone may not certainly imply obedience to the teaching to delay sex, and several young people who profess to be Christians still take part in premarital sex.

The Church cannot afford the nonchalant or hypocrisy of the society in showing a conservative posture toward an adolescent sexual activity while giving tacit approval by providing contraceptives and making them accessible to the youngsters.

There is no plan B for sin because plan A (redemption from sin by faith in the finished work of Jesus Christ on the cross of calvary) is so effective and dependable that you can't possibly miss it except by unbelief and lack of commitment.

People who maintain high Christian morals and high core commitment have more conservative sexual behaviors and smaller sexually permissive sentiments than their mates, which might lead to rarer sexual occurrences. More specifically, one or more causal factors underlying this observed trait may be connected to

(a) a personal resolve consisting of specific individual beliefs impacted and nurtured from childhood - bring up a child in the way he should go, and when he grows up, he will not depart from it. - Proverbs 22:6

(b) a family dimension, where certain values are socialized and or imposed through social control. Chastity is a Christian value that is passed down from godly parents from infancy and reinforced by the Church through the children's education department of the Sunday school.

Comparatively, spiritual parents talk little with their children concerning sexuality but more about sexual integrity. This should be expected because the Christian faith does not teach safe sex and the use of contraceptives for young people, rather abstaining from sexual activities. For the Christians, any compromise on the word of God on fornication and adultery does not only expose one to unwanted pregnancy and sexually transmitted diseases but to an additional horrific, the prospect of hellfire. As already indicated, sexual abstinence before matrimony is strongly encouraged by the Christian faith, and this belief could be sustained through church service attendance, along with vital social influence in families with moral and religious convictions.

Yes, Church service attendance and the thorough teaching of the scriptures hold the key to deterring our young people who are the Church of tomorrow from falling victims to the sex culture that is prevalent in the world today.

The concepts of homosexual, lesbian, bisexual, and gay must be confronted frantically with the truth of the word of God. The Church should not be reduced to a social crucible capable of holding every impure compound pretending to be ready for distillation. People become members of the Church because they heard the Gospel of Jesus Christ and accepted it to be true, and are committed to upholding the truth they heard by which they received redemption of their sins. They are not impurities waiting to be absorbed by the Church and preserved by fiat for further interrogation or social representation.

Neither is the Church a political party. Even political parties have ideologies and unique identities, at least in developed democracies, the Church cannot accommodate every shade of opinion nor seek to increase her numbers by recruiting rebels.

If crucible does discard earth impurities that did not conform to the appropriate treatment of temperature and pressure for usefulness and serious political parties don't go about amending and changing their ideological identities to accommodate every whimsical political opinion, why would the whole world bring the Church under undue pressure to modernize, to accommodate and condescend because they want the pastors' blessings over their contraption of marriage.

Matthew 23:16-19 NIV - "Woe to you, blind guides! You say, 'If anyone swears by the temple, it means nothing; but

anyone who swears by the gold of the temple is bound by that oath.: You blind fools! Which is greater: the gold or the temple that makes the gold sacred? You also say, 'If anyone swears by the altar, it means nothing; but anyone who swears by the gift on the altar is bound by that oath.' You blind men! Which is greater: the gift or the altar that makes the gift sacred?

The same goes for those who want the pastor and Church to bless their nefarious marriage of two men or two women, which is an abomination before the God of the Church. It is the hypocrisy of both the priests and the marriage clients to think that God will bless a union that is an aberration and sacrilege in His sight.

The priest has no authority except that given by God, and He will never honor the abuse of such authority by any priest. Remove the authority of the word of God, and the priest has no blessing to bestow, and when the precepts of the word are conveniently corrupted, the intended blessings will, of course, become curses. If the foundation is destroyed, what can the righteous do?

The Jamaican Church must be resolute in preaching, teaching, and defending the biblical perspectives on sex, marriage, and family. There is a heightened spiritual conspiracy against the Church by Satanic cohorts, and the strategy is to subtly undermine the holiness and power of the Church through the denigration of the word and tenets of the Christian faith. The enemy has chosen to start its vicious attack on the very foundation of our communal existence - the family.

- Sexual intercourse, which is an exclusive reserve for married couples, is being portrayed as a casual all-comers exercise without considering the implications. Satan calls it "lovemaking," a nebulous term intended to disguise the intrinsic intimacy and interchange of genes that is the consummation of marriage and reproduction.

Approximately seventy percent of sexual health problems the world is grappling with today could have been avoided by simple obedience to the biblical injunctions.

- Marriage is redefined to mean " the joining of two consenting adults in a marriage contract." Contrary to the word of God - Matthew 19:4-5: NIV: "Haven't you read," he replied, "that at the beginning the Creator 'made them male and female, and said, 'For this reason, a man will leave his father and mother and be united to his wife, and the two will become one flesh?

Where is this claimed ambiguity in the Scriptural lexicon that gave rise to the abomination of same-sex marriage? It is the devil's advocates who are promoting his agenda of deceit and destruction. Instead of accepting the word of God and repenting, the agents of darkness would rather have the priest interpret the scriptures to accommodate their sinful indulgence.

The popular excuse for not speaking, teaching, and preaching against LGBT is always " not to condemn them and allow them to change," but the real truth is their commercial value. In these days of measuring Church health and wellness economically, the offerings and freewill donations from this class of members can be considerable.

John 8:11 NIV: "No one, sir," she said. "Then neither do I condemn you," Jesus declared. "Go now and leave your life of sin." Talking about condemnation, this encounter with the woman caught in adultery reveals the ultimate desire of the Lord when He admonished the woman to desist from sinful life after she was saved physically.

We know that the Church is the body of Christ - the Assembly of believers when we come together and individual temples of the Holy

Spirit. It takes the hearing, accepting the Gospel, repentance, and confession of Jesus Christ as Lord and personal savior to be saved and be a member of the Church.

Assuming my sexual orientation was perverted like LGBT when I heard the Gospel and accepted it by faith, my repentance will necessarily include acknowledging my obvious sordid sexual State for which I'm remorseful and willing to joyfully forsake. Having accepted the Lord, should I still be identified with my former lifestyle.

Romans 6:1-2 NIV -What shall we say, then? Shall we go on sinning so that grace may increase? By no means! We are those who have died to sin; how can we live in it any longer?

I think the true position is that the people the Church is willing to accommodate are not ready to repent they want the Bible modified to make room for their sinful nature, and the Church must resist this attempt. It is intentional and aimed at destroying the Church doctrinally.

Romans 1:26-27 NIV - Because of this, God gave them over to shameful lusts. Even their women exchanged natural sexual relations for unnatural ones. In the same way, the men also abandoned natural relations with women and were inflamed with lust for one another. Men committed shameful acts with other men and received the due penalty for their errors.

There are still discussions in some Christian denominations on what to do with LGBT people in their midst. But I think it's cynical for a Bible-believing Church to adopt discussion as a solution to sin. Condemnation of sin is NOT the condemnation of the sinner. But the refusal to condemn sin is a disservice to the Lord and His Church.

Abnormal sexual orientation is not a physical deformity or an ailment; it is an attitude that can be changed if the individual is willing. The Gospel has changed lives, from serial killers to drug addicts and from armed robbers to drunkards and rapists. The question is whether the sinners acknowledge their dilemma and the readiness for repentance- turning away from the status quo.

The Church should ameliorate LGBTQ+ persons but must loathe and condemn the practice of sexual perversion on a biblical basis. Compassion and help are required to win them to Christ. Pastors should resist using the pulpit of power and influence to ignite division and disunity because such oratory suggests that it is alright to discriminate, that it is alright to throw out members of your household because they are going to hell is unbiblical. This concession would not muzzle clerics from denouncing the LGBTQ+ sexual orientation according to the word of God.

Opposition to LGBTQ+ sexual orientation does not necessarily ignite societal renunciation of the minority community because Jamaicans have been very passive as these individuals are not being discovered stoned in the several neighborhoods in which they stay. And there are no special vigilantes targeting gays, lesbians, and the rest of them.

The Gospel is effective when delivered truthfully but powerless when it is distorted to accommodate those who should be saved, and there are no available contemporary sexual issues that had not been practiced before and for which the Bible has no answer.

Within the first century AD, when the Apostle Paul wrote the book Romans, the first chapter contained specific mention of homosexuals and lesbians, but they were not in the Church then, yet they caught the attention of God.

Further back in history, in the days of Abraham and Lot, his nephew, the cities of Sodom and Gomorrah, where Lot resided, got the ultimate punishment from God for practicing homosexuality. The whole city and its entire population, including livestock, were burnt down by God Himself except Lot, the alien.

If we still pray to the God of Abraham, Isaac, and Jacob, it will be preposterous to think that He has changed His stand on sexual perversion. Therefore, the contemporary Church has got no basis for enlarging the sphere of acceptable sexual orientation and practice.

A fundamental notion in any conversation about gay and lesbian in the Church is the issue of tension. This conflict is the internal tension that is most likely to arise between gay or lesbian "Christians'" sexual orientation and their religious attitudes. But a deeper insight, however, reveals that the issue of conflict is not just about the clash of identity that can occur between gay and religious ethics but furthermore about the apprehension that arises in a gay or lesbian person undergoing such conflict. Where do such conflict and its resulting tension originate from? Six passages from the Bible (Genesis, 19:1–28; Leviticus, 18:22, 20:13; Romans, 1:26,27; I Corinthians, 6:9; I Timothy, 1:10) have typically been used to substantiate the contention that homosexuality is a sin. Based on these chapters, Christian doctrine has sanctioned homosexuality to be unusual, a perversion, and an abomination in the sight of God. While very few Christian denominations may view homosexuality in a more favorable light, the preponderance of mainstream Christian denominations does not. In one of the surveys, 72% of Christian religious organizations polled condemned homosexuals and homosexuality.

Besides, Christian doctrine insists that gays and lesbians are unnatural and willful, yet also declares that God loves you unconditionally, and every one of the children of God will gain a place in Heaven. Such dualistic information may build a sense of turmoil, self-loathing, and sadness in gay or lesbian persons. Yes, no one earns God's love, He loves us the way we are, and our response to God's love is obedience to His word. Accepting God's love is crucial to every sinner because, without a deliberate decision to acknowledge and accept the offer of love from God, there will be repentance and a change of attitude. John 3:16 NIV: For God so loved the world that he gave his one and only Son, that whoever believes in him shall not perish but have eternal life.

That God loves you unconditionally does not imply that He loves the condition He met you. His love is redemptive because our condition is precariously sinful.

However, despite such messages from Christianity regarding the sin of homosexuality versus God's all-encompassing love, many people who identify themselves as gay or lesbian still maintain strong religious beliefs.

This maintenance of an intense Christian religious belief and a strong feeling of being out considering one's gay or lesbian sexual orientation has assisted in creating feelings of tension between these two characters that are each essential to one's sense of self, as well as perceptions of apprehension within the individual.

Maintaining strong religious beliefs is a generic statement that anyone can use to placate a bruised conscience, but in Christianity, the basis of faith and a living relationship with God is not a strong religious belief but the "atonement for sin and a new life that Jesus Christ gives.

The Church is not an umbrella that shelters every lifestyle and facilitates the individual display of peculiarity and orientation. If obedience to the word of God is not part of anyone's resolve, such a person has no legitimate claim as a member of the Church.

LGBTQ+ (an endless acronym for sexual deviants) persons should be seen by the Church as part of the unreached community and be included in the work-in-progress of the evangelism drive.

CHAPTER 15

CHURCH IMPACT ON JAMAICAN FAMILY

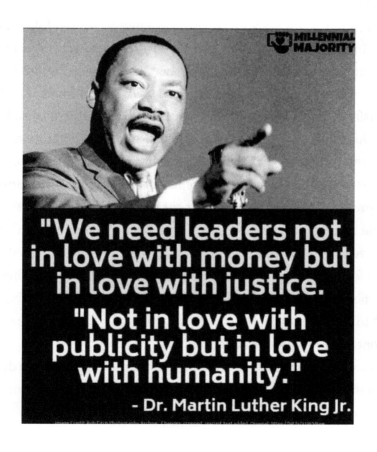

T he family remains the microsomal unit of the society and the bedrock of the Church.

Jamaican families have special bonds, and the entire extended family members have roles in the children's upbringing.

Even neighbors have substantial roles in overseeing the children as well. While parents are strict, they are also friendly and very active in all facets of their kids' lives, motivating them to excel in education and sports. Jamaican households continue to be the counseling impetus in their youngsters' lives sufficiently into adulthood. Parents often feel accountable for their children, irrespective of their age, and carry the responsibility seriously.

Siblings in the Jamaican household are motivated to look out for one another. In most cases, children are looked after by nannies or attendants, which is an instructive adventure for them as they are familiarized with how others live in settings beyond their own. Attendants tell children tales of island mythology, and they educate them on the basics, like how to comb hair and how to cook. Families and their attendants encourage the children to be coordinated and well-mannered at all times. A major ingredient in the life of Jamaican women and girls is how they appreciate paying attention to their physical appearance.

While attendants may be useful in a home, Jamaican children are however required to do domestic chores, such as preparing beds, fixing the table for dinners, preparing a beverage for dinner, or washing plates. During the week when schools are in session, Jamaican children are not allowed to watch television or socialize. Normally, Jamaican parents do not accept their children lazily socializing.

Religion is a crucial aspect of Jamaica's life, and parents are delighted when their children assist as altar boys and girls. Homes also ensure that children are never fatigued but always make sure they are creative with their leisure time and are well exposed to wholesome activities.

Festivals like Christmas, Easter, and Independence Day are very significant to Jamaican families, who commemorate by donning their best clothing and preparing special delicacies and drinks suitable for the occasion, such as sorrel or biscuit and cheese. Luxurious meals are prepared and relished on holidays, and families like to attend street proms and float at Christmas.

Jamaican parents want their children to agree upon a career or occupation after their introductory education. They are then required to decide on a suitable life spouse, marry and build their own families. All family members get involved in the marriage process, with fathers being conscious of their daughter's welfare. A father wishes for his daughter to marry a man that can provide generously and defend his wife. Parents expect their sons to marry creative, pleasant women who are nice cooks and who can sustain a household efficiently.

Families are tightly knitted in Jamaica, and even when kids start running their own lives, their families persist in presiding over and worrying about their best concerns and well-being.

Cultural life

Jamaica's cultural evolution has been deeply swayed by British traditions and exploration of essences in folk forms. The latter is founded chiefly on the brilliant harmonious vigor of the island's African ancestry.

Jamaican culture is a creation of the interchange between Europe and Africa. Terms like "Afro-centered" and "Euro-centered," however, are repeatedly used to convey the understood duality in Jamaican artistic traditions and virtues. European impacts continue in social institutions, medicine, Christian worship, and the arts. Nevertheless, African durability is present in spiritual life, Jamaican Creole language, cookery, adages, drum beats, the tones of Jamaican music and dance, traditional medicine associated with herbal and spiritual healing, and stories of Anansi, the spider-trickster.

Family life is important to most Jamaicans, though proper marriages are less prominent than in several other Caribbean countries. It is normal for three generations to live together in a home. Most women receive wages, particularly in families where men are lacking, and grandmothers generally take care of preschool-age children. Wealthier Jamaican families normally hire at least one domestic servant.

The major meal is virtually often in the evening because many people do not have time to cook a noontime meal, and children generally eat at school. Families seem to be too busy to have most weekday meals, but on Sundays, tradition demands that even needy families celebrate a huge and cheerful brunch or lunch, usually containing chicken, fish, yams, fried plantains, and the stable rice and peas (rice with kidney beans or gungo pigeon peas). One of Jamaica's very popular foods is jerk (spiced and grilled) meat.

Clothing styles differ. Rastafarians, who make up a tiny fraction of the population, normally wear loose-fitting clothes and long dreadlocks, a hairstyle connected with the Ethiopian emperor Haile Selassie I in the early 20th century.

Jamaican sovereignty from Great Britain on August 6, 1962, is celebrated annually. The Government champions festivals as part of the independence festivities. Though there is some commonality the National Day festivals have with the region's pre-Lenten Carnivals, the Festival is vastly wider in size, comprising street dancing and processions, arts and crafts presentations, and literary, melodramatic, and musical contests. Since the late 20th century, Jamaicans have also commemorated

Carnival, typically with processions, bands, and dancing. Emancipation Day is commemorated on August 1.

IMPACT OF CHURCH

The Church leads the campaign in facilitating and canvassing for a healthy family, referring to the lengthy responsibility between a man and a woman, bringing up children in a very credible nurturing home. We are the ones promoting that knowledge of the family.

The Church not barely shapes the ethical fabric of the family but also provides its strength, time, and resources in health care, education, and the family. When it gets to moral problems, society always requires a moral direction and ethical prophetic word to constantly prompt the nation about what is true and false.

The Church has constantly had an interest in the family because of the instruction of the Scriptures. The family is a constant topic throughout the Scriptures. Though the structure a family assumes is not specifically defined in Scripture, it is reasonable to assert that it was considered the basic institution for the society, and every action was made to maintain its integrity.

The Church is likewise called, as a component of its task, to protect the virtue of the family. Furthermore, the Church has remained attached to families because of its position in critical life cycle occasions such as christenings, marriages, and funerals. Also, the several pastoral attention and counseling matters that generally occur from family affairs have been another rationale for helping families. The Church is hailed to be a caretaker of family life, particularly if the structures of family life are injurious to the integrity of families, the integrity of people or jeopardize their moral fabric. What further became increasingly visible through research and out of knowledge was the necessity for more support systems for families in our nation today.

The compression of available support structures and the lack of initiatives to sufficiently address the problems of the family, especially in metropolitan areas, are swelling concerns. One of the significant sources of family help in Jamaica has foundationally been the extended family. This, though, is becoming less handy for a swelling multitude of inner-city families as additional females seek a livelihood. Moreover, the altering character of city life is diminishing the sense of communal responsibility and community child care that prevailed some years back and is still perceived in rural areas. In the dearth of a well-developed welfare scheme or community-based family reinforcement agencies, the Church embodies one of the rare institutions that can assist in handling the difficulties that confront the Jamaican family. If the Church stands to effectively offer solutions to family problems, there are three main challenges it must resolve, the ideational challenge, theological challenge, and ministerial challenge.

1. Ideational Challenge: Addressing the problems of the family in Jamaica implies confronting the challenge of expanding the nation's concept of family. The Church in Jamaica has traditionally retained a perspective of the family based on formal marriage and has always found problems recognizing non-legal unions and the family types that emerge from them. Clearly, for the most fraction, the Church has truly rejected these family types and has either disregarded them or segregated them. For instance, the practice of different baptisms and christenings for infants born out of matrimony. Calls for a widened perspective have emanated from several pastors and theologians in the country. A missive to the churches disseminated in the proceedings of a 1971 Caribbean Consultation anchored by the Planned Parenthood Program of Church World Service says:

"In our deliberations, we were encouraged by the churches increasing awareness of the problems raised by their traditional attitudes to the family in the Caribbean and their efforts to give serious attention to the State of the family in the region. However, we feel there is still room for the development of a more positive ministry to people who live in-legal unions".

This widened viewpoint on the family must be taught firstly by interchange with local research from supplementary professions such as sociology, psychology, and anthropology. Secondly, our perspective must be based on local theological research. Caribbean pastoral counselor Neilson Waithe, in the first chapter of his book "Caribbean Sexuality," bemoans the need for investigation of sexuality in the Caribbean from the philosophy of the pastor/minister. Pastoral practitioners must tackle theological investigation into the verities of family life in the particular context and not only echo the conclusions and viewpoints of other areas or other disciplines. Thirdly, it must be taught by perceptions of family evolution indicated in other cultures. By so accomplishing, we can help to eradicate some of the mindless prejudices we sometimes harbor about what is applicable or not. Finally, a fresh idea of the family must be taught by a fresh glance at the Bible. There are some unquestionable about family, which we keep as biblical, which are no better than European or American cultural adornments. It is when we take a closer glance at the scriptures, through the eyes of our cultural self-cognition, personality, and knowledge, that we uncover the explanations that apply to our context.

2. Theological Challenge: Attending to the problems of the family also compels us to formulate a Caribbean-based theology for the family. Such theology would give a rationale for how the Christian religion appreciates family structure in the Caribbean and how it connects to family issues. This reverberates a sentiment conveyed by Panton in his book "The Church and Common-law Unions. "If the Church in Jamaica must be real to its character and obligation in accomplishing its purpose, it must bring a fresh glance at the theology which buttresses its ministry and evolve a theology that is consistent with its character and its purpose within the ambiance of the Jamaican society. Such theology will necessarily prompt the development of different forms of ministry.

The strategy of evolving such a theology, though, is not without its difficulties. One difficulty that Panton pointed out is the ingrained conditioning of the wedding ring and what is an ideal family. Another problem is the friction between belief and culture. The problem of the family, like another aspect of Christian sociable ethics, is aggravated by the pressure that occurs between the Christian belief and the cultural circumstance in which it is practiced. This friction is inevitable because the Christian faith is not accountable to culture and must be prepared to challenge it. Still, the Christian belief must be lived out in a cultural environment, and consequently, it must be prepared to acknowledge and adopt cultural nuances. The faith of the family must steer through these complications. As this theology is forged, it must, on the one part, corroborate the wisdom of Scripture and the chronological habits of the Christian faith pertained to the family. For instance, the significance of a lifelong marriage is a vital aspect of fulfilling family life. On the other hand, it must reexamine its practices in light of modern verities. In this respect, we may wish to reexamine themes like male headship of family in favor of shared headship and larger gender equality in family roles. Even though the headship of the man per se is not the bone of contention.

The theology of family should deal with the problems of gender relations, especially in light of family researchers' indication that "a major problem area resides in the complex of factors related to the quality of gender relations within the household as well as within the society as a whole." No particular theology of the family will be approved by all segments of the Church, but any endeavor at such a program can help as valuable assistance to the Church's discussion about family and is imperative if a concordant ministry is to be practiced.

3. The Pastoral Challenge: Jamaican family life poses a challenge for pastoral activity. Introspection of the family has always tended to be hypothetical and not satisfactorily practical. This challenge engages the long-standing anxieties and ways of reflection about the family that has impeded the Church's ministry to Jamaican families. Panton tracks the history of the Jamaican Church's reaction to common-law marriages to illustrate how the Church, over the years, has held categorical the values of the colonial period. We have so admired the marriage within the nuclear family that we have flunked to recognize other family structures and have failed to develop practical means of ministering to them. Many of these are associated with the fear of appearing to reduce our standard, but conquering this fear and leaving the customers are critical barriers to cross if the practical pastoral effort is to be launched.

Besides, the Church requires to alter its strategy for family ministry. There is an urgent need to create a detailed standard for family pastoral supervision. Most of the time, the family ministry has been directed at church members or future church members and is always restricted to married couples. The usual outline of the woman who wishes to become a member of the Church but who is staying in a common-law marriage with a spouse and their children is so regular, yet few churches appear to have established a way of dealing with this circumstance that is extensive, appreciative of the woman's faith responsibility, considerate of the unit as a family and ready to voyage with the woman and her spouse. Nor have we established ways of reaching out to singles, divorcees, separated couples, or common-law partners and their families in the larger community who don't come to Church. These too need assistance to enhance the value of their family life. The outcome is that a vast plurality of people, especially in rural and inner-city populations, feel prohibited from Church. The family ministry also verges to pertain to issues of church discipline or a reaction to disasters, as very often transpires when a young, single member gets pregnant, or a couple separates. Also, family ministry is always ad hoc restricted to the unique family week/month ceremonies with little enduring effects. What appears to be needed is a strategy that integrates various age groups and extends beyond the church families into the larger community. It must be an integral part of the Church's teachings, discipleship, and outreach ministry. This, hence, needs a radical deviation from the manner things currently are and depicts another important obstacle to be crossed. Productive family pastoral interest in a context of insufficient resources may need careful examination of which is the most strategic part of family care to address.

Priority Areas for Family Pastoral Care

The scope of pastoral family ministry is vast and diverse. Therefore, what is proposed here is not by any means exhaustive. Not every denomination may have the capacity to implement these, but those who are not able to do it alone should examine how they can work together with other churches and agencies to deliver these ministries.

- The priority area suggested is relationship enrichment. This should incorporate an extensive program of training and education for children and adolescent people about relationships, sexuality, and marriage. A well-developed sequence of premarital counseling for all intending couples that come for marriage is also essential. Regular recreations for relationship enrichment that are not restricted to married couples but are available to other unions in the larger community should likewise be developed. Along with these, the organization of effective evangelism techniques for working with non-married couples and non-Christian spouses of members is an aspect that continues to demand serious attention.

-Male economic empowerment would be another priority area. Support groups created around helping men to develop self-awareness, spirituality, relational aptitudes, nurturing skills, and job innovation are challenges for every Church to ponder, especially those in the urban centers.

- Building parenthood skills is yet another priority area, and this should begin with adolescents. Young people have to be exposed more deliberately to what credible parenting entails early enough before they beget their first child. Also, there is a necessity to work with parents at various phases of family development in developing parenting strategies. Single parents and parents of young children are especially needy of this support. Connected to this is the aspect of teenage mothers. Every community should develop a program similar to The Woman's Centre directed at helping teenage mothers move on with their lives and education after delivery and avoid the pitfall of repeated pregnancies that hamper the life opportunities of so many. Churches should at the least work closely with members and youngsters of members who find themselves in this predicament but should aim to develop, in collaboration with other churches, similar assistance for teenage mothers in the larger community.

- Another priority, particularly in the face of the swelling band of single parents, is the necessity for educational support and administered recreational activities for children and youth. After-school clubs and homework clubs, sports clubs, and tournaments could go a long way to help parents find acceptable activities for their children and prevent the large-scale indolence or television obsession that many cultivate when they come home from school to an empty house, always because the single parent is out there all day striving to earn a living for the family.

The most outstanding challenges of the Jamaican family seem to be:

1. Family structure- The foundation of the family can vary from a conventional marriage that brings together the husband and wife to begin the family. Or the living together of a man and woman without any marital commitment. The latter arrangement tends to pose some challenges to Church where there is no Biblical basis for such union. Secondly, the offspring of such unions are not legitimately the heritage of the man though he is the biological father. Scripturally the living together of a man and woman without the marriage commitment is sinful. However, where this is the case, the Church should take necessary steps to encourage the partners to come forward to legalize their union as soon as possible and as simply as they can afford it.

It is irresponsible for a man to live with a woman and have children with her without any marital commitment. Such a man may walk away from one woman into the waiting arms of another, causing social and psychological problems for society. The prevalence of female single mothers in our nation is a direct consequence of unmarried union. Irresponsibility in the affairs of marriage will spill over to the children's upbringing and family life. In one of the research findings on the Jamaican family mentioned earlier, one of the problems highlighted is the dearth of father figures and role models in the family. The reason becomes obvious when the men behave like the ostrich that refuses to hatch its eggs and care for its young.

Today family advocacy groups are calling on the Church to recognize the unmarried union as members and to turn a blind eye to underlying deficiencies. But the Church does not send people away from fellowship and prayers. The truth of the Gospel is to convict the sinner and cause repentance. The Church will be failing in her duties to God and humanity if she fails to point out the truth of the Scriptures and uphold the tenets of the faith.

There is no statute book or legislation that allows a man to enjoy the intimacy and personal comfort of a woman ex gratia. Commitment to his wife and responsibility for the offspring of the union is what makes the man a father and husband.

2. Single parents and adolescents' pregnancy - The percentage of those who become single parents due to the death of a spouse is very negligible compared to the rate of divorce and teenage pregnancy. Of those who are single mothers by divorce, the majority of them are without support from their fathers since there was no marital commitment in most cases, so the man simply abandoned the ship and walked away. He goes on preying on the helpless woman with the attendant social consequences.

3. The Church - The Church most times seems to be more intent on finding balance and accommodation for the various shades of opinion and attitudes rather than changing lives with the Gospel. Our agelong Christian preponderance would have given us a robust Christian family foundation, but we seem too busy seeking ways of making people comfortable irrespective of whether they are growing spiritually or seeking sympathy for their perverse demeanor.

The Church must be firm with its doctrine and relationship with the sheep, but compromise on the altar of accommodation will harm the Church in many ways.

EFFECTS OF RELIGIOUS PRACTICE
ON FAMILY RELATIONSHIPS

1. Mother-Child Relations

When compared with mothers who did not deem religion as important, those who considered religion to be reasonably crucial valued their relationship with their children considerably higher, according to a 1999 research, when mothers and their children have the same degree of religious discipline, they share healthy relationships. For example, when teenagers observed liturgies with almost the same regularity as their mothers, the mothers revealed considerably better friendships with them, even several years after, demonstrating the impacts of similar religious exercises. Besides, mothers who became more committed religiously throughout the initial 18 years of their child's life revealed a better connection with that child, irrespective of the degree of their religious observance before the child was born. Mothers who observed religious duties less frequently over time recounted a poorer quality of relationship with their grown-up children.

Grandmothers' religious practice exemplifies an intergenerational impact. The more spiritual a mother's mother is, the more inclined the mother is to maintain a good connection with her child.

2. Father-Child Relations

The deeper religious exercise of fathers is related to better connections with their children, higher prospects for promising relationships in the future, bigger involvement in their relationships with their kids, an enormous sense of commitment to stay in steady communication with their children, and a greater probability of helping their children and grandchildren.

Brad Wilcox of the University of Virginia found that "fathers' religious affiliations and religious attendance were positively associated with their involvement in activities with their children, such as one-on-one interaction, having dinner with their families, and volunteering for youth-related activities ."Compared with fathers who had no religious association, those who observed religious duties repeatedly were more likely to scrutinize their children, applaud and hug their children, and spend time with their kids. Fathers' regularity of religious attendance was a decisive forecaster of paternal interest in one-on-one actions with children than were occupation and income—the components most frequently referred to in the academic works on fatherhood.

Wilcox also tracked the "pathways" through which faith influenced fathers' relationships with their children and surmised that religious cooperation and particularly religious attendance have personal effects that are unrelated to traditional habits of social engagement. The priority that religion generally puts on family life, together with churches' family-focused social systems of support and emotional support of fatherhood, helps to clarify why religiously enthusiastic fathers are more active in youth-related activities.

3. Domestic Violence

Couples who have the same religious responsibility are less inclined to perpetrate acts of domestic violence. Men who observe religious services even once weekly are less than half as likely to engage in the act of violence against their spouses as their counterparts who visit once yearly or less. Routine attendance at religious traditions has a powerful and statistically substantial inverse correlation with the frequency of domestic invective. Mothers who visited spiritual services less frequently over time recounted a lower integrity relationship with their grown-up children.

Compared to those who deem themselves very religious, those who are "not at all religious" are very much more inclined to bear children out of matrimony.

CHAPTER 16

ELECTION IS NOT WAR

By the Jamaica (Constitution) Order in Council of 1962, by which the nation attained independence from the United Kingdom, Jamaica is a constitutional monarchy with a parliamentary system of Government. Citizens 18 years old and above are qualified to poll. Jamaica has had universal voting since 1944.

The prime minister, who is the head of Government, is elected by the majority political party from its elected parliamentary members. The British monarch, who is the nominal head of State, follows the prime minister's suggestion to select a Jamaican governor-general who has mostly ceremonial powers. The principal policy-making organ is the cabinet, which comprises the prime minister and at least 11 other ministers.

The bicameral parliament includes the House of Representatives and the Senate. The house has 63 members, who are elected directly from their constituencies. The speaker, who is the leader of the house and his deputy speaker, is elected by the House members. The Senate, which is the upper chamber of the parliament, has 21 members, who are appointed (not elected) by the governor-general—13 by the recommendations of the prime minister and eight on the advice of the head of the opposition party. Senators are nominated to serve for the duration of a single parliamentary period. The president and deputy president of the Senate are elected by their members. General elections must be conducted at least once every five years, and the ruling party may decide to conduct early elections.

Electioneering campaign is synonymous with political democracy, especially in the adult suffrage general elections, and the participatory Government is hailed as the beauty of democracy.

Local Government

The country is divided into 14 parishes that serve as local government areas, two of which are amalgamated as the Kingston and St. Andrew Corporation, mostly conforming to the Kingston municipal area. Parish parliaments, whose members are directly elected from the wards, administer the parishes. The capital city of some parishes has elected mayors. Jamaica is also generally divided into three counties—Cornwall, Middlesex, and Surrey.

Political Process

The two major political parties are the Jamaica Labour Party (JLP) and the People's National Party (PNP), and between them, they have bestridden the Jamaican legislative environment since the country's independence winning all the elections to the virtual close out of any other party. The malicious nature of Jamaican politics cloaks widespread reform agreement on constitutionalism, public education, and social welfare.

The PNP, established in 1938 as a democratic socialist party, bends more to the left than the more moderate and conservative JLP. Ethnic minorities such as the children of Indian and Chinese settlers have taken part in politics at the highest levels. Women have served with reputation in the House of Representatives, Senate, and parliament, although men still dominate in their numbers. In 2006 Portia Simpson Miller was elected the first female president of the PNP and the first woman to serve as prime minister.

Our political background and structure ensure that the political environment will be very busy with electioneering campaigns, underground political horse-trading, and elections for various levels of political vacancy. In a constitutional democracy like ours, the major political stakeholders are the political parties, their candidates, the umpires, and most significantly, the voters.

Political participation encompasses a broad range of exercises through which people formulate and express their sentiments on the nation and how it is administered and try to take part in and mold the decisions that impact their lives. These activities vary from evolving thinking about disability or other common problems at the personal or family level, enrolling disabled people's groups or other communities and unions, and campaigning at the local, regional, or federal level, to the process of traditional politics, such as ballot, entering a political party, or standing for elections.

Ordinary people can take part in politics, and every person has the freedom to participate, plus the people with disabilities.

While the political parties engage the voting public in their campaigns for a vote, trying to sell their candidate and their manifestos, the voters should judge or assess the parties based on their performance antecedents and the content of their current manifesto. The party manifesto represents their statements of intent, promises, and proposed policies and programs based on which they are seeking power. The organized private sector, professional bodies, the Church and its agencies, academia, and labor unions must obtain the manifestos of the various political parties and analyze them in the light of the country's current pressing economic and social needs. The result should be communicated to the general voting public so that they can make informed decisions on whom and which political party to vote for.

As the political parties pursue their usual mostly baseless campaign, there should be an issue-based dialogue and exchange among the non-partisan stakeholders to help clarify the political space and influence a voting pattern that will ultimately benefit society.

POLITICAL VIOLENCE

The growth of Jamaican trade unionism and its complementary leadership produced the political architecture out of which Jamaica's two major political groups, the Jamaica Labor Party (JLP) and People's National Party (PNP), originated. Within the development of their support root, Jamaican politicians such as Alexander Bustamante employed their influence on local wards to create a military command form of lobbying that depended heavily upon violence.

The Jamaican political tension is a long-standing quarrel between right-wing and left-wing characters in the country that dates back to pre-independence, often erupting into violence. The Jamaican Labour Party and the People's National Party have fought for custody of the island for years since 1943, and the rivalry has promoted urban warfare in Kingston. Each side thinks the other is sponsored by foreign entities, the JLP is said to be supported by the American Central Intelligence Agency(CIA), and the PNP is said to have been supported by the Soviet Union and Cuba.

The election period in Jamaica has become associated with heightened apprehension and destructive violence that, in most cases, mar the elections. Political thuggery seems to be an integral part of our elections, with the political parties fighting to outdo one another in this shameful debacle.

This endemic violence has nurtured a volatile political environment that evolved out of a symbiotic alliance between Jamaican labor unions and political violence. Consequently, the political system was destabilized by the acrid influence of biased politics, whereby party loyalists hanging on political commerce were convinced by the parties to protect local constituencies and take part in political conflict. Within this network, the Jamaican general election procedure became startling and violent, illustrating how insufficient political patronage was distributed among loyal party followers.

The social and political association between local politicians and riots will be understood by examining how incidents such as the "Henry Rebellion" in 1960, the 1978 Green Bay Massacre, and the public killing of the PNP presidential hopeful Roy McGann in 1980 illustrate the failure of the formal Jamaican political patronage to curb extremist violence among grassroots followers, giving rise to general public displeasure with the traditional Jamaican leadership. This modification of the political system manifested in the formalization of political violence by the late 1960s and a habit of general elections disrupted by brutal confrontations between JLP and PNP gangs. This political violence was indicated in the rise of mob dons such as Jim Brown and Wayne "Sandokhan" Smith, who became self-reliant from the patronage system through their leveraging of the drug trade. Accordingly, contemporary Jamaican politics in the twenty-first century is splintered, and local political authorities have lost custody of the gangs.

Political violence exists in Jamaica for two main reasons. Firstly, to fortify its current territory and make it unsafe for members of the opposition party and their gang members. Secondly, the violence is meant to create tension and intimidate the supporters of the opposing party.

SOLUTIONS TO POLITICAL VIOLENCE

Electoral Reform - Jamaica has accomplished substantial electoral reform and modification in the last 30 years.

The country's achievements in this regard stand as an example for many countries internationally; some have come to explore our system while others have asked us to examine their national elections.

All this interest is because of the high degree of esteem and honor they have for what we have achieved in modernizing our electoral system and how satisfactorily this system has functioned during election after election.

This success has been feasible because of a diversity of reasons. We have withdrawn the electoral process from natural political interference, which has given a great measure of transparency. The way was cleared with the institution of the Electoral Advisory Committee (EAC) in 1979, which was modified in 2006 into the Electoral Commission of Jamaica (ECJ). This agency, which has the irresistible support of political authorities over the years, has been tremendously profitable in guarding and bolstering the country's democratic system.

1. Jamaica pioneered the use of biometrics (fingerprints) to clear the voters' list and develop a special ID card.

2. Electronic Voter Identification and Ballot Issuing System (EVIBIS), used in designated constituencies and voting areas for designation of the voter, not for voting goals. The application guarantees "one person, one vote" and 'same person, the same vote."This system has culminated in the virtually total exclusion of impersonation, curtailed the risk of vote tampering, substantially closed out over-voting, and diminished the possibility of intimidation related to communal voting.

3. Jamaica has incorporated the use of G.I.S. technology which enhances the accuracy of ascertaining electoral borders.

4. Jamaica has inaugurated the Constituted Authority, which promotes the voiding or halting of voting where certain situations warrant and then retaking the votes within 30 days.

5. The House of Representatives has recently approved great legislation to deal with campaign finance issues, modeled to

control the amount of spending on elections and restrain corrupt practices in this regard.

We should be excited by these accomplishments as a people and as a nation and, therefore, should not do anything to overturn the extremely hard task we have achieved to get to this phase. It is for this motive that every law-abiding citizen should oppose any attempt by anybody, anywhere, to initiate political-related unrest during the interval leading up to the subsequent general election or afterward.

We are pace-setters in electoral reforms; we must protect this achievement, this important milestone; we are politically developed as a country, and hence political-related turmoil must have no room in the continued advancement of our democracy and our electoral process.

We urge concerned groups and civil society to stand with us. In the same manner, the PSOJ, other business associations, and civil society lately called on the two major political leaders to dedicate themselves to favorable economic management after the elections. We urge the same stance about the warning for no political-related riot during the election campaign.

Our political authorities, and every individual candidate representing the nation's sixty-three constituencies, must speak up. They have an obligation to this country to openly declare their renunciation of political violence and any damage to the electoral system. This is a crucial symbolic signal as we must do whatsoever it takes to make the forthcoming general election one of the largely peaceful elections in the contemporary history of Jamaica. This is achievable, and we must make it come to pass.

We advise that this also be enforced by interest groups across all the parishes to emphasize the decisive stance of citizens of this nation. All chambers of commerce, resident associations, neighborhood organizations, the Church, service clubs, and professional and different organizations across the parishes should enlist jointly and send a warning to Jamaica that we will not be aloof and let the progress of the electoral reform policy to be destroyed. Jamaicans, we must not condone reversed strides in this regard. Let us move forth as a country to further bolster the electoral system; to enhance peace and vitality in the society.

A robust and autonomous electoral system is important for contemporary liberal democracies like Jamaica. Democracy is not only ideational; it is critical for the modification of a country. Democracy is a method that empowers its citizens with the most liberty, ample opportunity, considerable prosperity, and the most livable life. In other words, building a society in which to reside, work and bring up families.

The entire public, as inhabitants of Jamaica, must help to aggravate and strengthen Jamaica's democracy. To guarantee that democracy stays strong and in good form, every one of us as Jamaicans must become active. The aspect of this effective role is to oppose political violence in any mold or pattern. This is essential for political stability. This is essential for peace. This is essential for employment creation and economic advancement. This is basic for moving forward.

Public Enlightenment and Law Enforcement

Jamaica has been harshly challenged with the issue of crime and turmoil for more than 45 years. This problem has impacted the country negatively by impeding social, political, and economic development. The country is endowed with its strategic site in the Caribbean, beautiful setting, friendly people, and a culture that is cherished by citizens of the world. Many policies, methods, commissions, and proposals have been formed to deal with crime, but the disease of horrible and surging crimes goes on to escalate. The security troops, consisting of the Jamaica Constabulary Force and the Jamaica defense Force, have performed well with insufficient resources to stem the wave of crime. However, the problem appears to threaten the lives of citizens.

Creating a rapid response department (RRD)- The establishment of a rapid response department is significant at this time in the Jamaica Constabulary Force. An RRD is necessary because this is a major organizational thrust to impact positively on crime, which is threatening.

the stability of the country. The RRD should be supported by rapid response units at police stations in all parish headquarters and all major towns.

This approach to crime-fighting would not be an isolated response, but it would be sustained action that goes across the country to ensure quick apprehension of perpetrators of crime. The delayed apprehension of perpetrators of homicides strengthens the actions of criminals to continue their vicious acts. The rapid response method is practiced in First-World countries like the USA, Canada, England, and France. This involves a heightened awareness of law enforcement and citizens about crime, resulting in the quick apprehension of criminals.

The response involves immediate contact with police stations following a reported shooting or homicide. This is followed by increased police presence on major roadways leading out of the area where the report was made. Increased checks would be made on motorists leaving the area, and there should be a massive deployment of security personnel in the area. This rapid and aggressive response to shootings should be communicated to citizens, so they can cooperate with the police in their investigations. This rapid response will send a message to criminals that once a shooting act is committed, they will be caught.

The quick response and apprehension of the persons responsible for the shooting that occurred at a church in Trelawny on Sunday, January 31, is a good example of the effectiveness and success of the rapid response method. The sustained rapid response in solving crime will make a difference in addressing this problem that is impacting negatively on development within the country.

Conducting Sustained Public Awareness

The solution of intensified public awareness campaigns should involve improved advertisements on the tragic effects of crime. This should be done on radio, television, and social media. The Government and organized private sector should boost public broadcast on the adverse impact of crime and proclaim a zero-tolerance strategy going forward. The broadcast should persuade all Jamaicans to enlist and unify against the smudge of crime. There should be multiple multimedia displays of signs, banners, and billboards in cities, metropolia, villages, and communities condemning criminal acts and shootings. This heightened public attention would bring to the vanguard the gravity of criminal actions, and law-abiding citizens would be sensitized and cautioned. This would lead to increased teamwork among the population against criminal activities.

Undertaking inner-city renewal projects will make a substantial difference in dealing with this long-term problem.

Constructing community-renewal projects to tidy up and paint the communities, along with holding vocational programs at community centers, should be proposed immediately. There is existing vocational training in some areas, but it needs to be sweeping and deliberate for specific communities. The focus on bolstering communities through schemes would make a considerable difference in empowering and helping citizens within communities. This will give immediate jobs to the youths. Constant plans should be put together to maintain cleanliness and revive the confidence of the citizens within neighborhoods.

Rusty buildings should be destroyed and alternative locations made available to transfer poor individuals living in miserable communities. The Government should figure out long-term payments for these housing remedies. The teaching of trades and handcrafts should be given at community centers to the youth, so they can have options for guns, mobs, and drugs. The public and private sectors should educate the public about the rebuilt thrust and solicit cooperation. The timely execution and sustained assistance for these solutions will help extensively in solving the crime dilemma in Jamaica.

A cardinal standard of effective crime management is the linking of informal and conventional state control. This is crucial to any good strategy, especially where the legality and ethical authority of the state, including some of the organizations within the criminal justice process, is viewed as dubious.

Popular participation at the community level verges to strengthen the ethical authority of the state's managed institutions and enhances their effectiveness. The truth is that most conflicts are informally addressed with variable outcomes. Where there is an inability to deal with these conflicts in positive ways because of the lack of trusted third parties and so forth, these nonformal interventions tend to result in an escalation of violence. There is substantial room for creativity here and the establishment of a more adaptable criminal justice structure with a bigger capacity to make positive informal interventions, although the penchant for accumulating power through centralization surely militates against this.

A more adaptable and service-oriented strategy may be achieved through new and more sensitive institutions that incorporate the communities and are responsible to them. Community-based policing, community judiciaries and mediation and conflict administration institutions that can handle inter-group conflicts, and neighborhood verdicts and rehabilitation programs are some illustrations of this.

Reforming the criminal justice system may suitably begin with the initial point of contact with the system – the police. What is expected here is to implement a revolutionary change in the technique of policing. This will include redefining the relationship between the authority and the populace on a more democratic, liberties-safeguarding, and law-obeying basis. This implies, among other things, bigger attention to crime deterrence and perhaps a suitable model of community-based policing (not community policing).

Historically, in other (British) types of policing, the police deter crime by their strong presence in the communities and cooperating with the citizens, employing their moral authority to convince people to obey the standards and laws of the nation, maintaining order, and assuring a reduction in the chances for the crime. This implies a consensus model and admiration for police authority. In Jamaica, these cannot be presumed; the respect for the police has been poorly destroyed and has to be rebuilt through participation and modifications in the power structures between police and citizens. Except for this, anti-corruption campaigns and the deployment of new technologies for crime-fighting may usher in some positive outcomes, but these results are doubtful to be sustained if the basic relationships and policing techniques remain unchanged.

Therefore, a helpful starting step would be a reworking of the prevailing community policing drive-in ways that strive to strengthen community capacity and help to socially separate the criminals from the neighborhood. This should entail accepting more from the community beliefs and rendering policing more as a service to the communities in which the community members share with the police the obligation for the management of crime and the sustenance of order. The surviving Neighborhood Watch program, for instance, makes the residents the eyes and ears of the cops, workers, or informants for the police instead of someone merely working to ensure that their community is safer with the help of the police.

Similar changes to the courts would help to improve the effectiveness of the system.

The establishment by some inner-city communities of "codes of conduct and enforcement mechanisms" to regulate deviant and preying behavior within their borders is a result of the impotence of the criminal justice process and their estrangement from it and its description of problems. New ways are expected to enhance access to cheap and fairly quick justice, especially in the violence-prone neighborhoods of Kingston where these colloquial courts have developed.

It is hard to specify the shape that this would assume, but one likelihood is a modified petty court session that would be created at the community level, that would have broadened powers to handle some types of disputes and crimes that are now dealt with by the formal courts. Panels of lay judges drawn from the neighborhoods by either an explicit or indirect use of the election precept or some other applicable principle that is satisfactory to the communities could hold as a kind of communal judge.

This would probably require that they acquire some additional coaching to make them more skilled in handling more complicated cases. This could be difficult, but then there would invariably be the right of plea to a higher judiciary if the parties to the several disputes are not assuaged by the decisions of the community courts. The general sense here is that there are invariably lessons to be known from the informal formations and the challenge of the conventional system is how to adjust and react to these outcomes.

These measures could be supported by the employment of the communities in aspects of situational crime deterrence, beginning with physically tidying up the neighborhoods as a joint project with the cops and other state agents. As community power is built up through such small feats in situational crime deterrence, their actions could then be enlarged to more demanding projects such as demolishing drug cabins from their communities, putting coercion on young people to dissolve gangs, or at least averting gang wars and other violent disputes and to stimulate better restraint of illegal guns.

Community activism in the ambient of better relations with the police could influence an important role in preventing illegal gun possession. Some people who live in the embattled populations of inner-city Kingston buy guns for the "defense" of self and community. This is deemed justifiable. In a mood of community solidarity, Jamaicans in the Diaspora who may not be corroborative of ordinary criminality may have no moral irritation in assisting the struggles to buy guns for these purposes. In the lack of inter-community wars, effective community efforts to restrain these practices as an aspect of the process of ensuring abiding peace would isolate gun ownership and trafficking as ordinary crimes, thereby making such exercises more susceptible to law enforcement.

The neighborhood dons and other authorities have indicated that it is feasible to have more productive crime restraint at the community tier even without creating more employment opportunities. But much of this is not endurable without some developmental actions and social interventions that are particularly geared toward crime prevention. There are some 140

NGOs in the neighborhoods of Kingston doing numerous good things, such as operating after-school coaching centers for teenagers, providing shelters for women casualties of domestic violence, counseling, and so forth. All of this is organized to respond to the several demands of the citizens. But there is relatively little purposeful crime prevention.

For the community's ambition to work, they require to have a confirmational national environment. If a trial is to be made to strengthen the peace process and secure productive crime control in the metropolitan communities, then such a program could be expanded relatively by simultaneously striving to create order in some of the important public places in the towns and main cities.

The state of the major public spaces, that is, the junctures at which the commercial vehicles assemble and the main commercial and organizational headquarters, set the standards for what is considered tolerable behavior and verges to have a large effect on the psychology of the people. If there is a significant disorder in these public places, then it gives a feeling of failure and engenders impressions of hopelessness in respect of the fight against disorder and a lack of faith in the police and the ability of the state. The reverse may also be true. Reviving order in these same public places may bring positive signals, rebuild hope and serve to marshal the energies of the population for the larger battle with the crime situation. For instance, the major centers could be tidied up, beautified, then populated at given times with police officers and reasonable citizens auxiliaries and volunteer organizations such as the Cadet Corps, Boy Scouts, and Girl Guides to assure that people behave more logically, that they queue up to enter the buses, that street seller has respect for other stoners of the streets and so forth. Such a strategy would seek to depend not just on traditional law enforcement and police power but also on several informal shapes of social penalties and persuasion.

This point can scarcely be overemphasized. To return to the illustration of attempting to rectify the disorder in the usage of the public transportation structure, most of this disorder is prompted by the shortage of seats and the undependable nature of the busses. Compelling people to conduct themselves in an orderly manner when met face to face with such a disorderly duty could quickly lead to insults and the undue use of force and violence by greenhorn control agents. The purpose of the lesson is to get people to adapt to law-abiding behavior and not to further overpopulate the jails, and such actions are only endurable to the duration that they are developed to stimulate the timely internalization of such harmony.

A universal principle that could prove useful here and in other facets of crime management is the principle of boundary delineation. Given the prevailing social conditions, unlike with the zero-tolerance strategy, the target should not be to totally solve the issue of disorder or to solve it by conventional law enforcement but instead to alleviate the problem and to try to achieve this by integrating those who are presently part of the crisis as custody agents for the new modifications. For instance, street traders could be requested to meet stated standards and to comply with agreed rules as a requirement for continuing to ply business on the streets. They could be directed to use carriages that meet certain measurements of size and appearance, clean the streets after an agreed time of day, procure trash bins for their clients, and so forth. They could be comprised in the drafting of these regulations and made to have a representation in their enforcement. This may not solve all the problems related to street trading, but it would enhance the existing situation. The sense here is the establishment of acceptable thresholds that can be implemented unfailingly and sustainably.

For many decades, definitely before independence, the police have been struggling to solve this situation with an all-or-nothing attitude through periodic raids, which at times proved successful in removing the traders from the streets for a short while. Within a short period, the streets are once more taken over by the vendors in bigger numbers because the regulations handed down by the police are not sustainable. This approach of setting enforceable regulations may be expanded in different ways to curb violence and criminality. In this respect, the current codes that are functional among adept criminals in the tourist sanctuary of Montego Bay are informative. There, robbers who target the tourists tend to refuse to use guns and do bodily damage to their tourist preys. The gain for them is nominal stress from the police. This is not the result of a detailed arrangement with the police, and there could have existed nothing as such. However, it is still the result of police criminal interchange and the effective patrolling of this no-gun horizon by the police, which compelled the criminals to recognize the patterns of police attitude. Perhaps this code is transmitted in the socialization of new tourist robbers.

CHAPTER 17

CONTEMPORARY JAMAICA - POLITICS, AND CHURCH

Jamaica is an island country in the northern Caribbean Sea. It was first occupied by the Taíno, an Amerindian community that vanished under Spanish rule from 1509 to 1655. The British invaded the island in 1655, and it was a British province until its freedom in 1962. The population is mostly Black, having a descent of peoples carried from West and Central Africa, mainly for the slave trade on sugar.

Jamaica is today a passionately Christian nation that is mostly Protestant, evangelical, and charismatic. At the beginning of the twentieth century, European Christian denominations such as the Anglicans, Baptists, Congregationalists, Methodists, Moravians, and Presbyterians held sway among the middle class in especially, while the underprivileged practiced syncretic, indigenous religions such as Zion Revival. The twentieth century has witnessed the unprecedented growth of American denominations, particularly the Seventh-Day Adventists and Pentecostals, and more lately, those who profess no religion.

Pentecostals are the most rapidly-growing group of Christians in the world. Between 1970 and 1990, the number of Pentecostals rose from 4.4 percent to 26.9 percent of the world's population. The preponderance of Pentecostals and charismatics live in the Global South of Africa, Asia, and Latin America. Referring to a 2006 Pew Foundation document, nearly 25 percent of the world's population are part of these religious communities. The Pew research separates Pentecostals and charismatics, referring to them altogether as Christian renewalist traditions. Pentecostals, specifically, represent 36 percent of Christians in the Americas, which comprises Latin America and the Caribbean, and 43 percent of Christians in Sub-Saharan Africa. One scholar has described Pentecostals as "Christians who pertain to refined Pentecostal denominations and churches like the Assemblies of God, the Church of God in Christ or the Universal Church," whose church rites include "people exercising the gifts of the Holy Spirit, such as speaking in tongues, foretelling and praying for miraculous healing." Charismatics, on the contrary, have several diverse denominations and include Catholics and mainstream Protestants. Charismatics, like Pentecostals, axiomatic spiritual gifts or charismata such as speaking in tongues, supernatural healing, and prophecy. The terms employed in the Pew report reveal the challenge of developing an academic definition of Pentecostalism. According to Allan Anderson, it is preferable to refer to a "diversity of forms of 'Pentecostalism.'" The overlaps between charismatic churches that pertain to mainstream Protestant denominations, refined Pentecostals who track their heritage to North American crusades such as the Azusa Street Revival, and autonomous churches that exemplify Pentecostal-like worship styles complicate measures to refine the tradition to a major set of institutions, doctrines, and practices. Here, however, Pentecostalism relates to Christians who are members of churches that belong or belonged to classical Pentecostal denominations.

Theological Origins: Pentecost is the Greek term for "fifty days," and for Shavuot or the Feast of Weeks, a Jewish festival that is celebrated fifty days after Passover. Initially an agricultural festival, Shavuot commemorates the presentation of the first grain harvest by the Jews. Pentecost in the Christian culture came to represent the culmination of prophecy. According to the New Testament, after the crucifixion and resurrection of Jesus Christ, he told his disciples that they would shortly be "baptized with the Holy Spirit." This promise came to fulfillment on the day of Pentecost: "When the day of Pentecost came, they were all together in one place. Suddenly a sound like the blowing of a violent wind came from heaven and filled the whole house where they were sitting. They saw what seemed to be tongues of fire that separated and came to rest on each of them. All of them were filled with the Holy Spirit and began to speak in other tongues as the Spirit enabled them"(Acts 2:1-2).

Modern Pentecostalism is traceable to three religious' movements, German Pietism, Wesleyan Holiness, and nineteenth-century US revivalism. German Pietism underscored conversion through an individual encounter with the Holy Spirit. This message of being "born again" directly impacted the Wesleyan Holiness campaign, which preached consecration through the cleansing of sin and loving God and one's acquaintance. In the expressions of John Wesley, founder of the Methodist convention, "Entire consecration or Christian perfection is not more or less than pure love, love deposing sin and ruling both the Spirit and existence of a child of God.

The Wesleyan Holiness campaign grasped this message of full consecration. In addition to this message of consecration, the Holiness movement underscored biblical realism, the need for a personal, emotional, and individual knowledge of conversion, and the moral embodiment of holiness of the Christian person.

The message of moral rectitude, the experience of delighting worship, and baptism by the Holy Spirit commemorated revivals throughout the United States and Europe in the nineteenth century.

Revivals that illustrated Pentecostal characteristics were also recorded in India beginning as early as 1860, in Latin America by 1909, in China in 1907, and in Liberia, by 1914. The concurrent eruption of Holiness revivals in the United States and all the non-Western world also illustrate that Pentecostal inceptions are complex and several, polycentric, and diffused.

Azusa Street Revival

The Holiness revivals were followed by the Azusa Street Revival, the main turning point in the advancement of the Pentecostal crusade in the twentieth century. On January 1, 1901, in Topeka, Kansas, a woman listening to a Bible class taught by Charles Parham at Bethel Bible College was recorded to speak in tongues. In 1905, Parham toured Houston, Texas, to preach. While there, Parham authorized Blacks to settle outside his classroom during Bible study. One day, William Seymour, a Black evangelist from Louisiana and the descendant of three lineages of slaves, was attending and accepted the spiritual gift of speaking in tongues. Seymour later toured Los Angeles to evangelize under Parham's guidance. The week of April 8, 1906, Seymour directed a revival service visited by African Americans at 216 North Bonnie Bray Street. The revival was so tremendous that on the last night, while attendees stood on the street speaking in tongues, the terrace fell in. The police apprehended seventy-two people and compelled them under psychiatric attention for twenty-four hours. The police instructed Seymour to relocate his revival meetings, and the group shifted to 312 Azusa Street. The Los Angeles Daily Times published a news article characterizing the ongoing revival meetings at the new location as a "Weird Babel of Tongues," a group of zealots who worked themselves up "into a state of mad excitement in their peculiar zeal." With time, Seymour founded the first Black-led Pentecostal ministry in the United States. Charles Mason, an African American pastor from Tennessee, also visited the Church at Azusa Street, where he accepted the baptism of the Spirit. On Mason's return to his Church, he exhorted about the significance of the knowledge of the Holy Spirit and appointed the Church of God in Christ (COGIC) as Pentecostal. Mason's experience is significant here because COGIC is one of the biggest African-American Pentecostal Holiness denominations in the United States. The Azusa Street Mission was the outset of African-American Pentecostalism in North America.

Modern Pentecostalism is a mixed tradition with three main characteristics. The first is an end of time Messianic cataclysm conception, that is, a belief that the return of Jesus Christ, which will signify the end of historical time and the advent of eternity, is near and that these are hence the "last days" when the prophet Joel foretold that the world would see an outpour of the gifts of Holy Spirit. Peter's reference to Joel in the Book of Acts is significant to Pentecostals: "In the last days it will be, God declares, that I will pour out my Spirit upon all flesh, and your sons and your daughters shall prophesy, and your young men shall see visions, and your old men shall dream dreams."

The second characteristic is a priority on the recovery of the apostolic age. In other words, stuff that occurred in Jesus's time, such as supernatural healing and wonders, have contemporary similarities. Supernatural healing, both bodily and emotional, and reprieve from difficult situations serve as indications that the ability of the Holy Spirit that was illustrated in the days of Jesus still performs in the lives of disciples. Lastly, the third identifying feature of Pentecostalism is its egalitarian and representative ethos. Everyone can get the gift of the Holy Spirit, which gives all believers entrance to God's divine power irrespective of ethnicity, race, and gender.

Pentecostals spill into two main doctrinal classes: Trinitarians acknowledge that Jesus is the disclosure of God the Father and that the Spirit proceeds from the father and was expressed in Jesus. Oneness Pentecostals oppose the traditional Christian principle that God, Jesus Christ, and the Holy Spirit are "separate but equal." Oneness Pentecostals think that the same God that came across in the Old Testament as Yahweh was uncovered in the manifestation of Jesus in the New Testament, and God's preeminence takes present trait in the Holy Spirit.

History of Pentecostalism in Jamaica

A history of working-class cultural and political opposition gives Jamaican Pentecostalism its distinct form. Diane Austin-Broos contends that Pentecostalism on the island is a facet of a tradition of "fundamentalist religion historically interweaved with political problems of the poor. "The Native Baptist culture carried a strong bequest of direct social effort on the part of impoverished and working-class Jamaicans. The Baptist faith was initially introduced into Jamaica by George Liele, an African American Baptist pastor from Georgia who was authorized passage to Jamaica after the American Revolutionary War. In Jamaica, Liele started preaching in households and small congregations in 1784, and by 1791 he founded the first Baptist Church on the island. Liele's dynamic ministry spurred the advancement of Black Baptist churches throughout Jamaica. Black or Native Baptist ministries incorporated African religious beliefs with the Christian religion. The churches underscored the Spirit instead of the message of the Bible. Their practices involved speaking in tongues, providing metaphysical interpretations of Bible passages, and pursuing after the Holy Spirit through self-abasement, fasting, and sleeping in the open air.

The Native Baptists' liturgical and spiritual exercises reflected the cultural and civil history of enslaved Africans. Native Baptists perceived themselves as social equivalents to Whites and segregated themselves from mainstream Baptists, whom they deemed disseminators of the principles of White men. Native Baptist religion and institution-building were noticeably race-conscious, and Native Baptists also engaged the state through explicit action. An enslaved African and Native Baptist pastor, Sam Sharpe, steered the Christmas War in December 1830, also called the Baptist War. Utilizing the Baptist Church as an institutional headquarters, Sharpe orchestrated a rebellion that bolstered the call for the formal liberation of slaves in 1834. His revolution was counteracted quickly, however. More than two hundred slaves perished, and five hundred coconspirators were killed. More than thirty years after, Paul Bogle, also an Aboriginal Baptist minister, with evangelical leader George Gordon, oversaw the Morant Bay Rebellion of 1865, a violent revolution protesting unfair compensations and requesting fair rationing of land. The political and economic interests of the Afro-Jamaican working-class fueled both the Christmas War and the Morant Bay Rebellion.

These class interests were also in practice in twentieth-century religious campaigns in Jamaica. Alexander Bedward, a charismatic Afro-Jamaican, questioned the predominance of White influence and administration in Jamaican matters in the tradition of Sharpe and Bogle. Bedward, an Aboriginal Baptist preacher, established a church in St. Andrew that declared at least fourteen thousand members by 1895. There were also records that his Church comprised adherents in Cuba, Panama, and Costa Rica. He raised the resentment of White and middle-class Jamaicans and the Government for his capacity to reach many Jamaicans displeased with the inequities that prevailed after Emancipation. Temporarily confined for sedition, he was eventually charged with madness and later released.

During the same interval in which Bedward began his ministry, a White English minister from Bristol, Raglan Phillips, established the Light Brigade. Working in association with Baptist churches in Clarendon and Westmoreland, Phillips called revivals in 1906–1907 and 1915, in which attendees obtained healing and spoke in tongues. In 1924, Phillips toured Kingston and carried out similar revival meetings. The Light Brigade prospered and became City Mission, a Jamaican Pentecostal church. It developed into one of Jamaica's most outstanding indigenous Pentecostal churches, with an identical religious shape to the Churches of God. Comparing Phillips's success in founding a Pentecostal movement to Alexander Bedward's efforts highlights the significance of culture and religion in the early twentieth century. Whereas Bedward's influence was perceived as a threat, Phillips was worthy to eventually gain acceptance for his faith strategies. The authorizations Phillips received from Baptist authorities form a precedent of White male preachers from the United States selecting and ordaining Jamaican pastors. This contributed to what Austin-Broos labels the "pervasive indigenization" of Pentecostalism as local Black pastors founded churches across the island. Association with US-based church structures, such as the Church of God situated in Cleveland, OH, offered Jamaican Pentecostal churches aid and the legitimacy that accompanies ministerial credentials.

Pentecostalism in Jamaica arose from the Native Baptists, who severed from their White US counterparts and inaugurated the Jamaica Baptist Union in 1849. After this autonomy, pastors began normalizing their leadership through educational improvement and administrative strategies. The Church was generally rescinded from political activities but built schools and training institutions throughout Jamaica. Social change was now validated by social mobility through academic laurels. Consequently, what had prevailed as a working-class campaign was modified into a middle-class organization. During this period, American evangelists from the eastern coast, such as George and Nellie Olson, founded Holiness churches as early as 1907 in Clarendon and St. Mary parishes.

These parishes were primarily made up of peasants and small-scale growers. At this historical milestone, Clarendon, where the Olsons built their Church, was a transition site for emigres moving in from more far parishes and those relocating to Kingston. The Olsons' Church preached consecration or purity by the in-filling of the Holy Spirit. However, Holy Ghost baptism was distinguished by a silent receipt of the Holy Ghost and was an intellectual experience instead of blissful worship and speaking in tongues.

Austin-Broos contends that Pentecostal churches in the early twentieth century attracted converts from the same socio-economic group that the Native Baptists had in the nineteenth, but that the former could not generate the institutional scope of the Jamaica Baptist Union and frequently lacked the radical passion of the Native Baptists. In one aspect, the state was directly responsible for primary education, which withdrew an important sector of public life from the responsibility of the Church. Additionally, as opposed to Native Baptists, American Pentecostal preachers were vastly dissociated from Jamaica's colonial past. Newly arrived missionaries appreciated that churches should cease overt political involvement with the state. Yet, despite the lack of cultural and historical connections to the island, Pentecostalism gave a major status alteration to people disenfranchised by the upward outlook of the Baptist Church. Pentecostalism, in Austin-Broos's view, gave middle-class Jamaicans a religion focused on moral injunctions that would radically modify their status into that of a preferred spiritual elite, and all inside a church upheld by a metropolitan authority. Women comprised the majority of members, but men were selected as leaders. In this manner, the Church provided a means of promotion and integrity for men that was unreachable through formal economic and social means. Though early Pentecostal churches provided ministerial training for male supervisors, they did not compel ministers and preachers to illustrate proficiency in the word through strict training. Rather, Pentecostal belief, in its egalitarian strategy, distinguished leaders who were directed by insights from the Holy Spirit, whether or not they were properly trained.

Today Pentecostalism is the biggest tradition in Jamaica. Currently, 27.5 percent of Jamaicans who profess a religious association are Pentecostals and Church of God members, including the Church of God in Jamaica, the Church of God of Prophecy, and the New Testament Church of God. In Kingston, more specifically, 26.6 percent of religious cohorts are Pentecostal. In each denomination, women make up over 56 percent of the membership.

Pentecostalism circulates through both missionary structures and globalization. The advancement of Pentecostalism in the Global South is composed of an extended history of Christian missionary endeavors in the New World. European nations broadened their empires and amassed a fortune much early as the fifteenth century by wrenching resources through the slave labor of indigenous communities and enslaved Africans. Christian missionaries gave moral and ethical rationale for colonialism through actions to educate indigenous people and enslaved Africans.

In the New World, missionary breakout had contradictory outcomes. It further ingrained European authority yet furnished spiritual spaces for subjugated Africans to integrate their ancestral professions with Christian teachings. Through a method of assimilation and opposition, enslaved Africans developed life worlds that asserted their humanity and mechanism within tyrannical systems built on the commotion, economic exploitation, and denial. Twenty-first-century globalization, the strategy by which world monetary and political systems become merged under a neoliberal arrangement, delivered new structures in which opinions and goods traveled.

Most recently, colonialism assumed a new shape in structural adaptation and development drives. Economic improvement and social uplift were integrated into the soul of capitalism and worked in harmony with a reinvigorated Protestant ethic. Meanwhile, Pentecostalism circulates all through the Global South, employing modern communication technologies. Marla Frederick has discovered that modern evangelists who touch worldwide audiences through religious radio and television programs are as much concerned about how to subdue abuse, get out of deficit, and maintain family as they are about how to enter heaven. If nothing more, these messages illustrate the porous barriers between the spiritual and profane. Under democratic leftism, theologies pass through as fluidly over boundaries as principles over American capitalism.

The problem in the Field

Scholars of Pentecostalism always describe believers as alienated and uninterested in conventional politics. Many studies also depict Black Holiness beliefs in terms of concession or resistance. This contrast conceals myriad forms of purposeful action. The use of politics signifies all activities that promote individual and communal flourishing and not exclusively exercises of statecraft or electoral attitude. According to Amos Yong, politics and the political, when extensively conceived, deal with the structures, strategies, and relationships comprising the state and the public square. While conventional politics, economics, and community make up this public square, the project takes on a personal view of the lives of Pentecostals.

Political action comprises a host of actions meant to obtain material goods, encourage healthier public behaviors, and create favorable attitudes for civic engagement. Through these efforts, individuals and communities are made visible and their lives purposeful.

Two problems alter prevailing notions about Pentecostalism: an insufficient understanding of the belief's historical and geographical heritage and extremely narrow definitions of political activity. How we narrate the story of Pentecostalism and the phrases to describe believers' activities limit our opinions about the ways personal and collective religious obligations inform political action. Too frequently, the word politics is a synonym for electoral attitude, government activities, and the interchanges between the Government and citizens. Religion has often been deemed an opiate, diluting political activity due to its supernatural orientation. This is particularly the truth for the review of Pentecostalism. Questioning the stereotype that believers are apolitical, Yong contends that Pentecostals engage in a range of political activities. In disadvantaged communities, socio-economic existence has been the prerogative, and thus there has existed much less interest expressed in voting, lobbying, statecraft, etc. Other Pentecostal populations and organizations, however, reveal a much more formal interest in politics.

In Brazil, for instance, Pentecostal churches established an organization that vigorously campaigned for aspirants in national elections. Pentecostals and Evangelicals make up two-thirds of the recently elected Brazilian Protestant parliamentarians in 1998 and 2000. In between these two extremes, Yong contends that some Pentecostals are remotely political. For instance, Pentecostal leaders may give prophetic criticisms of the social arrangement. In Nigeria, for instance, before Obasanjo's election in 1999, charismatic churches across Nigeria had joined in national prayer meetings and campaigns in support of his candidacy. Yong asserts that such efforts by the Pentecostals and charismatics form an engagement with politics through lobbying, public acceptance, and critique.

Pentecostals may also connect indirectly with politics by creating spiritual communities that give alternate structures of care and resources. In nations where political clientele or the practice of peddling that ties citizens to a political party preside over citizens' access to goods, Pentecostal churches furnish alternative conduits to circumvent the clientele systems that political parties create and give free leeway to local organizations. Creating such alternative communities is the choice of political action of Pentecostals on the socio-economic fringes of society. While the magnitude of disenfranchisement makes them nonparticipants in conventional politics, Yong acknowledges that they are building life worlds that question the status quo of political patronage.

The relationships and engagements that happen within the space make up a type of politics. This may depart slightly from Yong's opinion of politics by locating the starting block of political activity elsewhere than in interaction with the state and its traditional mechanisms of representation. It is centered around the quotidian, close interactions that hit at the heart of what conventional politics seeks to achieve, that is, social engagements, decision-making, and rapports that create change. It corrects a restricted understanding of the character of politics by centering Pentecostalism, a religion mainly considered apolitical, amid the discussion on political activity broadly defined. It also offers a viewpoint on the Anglophone Caribbean that varies from the dominant one. Too often, scholars propagate a public perception of the anglophone Caribbean as a section of North America. Studies about areas take up the themes of economic growth, tourism, and multilateral actions to contain the traffic in drugs and guns, thus constraining our understanding of stories about political dysfunction and portrayals of pastoral beach resorts. On culture and the sculptures, the study of symbols, and African-derived religious traditions are mainstays.

The Anglophone-Caribbean offers a distinct context in which to investigate the political dimensions of the contemporary Pentecostal movement. The region has an abundant religious history, a multiracial society, and a long narrative of popular protest. The history and politics of the Anglo-Caribbean are distinct and cannot be encompassed in the religious history of Latin America. As William Wedenoja observes, "numerous scholars have elicited very enlightening studies of Pentecostalism in Latin America, but assumably, Pentecostalism has different shapes and purposes in Latin-Catholic cultures than in Anglo-Protestant traditions."Despite existing as a global campaign, Pentecostalism has to be examined regionally. Pentecostal self-expression adopts different valences based on the practitioners' social and political ambivalence. It is practiced in a specific way by Jamaicans residing on the island and those living in the Diaspora.

In 1962, Walter Hollenweger printed the earliest study of the coming of Pentecostalism. His theological narrative of the movement underscores the various derivations of Pentecostalism and its multivalent heritage. Using the portrayal of roots, Hollenweger views Pentecostalism's development as a rhizomatous process. The Wesleyan-Holiness campaign and the Protestant revivals of the late nineteenth century are part of the chronological and theological background of Pentecostalism. Hollenweger insists that the African-American slave religion and the Azusa Street Mission must as well be included in the movement's founding culture.

European and American White Protestant campaigns are antecedents but should not be the single standard against which to interpret and appreciate Pentecostalism in all its diversity.

In Pentecostalism, biblical instructions about the spiritual epitome organize the secular world. Baptism of the Holy Spirit and speaking in tongues substantiate God's direct and personal action in believers' lives. The cross symbolizes redemption, water baptism, and speaking in tongues signifies conversion. Dress codes and daily comportment distinguishes members of the beloved population from the communities around them.

Scholars have described these exercises and rituals as apolitical. This perspective, I contend, is a result of desultory processes that overstress the political as solely related to practices of statecraft. Asad's assertion of the importance of the historical and social context of symbols, rituals, and practices brings me to a more extensive interpretation of political activity and efforts on the side of Pentecostals toward social change.

Following Wynter's concepts of religion, we can make the significance of the discretions that Pentecostal believers use in their daily lives as a consequence of their faith obligations. In the ambient of Jamaican civilization and politics, Christianity gives the master protocol for right action.

Christianity in Jamaica educates ideas of right and vice, good and evil. In politics, Christian virtues and principles influence the language and emblems politicians use to pledge their claims on the best programs of strategy for Jamaica's future, even when these declarations also serve to further relegate vulnerable neighborhoods and justify state-sponsored violence.

Asad's historical actuality of religious emblems and procedures and Wynter's remark that religion approves action to mix up common affirmations about Pentecostals and political activity.

Assertions about Pentecostalism's apolitical character may merely reflect slim assumptions about what tallies as political action. Defining politics as conventional processes of statecraft limits our interpretations and conceals a multitude of other activities and qualities which comprise a type of politics, even if the actions themselves are not expressly related to state processes. With Yong, I insist that political involvement falls on a range and is not restricted to the practices that rapidly engage the state. I conceptualize politics as encompassing all social actions and attitudes geared towards human thriving, whether or not they include direct interaction with the formal mechanisms of the state. For instance, a church feeding scheme or a youth career development conference drawing on Bible tales may fulfill the same needs as a government food donation program or reserved government funds for in-school vocational programming. The latter requires a compromise between state power representatives, while the former depends on intentions of Christian philanthropy and excelling in secular endeavors using biblical doctrines, but the Church's action is targeted toward the same objectives as the interchanges with politicians and state establishments. Here, Michael Oakeshott's definition of politics is useful:

Politics, it appears, are a form of practical human activity; they are practical activities concerned with the arrangements of society. Those who engage in this activity seem to be moved by a desire to impose upon the human world as they find it a character that it does not already possess. The world which consists of what is good to eat and what is poisonous, the world in which the sea incites to navigation and the earth to cultivation, a world in which everything exists to be made use of, is the world of politics.

Oakeshott's understanding of politics as the exercise of tending to social agreements highlights the political significance of practical, everyday activities.

Reflecting on the past five decades, the "five literary pioneers" credited post Emancipation improvement to the labor of the churches. They also condemned the British colonial authority as having flunked to launch any program that would contradict the destabilizing impacts of slavery. The authors' conception of progress concentrated on two areas: enhancing the island's infrastructure and reinforcing Jamaicans' moral values. The economic growth of the country required creating better roads to stimulate internal trade and improve the country's dependency on locally cultivated goods. Their vision for ethical progress depended on frugality and industry.

Working the land as sovereign farmers as contradicted to laboring on the sugar farmsteads would result in an honorable peasantry that was economically self-sustaining. Integrity, argues Deborah Thomas, was defined as holding a small plot of land on the cliffs, being qualified to assist a family through small-scale agrarian production, having a quiet personality, and living simply. The relationships between disposition, values, personal effort, and national advancement were made obvious in the concluding chapter of JJ. The "path to blessedness," proclaimed Dingwall, compelled "enlightenment, enterprise, persistence, thoughtfulness, economy, and unity.

The history of social transformation in Jamaica was associated with Christian denominations that either assisted or provided a vocabulary to critique slavery, labor, and land ownership, as was the example of the Baptist War championed by Sam Sharpe in 1830, and the Morant Bay Rebellion steered by Paul Bogle and George William Gordon in 1865. Jamaica's history of religion and revolution depicts a battle for improvement and economic privileges that was always associated with Christian worldviews. In the issue of Garveyism, Rastafari, and the International Peacekeepers under Claudius Henry, extremism was never too disconnected from the already rooted beliefs about God; religion was often a servant to progress.

The historical and political examination conceptualized the effect of Jamaica's religious history and Christian verbiage on public life. Thinking about politics and faith in this way nudges against larger descriptions of secularism. It underscores how the nominal separation between Church and Government in modern democracies works more like an ambitious prescription for governance than as a valid definition of public life. In Jamaica, public verbiage and political policy have been imbued with Christian speech since colonization. Religion furnishes a means and language to accomplish social progress and solve moral ills. To tell the tale of Christian values and verbiage in the building of the Jamaican state, I have concentrated on key historical standpoints of social change, the stop of slavery, the 1972 and 1980 elections, and the 2011 attack on Tivoli Gardens. At these crucial moments, politicians and citizens pulled on religious values to enunciate remedies for the state's negligence. Dingwall's manifesto, Jamaica's Greatest Need, was written in the fallout of the stop of slavery in 1834 and the shade of the Morant Bay Rebellion of 1865. The rebellion, organized by Native Baptists, compelled colonial authorities to pay interest to Afro-Jamaican contends for fair wages and impartial access to land. "So help me God I will fight for my country" the oath sworn to by men at a Baptist cathedral before the upheaval revealed the theological bases of the uprising and the values that encouraged its participants. Afro-Jamaican laborers' request for rights as a consequence of slavery questioned a consistent pattern of negligence by the colonial Government. Dingwall's polemic kept on this tradition of Christian opposition. His signal for God-ordained loyalty was a request for Christian virtue among Jamaicans and an accusation of the colonial governments' continued relegation of Afro-Jamaican privileges and claims. What emerged was a complicated vision of national personality based on Christian doctrines and Afro-Jamaican solidarity as prescriptions for compensation and social uplift.

The national conversation around improvement and social elevation in the twentieth century would be influenced by the cliche introduced in Dingwall's manifesto. Norman Manley's 1972 election crusade drew greatly on the counter domination structures of the Black Power campaign and Rastafari, challenging government economic policies that aggravated class imbalance and as well the Creole jingoist denial of the importance of class and race in ascertaining access to the privileges of development and social uplift.

The Claudius Henry disagreement illustrated that the ideological domain in Jamaica, deeply conditioned by Christian virtues, could not adopt a radical concept of community and Afro-Jamaican elevate. Manley's victory and the execution of democratic socialism illustrated the effect of counter-domination cultural activities on the national program. Manley's third path introduced opportunities for Jamaica's disadvantaged and attempted to shift the country from its fringe stature in the global economy, and the PNP strived to communicate the Christian principles expressed in its variety of democratic socialism, but a plurality of Jamaicans found democratic socialism incompatible with their understanding as a Christian country. The contentions on singing the "Red Flag" in a church at McGann's funeral bespeak the ideological conflicts between the PNP's socialist disposition and the opinions of Jamaican aristocracies who deemed the song an insult to the country's Christian moralities. Finally, the third path and democratic socialism were paralyzed by Cold War apprehension about the reach of Communism and the cynicism about its menace to the Christian moralities that dominated Jamaica's national advertence.

During the 1980 elections, idealistic clashes burgeoned into armed battles between political parties. The country decided eventually to seek the Christian pledge of "deliverance." Seaga and the JLP beneficially utilized Christian cliches to end the country's unholy experiment with democratic socialism. The congratulatory messages written to Seaga talked to the significance of his party's triumph as one that had saved Jamaicans from what a writer depicted as "communism slavery and cruelty." Seaga was compared to Moses and characterized as having steered Jamaicans out from the hold of the terrible authority of communism of vicious Manley. Seaga also sent the country into "structural adjustment programs" that compelled Jamaica back to reliance on the United States. This fresh order reasserted the Creole patriotic tendencies that had rationalized suppressing economic strategies in the past, but many thought that this shift was equivalent to asserting the country's Christian virtues.

Once again, Jamaicans, especially the poor and disadvantaged, were made to assume the burden of reliance. Structural adjustment eliminated protections and safeties that would have guaranteed that Jamaicans from every social class could appreciate the dividends of progress. Meanwhile, gunmen, no more the armed hitmen of political parties, became semi-independent agents who fastened the barriers of belonging through turmoil and patronage in their particular neighborhoods, taking on responsibilities that the state neglected to carry out. The fall of the traditional state and the tensions that are associated with garrison life cultivated moral malady for which there existed few remedies.

During this period, Pentecostalism appeared in the Global South as a spiritual remedy for those who were affected by the discontents of adjustment.

Contemporary Jamaica is a nation intrinsically interwoven with its history, culture, civilization, and religion; the Christian faith is the nation's subconscious bedrock of last resort almost in all endeavors.

CHAPTER 18

PRODIGAL FATHERS

One day you'll
be just a memory
for some people.
Do your best to
be a good one.

Helen Barry
www.helenbarry.ie

The story of Jamaica and its endemic vices of violence, absentee fathers, and high rate of teenage pregnancy is akin to the story of the children of godly parents becoming delinquent.

The Church must be at the forefront of every effort geared toward the recovery of the Jamaican family because there is a disconnect between the preponderance of Christian background and the reality on our streets and hamlets.

Slavery and colonialism have had their toll on the psyche of the Jamaican man, and that is the root cause of the ugly malfeasance prevalent among the male folks. One of the sins of slavery is deprivation, the deprivation of dignity and honor that debased the victims whereby they are hushed, assaulted, and compelled to accept to live in depravity and inconsequentially.

Yet slavery formally ended In 1834, but the descendants of the victims are yet to purge themselves of the anachronistic effects of the worst man's inhumanity to man. Through our culture, politics, and music orientations, we continue to subconsciously exhibit the tendencies of a people struggling for self-actualization and prominence - real freedom.

The Church must do more to minister to personal rediscovery and affirmative action for self-actualization. When the Israelites left Egypt led by Moses under the mighty hand of God, they did display similar attitudes of lack of self-esteem and trust in the reality of their freedom in the wilderness. Though God was obviously in their midst, pulling every stunt to ensure their safety and welfare, they could not muster up enough trust and commitment to the reality of their freedom from the Egyptian bondage.

The Jamaican Christians, especially the men, must come to terms with their new and unique position in Christ, the double freedom from physical and spiritual slavery, and Emancipation from colonialism.

Family is significant as an objective in Jamaica, but the marriage status, especially among the underprivileged, is a matter of social interest for Jamaicans. This concern spans back to the period of the first Christian missionaries, but many watchers cite it as a bequest of slavery. Marriage has long been recognized as a characteristic of middle-class stature, but middle-class interviewees fussed that marriage was presently too rare there. In recent years, nearly 85% of deliveries in Jamaica occur to single mothers. In poor neighborhoods, one always hears of women relating to a "baby fada," the man who is the daddy of her children.

One of the contradictions of Jamaican society is that prominent Christian moralities continue to demand bigger adherence to matrimonial family life, but the Jamaican culture can be archly sexualized, and unmarried families are the standard. The marriage status in the last decade has decreased, while the divorce percentage increased.

Several Pentecostal churches are reported to send away unmarried women in romances with men, but Catholics assert that single women bringing up children can find a satisfactory home in the churches. Priests and others discourse on the value of nuptials, but women always say that they discover too few good choices among the men they come across and that men are extremely fearful of commitment.

Every Church in Jamaica remarks a particular problem in drawing in and keeping men in the congregations. According to the 2011 survey, women outnumbered men in every one of the Christian denominations. However, Catholic membership is almost equalized, at 47% male and 53% female. Two-thirds of the non-religiously related persons in Jamaica are men, and in the last decade, that proportion has risen. While the number of persons who identified with no faith or denomination rose by about 26,500 people between the 2001 and 2011 surveys, men made up 88% of that differential.

For as far as I know, Jamaica has remained a country of fatherless children. It is not heartbreaking or depressing; it was not until I moved out from home for the second period that I understood how unusual that was. Much of the nation sees it as normal. When I was growing up, virtually none of my elementary school friends resided in two-parent households. Like myself, several of us knew who our papas were, but they just were not at home. For better or worse, that is how the situation was, and we did not challenge it; no one did.

Fatherlessness is so extensive that many infer it. For much of my existence, the TV shows I watched with perfect two-parent homes were just American fiction. Like many other children my age, the idea that my parents could be heartily married, or even co-parenting, was exotic and incomprehensible. Of my ten intimate friends in elementary school, merely three of them had their papas in their lives.

Nationally, the statistics tell a scarcely different story. While there have been relatively few reliable studies about the matter of fatherlessness, it is reckoned that 47% of Jamaica's children stay in single-parent homes with their natural mothers. Besides, the number of homes led by women continues to soar as men erode completely from the family structure.

The effect of this on children, their social life, and the country's prospects has been a theme of discussion for several years, but it's always tabled in favor of trying to address more serious matters, like crime. In 2014 when Peter Bunting, the Minister of National Security, announced that fatherlessness was steering much of the criminality that bedevils Jamaica's streets, it seemed evident that this burgeoning problem was under the Government's purview.

The dilemma is that no legislation or policy could be established to change the fact for Jamaican children. These are issues that implore inquiries of tradition and culture. Those are aspects the Government cannot merely decide to reverse at a stroke, but it is obvious that until something changes, the mounting problems that are associated with fatherlessness will only rise.

Yet, this asks the question - why? In his article on Black fatherlessness in the Caribbean, Green identifies colonial intimidation during slavery as the first tear in the structure of Black households. During the period, men were not permitted to form families, and if we insisted, plantation holders would auction one or both of the parents to make sure those ties were severed. Consequently, Jamaican men have long been disillusioned with the concept of fatherhood. As fatherlessness breeds fatherlessness, the crack that was chopped open centuries ago has expanded and deepened into the current chasm that now splits our homes. Women, nonetheless, have always been adorned with the commitment of motherhood, so when men abandon, they are required to pick up the stretch.

Jamaica has constantly revered the portrayal of a strong, steadfast woman. Our only female national idol was best recognized in her time for her prognostication and unwavering commitment to the freedom of her people. "Nanny of the Maroons" is said to have been a nurturing dignity. She dwelled in the mountains that thronged British plantations and assisted hundreds of slaves on their journey. As they went up from the plantations, barely dodging the Redcoats that pursued to re-enslave them, she would accept them into the neighborhood she built. There are many stories about her part in those early days of anti-slavery opposition, including tales that she had extraordinary powers that enabled her and her neighborhood to win their persistent fighting against the British colonizers. Though it is difficult to know the full magnitude of her capacities, one thing is incontestable; she was fierce and stringent in her quests.

Certainly, with predecessors like her, the bar is fixed high for Jamaican women. To this day, we yet require the same strength, determination, and fervor from our female companions. Whether it is in the sphere of political activism or our families, women are reckoned to fill the voids where men are ceasing to function. As more men are abandoning family life behind, we are imploring mothers to still again fill the void.

When I was younger, my mama was my entire world. She was the only individual I could look up to for direction since she was the only person available. In retrospect, I can observe that this was not merely something she committed to out of love. She, like several women in our nation, had to love absolutely and mother responsibly by necessity. There was nobody else to help to make the task easier. But I was fortunate, my mama had a good job, and we stayed in a good neighborhood. We surmounted fatherlessness in the most aspect, but there are so numerous children growing up in households that cannot.

In Jamaica's main cities, where gang unrest is decimating any facade of stability, the toll of fatherlessness has never occurred more noticeable. One effect of the swelling number of single-parent homes in poverty. In 2014, Bunting indicated that this directly relates to increases in criminality as youngsters continue to enlarge gang populations. As more mothers are unable to make ends meet, the burden falls on their young children to assist. Often this exemplifies in elementary school-aged boys handling drugs and doing other servile tasks for more dominant gangs and gun go-betweens in their areas.

Bunting advocated for decent housing developments in low-income neighborhoods, but these efforts cannot possibly result in the transformations we need to see. Fatherlessness has become a platitude in Jamaican society, and with it appears challenges the Government cannot purposefully solve. We need to begin to implore more of our men at every twist to embrace fatherly responsive life.

Jamaican men are applauded for even cursory involvement in their children's lives, while our women are disgraced and rejected for an inability to evade their responsibility and the various economic limitations that prevent them from accomplishing them.

For my whole elementary school career, my mama would pay somebody to pick me up after school daily. Occasionally there would be slating conflicts, so she would beg my dad to come for me. Even though he never arrived on time or attended any other occasion at the school except for these brief frolics, my teachers would gather around to heap him with applause for being such a credible father. They would inform me in private discussions that I should be delighted that my father was so concerned and loving, though they understood it was still difficult for my mama to pay for me to attend this school because he was without. They were well familiar with his many negligences and other children, and yet, they honored him.

It infuriated me then, and it still does. No one ever thought it wise to compliment my mama and commend her for doing a wonderful job since that was what she was presumed to do. It is not as if she was not supposed to be a great mama. That would have often been her duty, but the truth that no one required the same sense of duty from my papa, who I hardly knew, is expressive of a vastly more significant issue.

Nothing has improved since I was a child. When I got home last November, people still feigned as though my papa was some outstanding patriarch. They still do.

As this problem only continues to thrive, something has to submit. Men must go back to their homes. Women need to be alleviated of this back-cracking responsibility. They are bearing the burden of a new age on their shoulders alone, and it is not acceptable.

A great many problems are confronting the Jamaican nation, but this one has been ignored for far too long. This ostensibly insignificant crack that first slashed open at the root of our nation's colonial outsets is threatening the fate of the nation as a whole, its women, and its youngsters. Jamaicans have to be performing better; we have to be more distinguishing and understanding of what it implies to assign all this burden to the women of this nation. If we expect to see real significant change, men require to start to assume a bigger function in family life.

The Good Father and the Ideal Child

Through both communities, there was a robust identification with the papa role, as men generally conceded that they preferred being recognized as a father, that they were currently ready to sacrifice for their children's necessities, and that they deemed it important to establish a standard for their children. When invited to interpret the word "father," respondents had no problem pointing out that a father was a trustworthy person, one who furnished his household, a devoted man who looked after his family, a man who established an example and provided guidance, and a man who gave emotional assistance to his family. A similar pack of qualities was recorded when men were inquired about what a good father should accomplish. It was apparent that Jamaican papas did not discern their role as restricted to being merely the financial provider, as recapped in the statements of a youthful construction worker: "Be good to the children. Take care of them. Own the children. Be there for them. Talk to them. Eat with them. It's not just about giving them money". When invited to define the true mother, there was the usual emphasis on giving emotional support and attention to the children. In addition, Jamaican mamas were often required to partake in the financial assistance of children, as approximately a quarter of papas listed this among the obligations of mothers. The specific traits which fathers believed were important to motivate children reflected both vast cultural qualities as well as gender-differentiated standards. In general, fathers conceded that the most crucial qualities which should be motivated in children were: exhibiting good manners, being respectful, showing loyalty, appreciation for others, sincerity and integrity, being caring, self-discipline, the belief in God, and obtaining a good education.

Despite these common consensuses, it was evident that papas in each community attached relatively different values to what were deemed the most important standards. In the middle-income neighborhood, the traits which were referred to most repeatedly were honesty and innocence (20.6 % citing this), appreciation for others (15.8 %), and the belief in God (13.6 %). In the low-income neighborhood, the significance of having good behaviors was identified most repeatedly (35.5 %), and this was proceeded by an appreciation for others (21.6 %) and by the desire for children to know to be caring and kind (8.7 %). In the inner-city neighborhood, substantial importance is dedicated to having good behaviors, a condition that may be handily appreciated within the background of a highly irritable environment where showing rudeness may lead to brutal confrontations. Traditionally, in both rustic areas and poorer neighborhoods, Jamaican children are instructed early to be well-mannered. These expected manners may be less significant in middle-income neighborhoods. It is also apparent that in the low-income neighborhood, there was a precise mention of children knowing to value education, as these papas were twice as inclined as those in the middle-class neighborhood to list this among the most crucial principles. Self-direction was underscored by papas in both communities and among both boys and girls. This comprised a range of traits, of which the most repeatedly cited were to have self-esteem and self-discipline, knowing the value of education, and to have a purpose, commitment, independence, and responsible. Irrespective of social standing, papas placed particular priority on children's knowing how to become dominant and self-directing. This was seen as especially important for girls, and it may be appreciated given the family arrangement and the major financial responsibility that several Jamaican women carry for their children. For these papas, there was no incongruity between insisting that women should become self-organized and, at the same time, stipulating the traditionally female traits of being ladylike. It was remarkable that among low-income papas, almost a quarter (23 %) emphasized that girls should recognize education and perform their school work, while this was cited as an important trait for boys by merely 8 % of these papas. In the middle-income neighborhood, 7 % of papas specified this as crucial for boys, while 5 % cited this for girls. The stress on educational achievement by papas of low-income girls is to be appreciated, given the potential for conventional educational qualifications to salvage these inner-city girls from their hampered occupational opportunities and to draw them away from early pregnancies. When inquired if there were any particular qualities that they believed were crucial for boys and girls, between a quarter and a third of the papas said they did not remember any other qualities apart from those recorded for all children. The moral standards identified by papas were generally communicated as "Do the moral thing" and "understand right from wrong. "For boys, it also comprised specific charges such as "Not to defraud or thief" and do not take to the gun. "Where gender-specific traits were identified, it was remarked that those boys need to be nurtured to be courageous, and in particular, this implies that they should be tough and prepared to rugged it out, participate in sports, and be the workers. Almost equal significance was allocated to their being groomed not to exploit women, to look after their sisters, and to care for and honor their wives. Additional minor concerns entailed avoiding homosexuals, and in this respect, boys should be educated not to permit themselves to be caressed inappropriately, not to relax in a man's lap, or let a man kiss or cuddle them. Being a nice papa, safeguarding the home, and not living promiscuously were also aspects of the charges for boys. Where specific gender functions were noted for girls, these were focused primarily on motivating them to be self-disciplined and to delay involvement in sexual relationships or resist having many boyfriends. Other principles involve being neat and learning how to dress. Girls were moreover to be exhorted to be reasonable and respect their family, to be trustworthy and loyal, and to conduct themselves in a manner that men will esteem them.

The habit of multiple conjugal romances, which is prevalent among Jamaican men of every social class, heightens the likelihood that most children will not grow up in the same homes as their fathers. But fathering actions do take place across family boundaries, and children naturally know who their papas are. It is also deemed important that fathers should admit paternity. As reported by Raymond Smith (1982), the Caribbean household is characterized by a household structure that does not restrict relations within a handily defined and bounded home. This is apparent from data released by the "Jamaica Survey of Living Conditions," which has unfailingly reported that many families receive income as child assistance from parents residing elsewhere. These are normally fathers. In 2009, the proportion of households receiving these revenue transfers from parents who lived in Jamaica was calculated at 23 %, while 11 % also earned child support from parents living abroad.

PARENTING

Any man can father a child, but being a dad is a lifetime endeavor. Fathers play a unique role in every child's life that is peculiar and cannot be fulfilled by others. This role can possess a large influence on a child and assist in molding him or her into the individual they become.

Parent-child communication and interaction are essential ingredients of positive parenthood and the opportunity for improvement and personal development for both the parent and child. For Jamaican papas, however, these interactions are not reliable, as they are moderated by the family pattern, which is characterized by substantial variability. In some examples, the Jamaican father is placed within a formal two-parent family, while in different cases, he maintains a distant or visiting position, with little presence or opportunity to shape the development of his child. Consequently, the outcomes for papas and children may become a source of delight or may lead to much disappointment. The Afro-Caribbean household has been the topic of significant study, and like the Afro-American household, its distinguishing characteristics have been a great incidence of female-headed homes, children born outside of legitimate unions, multiple spouses over time, and families that may include various sets of offspring who are the outcome of previous unions. Historically, these characteristics have been elucidated in terms of the dislocation effects of slavery (Frazier 1939) or are credited to the inheritance of special African cultural habits (Herskovits 1941; Robotham 1990). However, their continuation is strengthened by both cultural and financial factors. The sometimes-tenured relationship between papas and offspring has often set the basis for indictments of male irresponsibility (Barrow 2001), and it is just from the early nineties that there has occurred any systematic research on men's parenting attitude and their dedication to their fathering functions. These more recent examinations have sought to seek directly with men their opinions of the fathering function, their method of the socialization of offspring, and the degree of their real "father work. "As an outcome, a finer picture has occurred in which it becomes evident that Jamaican men at all social levels have a deep regard for their personality as fathers. There is also broad agreement among papas on the virtues that children should be facilitated to cultivate, as well as the techniques of child-rearing approved. However, in many circumstances, economic conditions, as well as family patterns, impede the satisfactory achievement of these roles.

Family Structure

Jamaican children may be raised within a diverse spectrum of families and homes, as these social patterns are closely associated with the alternative kinds of conjugal unions that their parents create, both at the period of the child's pregnancy and all through their growing up. These conjugal union kinds include visiting partners in which there is no formal residence, common-law or consensual partners in which there is formal residence, and legal marriages. It has been indicated that in several instances, these unions observe a cyclical pattern associated with rising age so that spouses move from their original visiting union to common-law partners, and ultimately, they may normalize the union through formal marriage (Roberts 1957; Priestley 2010). Data from the 2001 survey revealed that among males 20–44 years, only 18 % were in legal marriages, while 24 % were in common-law partners, with the rest (58 %) not living in any residential unions. These males either signified that they were unmarried or in a visiting partnership. In contrast, among men 45 years and above, 46 % noted that they were lawfully married, 14 % retained common-law marriages, and 40 % were not in any residential union.

The vitality of these patterns varies significantly in rural and metropolitan areas, and the foundation research has always shown that variations in connubial patterns are often correlated to the availability of financial support (Clarke 1957; Blake 1961). Educational achievement and other social class conditions also serve to differentiate the type of connubial union and the kind of family that is created (Roberts and Sinclair 1978). Early surveys of the Afro-Caribbean family indicated that as women changed positions through a series of conjugal unions over their childbearing interval, the family became increasingly matrimonial-focused, and male partners always became detached from this female-centered view (Smith 1973; McKenzie and McKenzie 1971).

Data from the "Jamaica Survey of Living Conditions" persists in highlighting the impact of financial factors on family headship, indicating that whereas 45.5 % of all families were headed by women in 2009, among the impoverished quarters, the percentage with female heads stood at 50.2 %, as compared with 36 % among the wealthiest quarters (Planning Institute of Jamaica 2010).

The results for children are likewise certainly evident according to data from this annual census which documented that in 2009, 34 % of all children 18 years and below resided with both of their biological parents, while 45 % resided only with their biological mother, and 6 % with their papas only. In addition, 15 % lived with none of their biological parents. Among those in the indigent quarters, 34 % resided with both parents, indifferent to 42 % of children in the wealthiest quarters.

In Jamaica, masculinity philosophies emphasize sexual prowess, as demonstrated through keeping multiple companions, and since childbearing is always viewed as evidence of manhood, several Jamaican men will reveal having several baby mamas over time. This priority on fertility which has been repeatedly reported among Caribbean women as the main ingredient defining their personality (Powell 1986), has similarly been observed by investigators who have evaluated masculine identity. Based on his research in a rustic Jamaican community, Whitehead (1992) discovered that men at every social took prestige in both their "inside and outside" children, as these filled as a testimony both to their masculinity as well their relative freedom from their female companion. He surmised that there was significant support for Wilson's contention that children are proof and the manifestation of a man's adulthood and manhood, earning him honor both in the larger society and among his associates (Wilson 1973). Although abidance to this macho philosophy is stronger at poorer social class levels and at young ages, it is still evident across all levels (Anderson 2012). Children who are bred outside of a prevailing co-residential union or who later become detached from their fathers as the outcome of the disturbance of a union often come to acquire the marginalized reputation of outside children (Barrow 1996, 2010). The degree of their relationship with their natural father may become weakened over time, while in contrast, the father may discover that blockages are set in the way of interchange with these first children, depending on his liaison with his children's mama. Therefore, while Jamaican men recognize their father's position strongly and have an increased passion for playing a positive part in their children's lives, these actions are often belated and not always profitable.

Church to the Rescue

The Church in Jamaica is capable of helping the men and their families. From research and observable trends, it is obvious that there is a need for social structural adjustment for the Jamaican man. It is pertinent that they are strongly inclined to their fatherly roles but are handicapped by their own misguided opinion of self-esteem.

The church and Christian doctrine should not be sacrificed on the altar of inherited culture and conveniences. The Scripture is very clear on the formation and structure of a family, and this is not optional.

Ephesians 5:23 NIV -For the husband is the head of the wife as Christ is the head of the Church, his body, of which he is the Savior.

Multiple partners will not find any place in the scriptures, and it negates God's plan for a healthy family; which of the wives is the head? Teaching them to observe all things whatsoever I have taught you is the responsibility of the Church. If the Church teaches the men what godly virtues are and reorientate them accordingly, then the children and the women will have hope, and the society will be better off.

Having several sexual partners is not different from adultery, which is sinful before God and capable of sending one to hellfire.

Slavery indeed had inflicted dastardly malfeasance on the Jamaican family life that tends to swap the role of parents in the family. While the man is supposed to own the home and provide both physical, emotional, and spiritual support for the well-being and stability of his household, in our clime, he has assumed a visiting role, basking in a curious euphoria of multiple partners, improperly trained children, and violent prone society.

Ephesians 5:31 NIV: "For this reason, a man will leave his father and mother and be united to his wife, and the two will become one flesh."

When a man is united with several wives, he cannot become one flesh according to the scriptures, and this puts the rules on its head, resulting in disorder and chaos as being experienced in our nation. God is the author of the family, and He did not fail in providing adequate guidelines for the proper and efficient running of the home. The Church should assist the members by ensuring that they are in tandem with the Biblical concept of marriage and are committed to the new life in Christ Jesus. Whenever there is a conflict between culture or tradition and the word of God, the Church does not stay passive nor compromised but acts in the interest of the biblical culture. The concept of the white wedding, for instance, was a fallout from the refusal of the unbelievers to allow converts who were ostracized from the community for their faith to conduct marriages for them. The early missionaries, who were predominantly white people, decided to be conducting the marriage according to their tradition. Therefore, the Church in Jamaica should create a Christian marriage culture that is less expensive and cumbersome that confers legitimacy by the Bible standards to the union of one man and one woman, which is separable by death. The Church should be bold and very loud in discouraging men from multiple unions.

Genesis 18:19 NIV: For I have chosen him so that he will direct his children and his household after him to keep the way of the LORD by doing what is right and just so that the

LORD will bring about for Abraham what he has promised him."

Homes, families, cities, and nations are built by men and not women, and this is not to belittle the incredible contributions of women in the building process. But enduring legacies are championed by the determination and sagacity of the man, who was endowed with the wherewithal for the tough task of building. The man's presence in the home provides emotional security and courage to the household, which is necessary for effective articulation and courageous actions by the members of the family. It is empirically proven that children who grew up under the watchful eyes of their fathers are more daring and resilient than those who grew up without their father's presence. That Jehovah is called the God of Abraham, Isaac, and Jacob does not imply that there were no women within the scene, but that nations, families, and homes are reckoned by the men.

In all of Abrahams's busy schedule, God did not relegate the training of the children to his wife but insisted that it was the man's responsibility to train his children.

Proverbs 22:6 - Train up a child in the way he should go; even when he is old, he will not depart from it.

As human beings, especially at a tender age, we learn by imitating the attitude of those around us; that's the way we learn to act in the world. If a father is loving and treats people with regard, the young lad will grow up largely the same. When a father is nonexistent, young boys depend on other male models to set the requirements for him how to function and overcome in the world.

There is a positive correlation between children's upbringing and what they turn out to be. Women, by their nature, are soft and tender, and this also shows in the life of children trained by their mothers alone. Sparing the rod and spoiling the child is a biblical assertion. The boys tend to extreme behavior because they grow up to wrongly or rightly believe that they are not masculine enough, and to prove to their peers and convince themselves otherwise, they become wild. The presence of the father would have given assurances and practical experience of the masculine world, and that would suffice.

The girls, in their search for the much-needed positive affirmation and acceptance, fall into sexual traps because the father is gone prodigal. The girl's self-confidence and courage are built on the foundation of the father, who is loving and always there. A teenage girl was approached in the school by a guy who told her "I love you," and her response " come and see my dad" jolted the guy who thought she was kidding, but when her answer became consistent, the guy backed out, but the girl told her father and promised to show him the pest. So on a good occasion, when the father visited her at the school, she called the guy to come and meet her father and repeat the words he said to her in the father's presence. Of course, the guy did not come, and that marked the end of the pestering. Her closeness with her father became her defense anywhere.

The culture of violence in our nation is a direct result of the failure of fathers. The children need training, and balanced training is anchored on responsible fatherhood.

Fathers not only impact who we are inwardly but how we maintain relationships with people as we develop. The way a father deals with his child will affect what he or she seeks in other people. Friends, lovers, and marriage partners will all be selected based on how the kid understood the significance of the relationship with his or her father. The examples a father sets in dealing with his children will influence how his children associate with other people.

Training children is not possible by proxy; it is practical, emotional, and spiritual. It does not end in sending things across or paying school fees but physical presence as much as possible and personal involvement in their lives. The formative years of 0-6 are very crucial for the overall development of the children; it is during this period that habits, personality, and character are formed. Therefore, the parents must be deliberate and smart in selecting what and who the children are exposed to during the formative years, and the father, in particular, should be involved in regular supervision and physical interaction with them. Whatever influence and traits or skills you desire to see as they grow up should be introduced within this period. There was an assertion in the long tennis sports world that if you have not played tennis at six, you cannot win the Wimbledon.

The Church, as the single dominant influencer, has the capacity to correct the ills of the society that are mostly members of one denomination or the other.

2 Timothy 3:16 NIV - All Scripture is God-breathed and is useful for teaching, rebuking, correcting, and training in righteousness.

Much as there is an intense desire by most parents to spiritually foster their children, many fall out of their spiritual direction, and by the time they become teenagers or grown-ups, the lives they are living are deficient. In this nation, statistics on child marriage are shocking. Drug abuse is on the increase among children, teenage pregnancies are widespread, children are fleeing from homes, and we are left to raise a question, what is the position of the Church in fostering children?

Sunday school is an event that children love to attend every Sunday. For many, it is a routine exacted on them by their guardians or parents.

For others, it is to sing harmonious songs; others are to pray, while others are merely accompanying their older siblings to Church. For whatever reason they come, it is the beginning of wisdom, and the word of God planted early in the life of children is a restraining force against evil.

Parenting, more than anything else, is training in leadership and reliance on God. We must withstand the temptation to seek an overly precise and precise footpath of biblical parenting that will ensure specific results for our kids and teens. Contrarily, we cannot be sluggish and adopt whatever parenting technique we believe is best. The Bible gives us some essential wisdom related to child-rearing at all ages, but this must again be supported by intelligent and spiritual rigor. This veracity embraces the challenge of enabling the next generation of character bearers to become everything that God plans for them.

The Church has a huge aspect in fostering the development of children. Children must grow up with integrity, and the Church is in a very strategic position to provide that. Today the Church is being reminded of its divine function, especially now when there are various conflicting challenges facing the children. The Church should reach out to people and particularly the children, in a holistic manner, spiritually, physically, socially as well as economically.

The Church can as well support or sponsor legislation that would make it difficult for men to have multiple partners. The child right act can be strengthened through policy initiatives and programs that provide education, health care, and counseling for the children.

Every nation rises or falls on the strength of its human capital, and Jamaica is not an exception to the rule. We as a nation must urgently chart a new and honorable course for our children. The Church and State must work together to procure an environment that is conducive to the overall development of the children.

SOURCES

Andrews University Digital Library

Caribbean Group for Cooperation in Economic Development (CGCED)

Journal of Homosexuality

Union Theological Seminary

https://www.kitlv-journals.nl/

https://christianhistoryinstitute.org

https://jamaicanobserver.com

https://thegospelcoalition.org

ABOUT THE AUTHOR

Dr. Donette S. Wright Is a phenomenal Minister of the Gospel and the proud mother of three amazing children and grandmother to one grandson. She has been in Ministry for over twenty-six years. This woman of God is an author, speaker, teacher, and preacher and celebrates her second book, *The Balances Between Church & Politics*.

Dr. Wright has traveled globally to share the message of hope, love, and healing. Currently, she is a part of an International Ministry called Faith Mercy & Truth and the Open Doors Ministries International.

Ms. Wright accepted the office of the Apostleship over twelve years ago and is a bold servant of her global community. Though she is not a "Politician," she was compelled to write this book, *The Balances Between Church & Politics*.